RELIGION AND THE OBLIGATIONS
OF CITIZENSHIP

In *Religion and the Obligations of Citizenship* Paul J. Weithman asks
whether citizens in a liberal democracy may base their votes and
their public political arguments on their religious beliefs. Drawing
on empirical studies of how religion actually functions in politics,
he challenges the standard view that citizens who rely on religious
reasons must be prepared to make good their arguments by appealing to reasons that are "accessible" to others. He contends that
churches contribute to democracy by enriching political debate and
by facilitating political participation, especially among the poor and
minorities, and as a consequence, citizens acquire religiously based
political views and diverse views of their own citizenship. He concludes that the philosophical view which most defensibly accommodates this diversity is one that allows ordinary citizens to draw
on the views their churches have formed when they vote, and when
offering public arguments for their political positions.

PAUL J. WEITHMAN is Professor of Philosophy at the University
of Notre Dame. He is editor of *Religion and Contemporary Liberalism*
(1997) and coeditor of the five-volume *Philosophy of Rawls* (with
Henry Richardson, 1999). He has also published articles in medieval
political thought, religious ethics, moral philosophy, and contemporary political philosophy.

RELIGION AND THE OBLIGATIONS OF CITIZENSHIP

PAUL J. WEITHMAN

CAMBRIDGE
UNIVERSITY PRESS

PUBLISHED BY THE PRESS SYNDICATE OF THE UNIVERSITY OF CAMBRIDGE
The Pitt Building, Trumpington Street, Cambridge, United Kingdom

CAMBRIDGE UNIVERSITY PRESS
The Edinburgh Building, Cambridge CB2 2RU, UK
40 West 20th Street, New York, NY 10011-4211, USA
477 Williamstown Road, Port Melbourne, VIC 3207, Australia
Ruiz de Alarcón 13, 28014 Madrid, Spain
Dock House, The Waterfront, Cape Town 8001, South Africa

http://www.cambridge.org

First published 2002
Reprinted 2004

Printed in the United Kingdom at the University Press, Cambridge

Typeface Baskerville Monotype 11 / 12.5 pt   *System* LaTeX 2ε   [TB]

A catalogue record for this book is available from the British Library

Library of Congress Cataloguing in Publication data

Weithman, Paul J., 1959–
Religion and the obligations of citizenship / Paul J. Weithman.
p.   cm.
Includes bibliographical references and index.
ISBN 0 521 80857 X
1. Religion and politics.   2. Citizenship – Moral and ethical aspects.   I. Title.
BL65.P7 W45   2002
291.1'77 – dc21   2002016594

ISBN 0 521 80857 x hardback

For Maura, with love

Contents

Preface and acknowledgments

Philosophical problems about the proper role of religion in democratic decision-making are problems I have been thinking about for a long time. I wrote this book because I became interested in rethinking them by asking questions which I believed philosophers had not investigated sufficiently: questions about the role churches actually play in preparing people for citizenship and in furnishing them with religiously based political arguments and religious reasons for political action. It is surprising that philosophers have not attended more closely to these questions. Recent years have seen a resurgence of scholarly interest in civil society across the disciplines. They have also seen a great deal of interesting philosophical work on the formation of citizens by other institutions, most notably public schools and, thanks to feminist critics of liberalism, the family. Contemporary political philosophy is deeply indebted to those who have produced this work. They have reminded us that citizens are made not born and that how they are made is of great philosophical interest. This book would not have been possible without those compelling reminders.

I began this book hoping to make room in the theory of liberal democratic citizenship for saints and heroes of the religious left, such as Dorothy Day and Martin Luther King. I was troubled by theories which seemed to imply that such people violate their civic duties by engaging in religiously motivated activism or by putting forward exclusively religious arguments. I was also troubled by the thought that theories which do seem to accommodate them do not do so in the right way. Much to my surprise, I felt driven to different answers about religion's role in democratic politics than those I had previously accepted and to a much less moralized view of citizens' proper relations to one another. I put my conclusions forward with some trepidation, mindful that the answers I am rejecting are powerfully defended in the contemporary literature. I also recognize the preliminary character of the book. Much empirical

ix

work still needs to be done on the political role of churches and other secondary associations, both in the United States and in other liberal democracies, before an argument of the sort I have made here can be regarded as complete. Finally, I recognize that there is also an increasingly large and interesting body of literature on the artifactual character of secondary associations, and on the extent to which it is legitimate to shape them for democratic purposes. Regrettably I have been unable to take full account of that literature here.

In writing this book, I have incurred a number of debts which it is a great pleasure to acknowledge. Early work on the book was supported by a grant from the Pew Charitable Trusts. Much of the final draft was written at the National Humanities Center in Research Triangle Park, North Carolina. There I held the Walter Hines Page Fellowship, endowed by the Research Triangle Foundation of North Carolina. The entire staff of the center deserve my thanks for their provision of warm hospitality and ideal working conditions. I have benefitted from invitations to a number of conferences, at which I was able to work out some of the ideas for the book. I am grateful to Robert Audi for an invitation to speak on religion and politics at a conference at the University of Nebraska, to Christopher Wolfe for an invitation to participate in a session on public reason at the American Political Science Association, and to the Philosophy Department at St. Louis University for inviting me to a Henle Conference on religion and democracy. I am grateful as well to Michael Perry for his invitation to speak at a conference at the Wake Forest University Law School, to Thomas Schmidt for his invitation to speak at a conference at the Johann Wolfgang Goethe-Universität, Frankfurt-on-Main, and to Brad Lewis and William Wagner for their invitation to speak at a conference that was jointly sponsored by the Department of Philosophy and the Columbus School of Law at the Catholic University of America. Parts of the book appeared in the published proceedings of the conferences at Wake Forest and St. Louis University: some of chapter 1 appeared in my "Religious Reasons and the Duties of Membership," *Wake Forest Law Review* 36 (2001): 511–34 and some of chapter 7 appeared in my "Citizenship, Reflective Endorsement and Political Autonomy," *Modern Schoolman* 78 (2001): 135–50. I am grateful to the editors of both journals for permission to reprint small portions of these articles. The Chicago Law and Philosophy Group has been a source of philosophical stimulation for some years. I am grateful to the members of the group, and especially to the convenors Martha Nussbaum and

David Strauss, for the opportunity to participate and for the invitation to present part of the book at a very early stage.

A number of people have improved this book by their comments or their conversation: Geoff Bowden, Thomas Christiano, Christopher Eberle, Mark Jensen, John McGreevy, Lisa McLeman, Christian Miller, Lawrence Solum, Rebecca Stangl, Joseph Syverson, Michael Thrush, David Thunder, and two anonymous readers for Cambridge University Press. Special thanks go to Robert Audi, Kent Greenawalt, David Hollenbach, Martha Nussbaum, Michael Perry, Phil Quinn, John Rawls, David Solomon, and Nicholas Wolterstorff for the insights they have shared into the topic of this book and for the encouragement they have given me over many years. Their generosity of spirit exemplifies what is best in the academy. It was not possible for Rawls to comment on the manuscript but his own work and his example have been an inspiration to me, as they have been to many who know him and to all who have been privileged to work with him. Phil Quinn read a draft of the whole book at a crucial moment. I shall always be grateful for his acute comments and criticisms, which saved me from many mistakes. Hilary Gaskin has been a model editor, holding me to deadlines, providing timely encouragement and shepherding the book through to publication. My adored twin daughters, Anne and Meggie, grew from infants to toddlers while I completed the book; they are daily sources of wonder and delight.

Finally I would like to thank Maura Ryan, my wife and constant companion, whose keen mind and discerning heart summon me to higher things and whose presence in my life makes all good things possible.

Introduction

Religion is one of the most potent political forces in the contemporary world. The recent emergence of religious fundamentalism in many parts of the globe and the rise of religious conservatism in America are developments the political significance of which can hardly be exaggerated. Religion's power to stir passions, nourish social ideals and sustain mass movements makes it of obvious interest to students of politics. My concern is with contemporary liberal democracies and with the many questions we can ask about what role religion may play in their citizens' political decision-making. These are moral questions. The task of answering them falls to political philosophy.

These questions get their purchase because a society's commitment to liberal democracy entails certain moral commitments, commitments which are in some way normative for its citizens. Among the most important of these are commitments to liberty and equality, religious toleration, self-government, majoritarianism, the rule of law, and some measure of church–state separation. The precise content and implications of these commitments are matters of disagreement. Still, I shall assume they are clear and familiar enough that we can see how moral questions about religion and democracy arise, and compelling enough that we do not dismiss the questions out of hand.

Questions about the proper role of religion in liberal democratic decision-making fall into two broad categories. Some seize on the effect religion may have on political *outcomes* and ask how those outcomes square with the commitments of liberal democracy. Thus we can ask quite general questions, like whether state support for a religion, or for all religions equally, or for religion as such, is consistent with liberal democracy. We can ask whether it is permissible for a liberal democratic government purposely to encourage religious belief or the conduct demanded by a particular religion, or whether it may permissibly enforce religious codes of conduct. We can also use questions about religion and political outcomes to illustrate puzzles about liberal democracy. Thus we can ask whether public school prayer should be permitted if the majority favors it. If so, then it seems that measures which threaten the liberty of the minority can be allowed in the name of a democratic commitment to majoritarianism. If not, then it seems that measures which the majority would like to enact can be frustrated by a liberal commitment to freedom of religion. Or we can ask whether some citizens should be allowed to make ritual use of drugs which are generally proscribed. If so, then it seems that the commitment to the equality of all before the law can, under some circumstances, give way to religious liberty. If not, then it seems that religious liberty can be restricted in the name of treating all as equals before a law which the state has an interest in enforcing.

Another set of questions seizes on religious political *inputs*. Liberal democratic commitments to religious toleration and church–state separation are sometimes thought to be incompatible with citizens' taking their religiously based political views as the basis of important political decisions. Those who publicly attempt to persuade others of their political positions using religious arguments, who base their own votes and political activity on their religious convictions, and churches and religious organizations which try to form the political preferences of their participants, are all said to betray these commitments and to violate their moral obligations by doing so. And so we can ask: on what grounds should citizens cast their votes? What sorts of arguments and reasons *may* ordinary citizens offer one another on those occasions when they speak in the public forum? What sorts of reasons *must* they offer one another, or be prepared to offer one another, on those occasions? What, if any, relevant differences are there between the public forum and other fora in which citizens express their political views? May religious arguments for policy be offered in public by those who occupy influential social roles like opinion-maker or religious leader? May they be offered by those who seek or who have been chosen for special political roles, like judge, legislator or executive? If ordinary citizens may offer such arguments and public officials may not, what difference between them explains *this* difference?

These questions about religious political inputs are questions about the ethics of citizenship. They are questions about how those who occupy a certain social role – that of the citizen in a liberal democratic society – are to treat one another as they exercise political power to conduct their common business. They are the questions I take up in this book. These questions about the *ethics* of citizenship force us to confront deeper questions about the *nature* of citizenship. Indeed, as I shall explain shortly, one of the reasons they are so interesting and important, and one of the reasons I pursue them here, is that by forcing us to confront these deeper questions they shed light from a fresh angle on some of the most fundamental issues in political philosophy.

OVERVIEW OF THE ARGUMENT

The conclusions I defend are that citizens may offer exclusively religious arguments in public debate and that they may rely on religious reasons when they cast their votes. More specifically, I shall defend the following two claims, the "provided" clauses of which express prima facie obligations of liberal democratic citizenship:

(5.1) Citizens of a liberal democracy may base their votes on reasons drawn from their comprehensive moral views, including their religious views, without having other reasons which are sufficient for their vote – provided they sincerely believe that their government would be justified in adopting the measures they vote for.

(5.2) Citizens of a liberal democracy may offer arguments in public political debate which depend upon reasons drawn from their comprehensive moral views, including their religious views, without making them good by appeal to other arguments – provided they believe that their government would be justified in adopting the measures they favor and are prepared to indicate what they think would justify the adoption of the measures.

These are principles of what I shall refer to as "responsible citizenship." I shall argue that liberal democratic citizens are sometimes under a role-specific duty to vote and advocate responsibly. These principles say what they are permitted to do consistent with that duty. The guiding idea in the argument for them is that how citizens discharge their duty to behave responsibly depends upon the circumstances of their society. This is because voting and advocacy are collective enterprises. What constitutes responsible participation in collective undertakings depends, in part, upon how it is reasonable for participants in it to regard themselves and upon what they may reasonably expect from one another. Citizens of contemporary liberal democracies like the United States are deeply divided on the nature and demands of citizenship, hence deeply divided on how to regard their own citizenship and on what they can expect of each other. Some of their disagreements concern the sort of reasons that can justify political outcomes. Some of *these* disagreements result from the political activity of churches and religious organizations. In some societies the political activities of churches and religious organizations are very valuable. They are valuable because, to take a phrase from contemporary political science, they are part of what makes liberal democracy "work." In societies in which this is so, the disagreements that result can, I maintain, be reasonable disagreements. Where such disagreements are reasonable, principles of responsible citizenship should allow citizens latitude in the reasons on which they may rely in voting and in public political advocacy. This is done by (5.1) and (5.2).

Clearly a crucial step in this line of thought is the claim that in some societies churches make valuable contributions to liberal democracy. The arguments I offer for the value of churches' political activities rely upon claims about what in chapter 1 I shall call "participation" and "full participation" in a liberal democratic society. One argument for the value of churches' contributions to liberal democracy begins from the value of being able to and knowing that one is able to participate in one important sphere of a liberal democratic society: its political life. In some societies, churches provide the means by which many people gain access to realistically available opportunities to participate in politics and develop a sense of themselves as citizens. A second argument begins from the value of debating the conditions of participation, including full participation, in other spheres of one's society. Many political debates – including those about abortion and the rights of women, affirmative action, homosexual marriage and domestic partnership benefits, welfare rights, the right to employment, how to treat prisoners, immigrants and the disabled – can, I shall argue, be seen as debates about who should be a full participant and about what goods various levels of participation should confer. There is a great deal at stake in these contests, for their outcomes determine who is accorded full participation, what rights, duties and privileges that status carries with it and what is conferred on those who are participants but not full participants. Vigorous, open and informed contests help to insure that no one is excluded from full participation who deserves to be accorded it and that those who are not full participants are treated with dignity. Churches and their representatives have defended the rights of slaves, immigrants, the poor and the marginalized. In doing so, they have often drawn on interpretations of participation which otherwise would not be articulated. These arguments can, therefore, be valuable contributions to public debate.

Showing how people gain access to opportunities for full participation and develop a sense of themselves as citizens, and showing how churches contribute to debates about participation, requires the presentation and analysis of empirical material about churches, religious organizations and their role in politics. My arguments for the principles therefore requires a departure from methods which are standard in philosophical inquiry. Philosophy typically proceeds by conceptual argument, by testing definitions, premises and inferences against our intuitions. Argumentation of this kind can take us quite far toward the solution of some philosophical problems. Much of the best work in political philosophy, including work on questions about religion and political decision-making, relies exclusively upon it. But I do not believe that exclusive reliance on conceptual argumentation is the best way to appreciate the role religion may permissibly play in democratic politics. I shall have more to say about my use of empirical data in chapter 2. For now, note that while empirical data cannot solve normative questions, they can suggest that some solutions to those questions are less reasonable than others because of the costs they would exact. They can be used to query presumptions about standard conditions which are implicit in some seemingly plausible solutions. They can also convey information needed to assess the reasonability of deep disagreement.

My defense of (5.1) and (5.2) points to the importance of distinguishing those who violate the obligations of citizenship from those whose politics we dislike. There may be many people who use religious arguments to support positions with which we vehemently disagree and candidates whom we hope will lose. It does not follow from this that they violate some obligation of citizenship. This point, though obvious, is worth bearing in mind. Though the philosophical arguments used to defend restrictions on religious political argument and activity are very powerful, the intuitive appeal of these restrictions depends, I believe, upon unspoken assumptions about the policies that religious citizens advocate and vote for, and upon opposition to those policies. In the second chapter I will try to undermine these assumptions by showing that churches and religious citizens of the United States defend a much wider range of positions than popular portrayals would have us believe. Still, there is no doubt that some citizens use religious arguments to defend political positions that others, including myself, consider illiberal or unjust. The fact that they do so shows, not that obligations of citizenship are frequently violated, but that modern societies are characterized by deep disagreements about the primacy of justice, about what justice requires and about what sorts of reasons are good ones for enacting public policy. An account of the reasons on which citizens may rely must take proper account of these disagreements.

THE STANDARD APPROACH

There is an approach to questions about religious political inputs that has become standard. That approach begins with a fundamental claim about the nature of citizenship: citizens of a liberal democracy are free equals. They can enjoy their freedom and equality, it is said, only if government justifies political arrangements, or basic political arrangements, or coercive arrangements, by reasons which are accessible to everyone. For if the reasons provided for these arrangements are accessible to some but not others, those to whom the reasons are not accessible will not be treated as the equals of those to whom they are (because they are not treated as persons to whom accessible reasons are due). Nor will they realize their freedom (because they will perceive basic arrangements as brutely coercive in the absence of a justification accessible to them). Having argued that citizens' freedom and equality require the provision of accessible reasons, those who follow this approach then isolate a class of reasons which, they claim, are accessible to everyone. These are reasons which informed and rational persons recognize or would recognize as good ones for settling questions of the relevant kind. Because these are the reasons government must use to justify political arrangements to citizens, we can call reasons in this class "justifying reasons."

Proponents of this approach go on to argue that whatever other reasons citizens offer each other when they deliberate and whatever other reasons they rely on when they vote, they must also have and be prepared to offer one another justifying reasons. This is because it is incumbent on citizens to participate in politics responsibly. By participating responsibly, they do their part to bring it about that their relations with one another are marked by civility, trust and mutual respect. Participation can be responsible and the quality of citizens' relations maintained, it is said, only if citizens rely and know that everyone else relies on accessible reasons, on reasons that they all recognize or would recognize as good reasons for deciding fundamental questions. Since religious reasons are not accessible to everyone in a pluralistic society, they conclude that appeals to them must be made good by appeal to reasons which are.

The standard approach is a very attractive one, for it is premised on a number of convictions which exercise a powerful grip on modern political thought. Indeed their grip is so powerful, and various elaborations of them so compelling, that the conclusion of the standard approach can seem inescapable. The claim that reasons for political arrangements *can* be made commonly accessible responds to the conviction that human beings share a common rational capacity. The claim that they *must* be, that the provision of accessible reasons is at the heart of equal treatment, responds to the conviction that that common capacity is what gives us our dignity.[1] The claim that the availability of such reasons is also at the heart of political freedom responds to the conviction that true freedom is realized when we act for reasons we can grasp using the common power of reason. The claim that policy must be supported by accessible reasons responds to another conviction. Exercises of political power are legitimate only if they are transparent to reason's inspection; they are not to be shrouded in mystery, obscured by "reasons of state" or hidden in the manner of government house utilitarianism.[2] The claim that citizens must be ready to offer one another reasons of the sort the government must offer them – that citizens should conduct themselves as if they were government officials – responds to still another: in a liberal democracy, citizens are really the governors and public officials act on their behalf. Finally, this approach answers to our desire for community amid pluralism. If a liberal society cannot be unified by a shared conception of the good life or by commonly acknowledged ties of blood, it can be held together by citizens' respect for one another's reason. It can be a society in which citizens respect one another as reasonable and show that respect by offering one another reasons they can share.[3]

These convictions and their implications for political argument seem so compelling because of the view of citizenship that underlies them: the view that citizens are cosovereigns who govern their society collectively using their common powers of reason. When citizens adopt this view of themselves, they develop certain expectations of one another. Thus when they think of themselves as governing their society collectively by their rational powers, it is natural for them to expect that others will offer them arguments which are rationally accessible, to feel disrespected when they are not offered such arguments and to react by withholding trust and civic friendship. Because these expectations are said to be reasonable, others should strive to satisfy them. Hence the standard approach's

---

[1] See Jeremy Waldron, "Theoretical Foundations of Liberalism," in his *Liberal Rights: Collected Papers 1981–1991* (Cambridge: Cambridge University Press, 1993), pp. 35–62.

[2] The phrase "government house utilitarianism" is Bernard Williams's; see his *Ethics and the Limits of Philosophy* (Cambridge, MA: Harvard University Press, 1985), p. 108.

[3] The phrase "reasons they can share" is adapted from the title of Christine Korsgaard's article "The Reasons We Can Share," *Social Philosophy and Policy* 10 (1993): 24–51. Korsgaard uses the phrase in another connection. My adaptation of the phrase here does not imply that she endorses what I am calling the "standard approach."

conclusion that citizens are obligated to offer one another accessible reasons.

The standard approach is a familiar one to questions about religion's place in political decision-making. Indeed I assume it is so familiar as to be immediately recognizable from the rough profile I have sketched. In one form or another it is amplified, laid out and defended by a number of thinkers in philosophy, law and political theory. John Rawls,[4] Cass Sunstein,[5] Joshua Cohen,[6] Bruce Ackerman, Amy Gutmann and Dennis Thompson,[7] Charles Larmore,[8] and Stephen Macedo[9] all argue that citizens should rely on accessible reasons or connect the use of reasons they regard as appropriate for political argument and action with the legitimacy or justifiability of political outcomes, the maintenance of good relations among citizens, or both. Not all these thinkers address questions about religious arguments and public political debate. But by offering compelling visions of how democratic deliberation should proceed in a pluralistic society, their work forces us to ask whether religious considerations should be accorded any reason-giving force in democratic politics. Reflection on their work, therefore, shows just how high the philosophical stakes are once the status of religious arguments *is* in question.

Despite its many attractions when sketched in broad outline and the many convictions to which it responds, I believe this approach is prey to serious and ultimately telling objections. It attaches far too much importance to maintaining what I have elsewhere called citizens' "reasoned respect" for one another,[10] sometimes using arguments of dubious psychological merit. It attaches very great value to a form of autonomy that is available only when government action is not premised on *any* thick conception of the good life. It does so while ignoring both the fact that some conceptions are more controversial than others and the possibility that *this* form of autonomy, though important, may be less valuable

---

[4] John Rawls, *Political Liberalism* (New York: Columbia University Press, 1993), pp. 212–54; also his "The Idea of Public Reason Revisited" in John Rawls, *The Law of Peoples* (Cambridge, MA: Harvard University Press, 1999), pp. 129–80.

[5] Cass Sunstein, "Beyond the Republican Revival," *Yale Law Journal* 97 (1988): 1539–1590; also his "Naked Preferences and the Constitution," *Columbia Law Review* 84 (1984): 1689–1732.

[6] Joshua Cohen, "Deliberation and Democratic Legitimacy," in Alan Hamlin and Philip Pettit (eds.), *The Good Polity* (Oxford: Basil Blackwell, 1989), pp. 17–34, at p. 21.

[7] Amy Gutmann and Dennis Thompson, *Democracy and Disagreement* (Cambridge, MA: Harvard University Press, 1996), p. 57.

[8] Charles Larmore, "Public Reason," in Samuel Freeman (ed.), *Cambridge Companion to Rawls* (Cambridge: Cambridge University Press, forthcoming).

[9] Stephen Macedo, *Liberal Virtue* (Oxford: Oxford University Press, 1985), chapter 2.

[10] See the introduction to Paul J. Weithman (ed.), *Religion and Contemporary Liberalism* (Notre Dame, IN: University of Notre Dame Press, 1997), pp. 1–37.

than forms of political freedom which are available only when it is not. Finally, the crucial notion of accessibility is hardly self-explanatory. The most promising attempts to explain it and to isolate accessible reasons are, I argue, ill-specified or highly controversial.

That there are problems with citizens' purported obligation to rely on accessible reasons can be brought out by counterexamples. These counterexamples show that our intuitions about the propriety of using religious arguments in politics are sensitive to contextual features of which the standard approach is unable to take account. Thus our judgment about someone's use of a religious political argument can vary depending upon his religious background, the outcome for which he argues, the use to which similar arguments have previously been put and even upon whether we think his argument is likely to prevail. I have developed these counterexamples elsewhere and do not want to rehearse them here.[11] But while the bulk of this book is devoted to developing arguments for my own view, it will be important to confront the standard approach in its most sophisticated forms. I do this in chapters 6 and 7. There I argue that the accessibility requirement on reasons cannot plausibly be spelled out.

THE PHILOSOPHICAL AND POLITICAL SIGNIFICANCE OF THE PROBLEM

One of the reasons for my interest in the standard approach and its shortcomings is that proponents of the standard approach offer powerful and systematic defenses of their restrictions. The second reason is related to the first. The standard approach is the one that can be most systematically defended because, as I said when I introduced it, it is the approach which follows most directly from views at the heart of much contemporary liberal political philosophy. The connection between the standard approach and the core commitments of liberal political thought therefore make it the most philosophically interesting rival to the view I want to defend. Because this approach is tied to accounts of political legitimacy and civic friendship, modifying the account of what public deliberation can look like may lead us to rethink our views about what democratic legitimacy and civility require.

Questions about religion's role in political decision-making are important for another reason as well, one that is more social and political than

---

[11] Paul Weithman, "Citizenship and Public Reason," in Robert P. George and Christopher Wolfe (eds.), *Liberal Public Reason, Natural Law and Morality* (Washington: Georgetown University Press, 2000), pp. 125–70.

philosophical. This is a reason which can be illustrated by episodes in American history. In the course of that history, doubts have been raised about the good citizenship of many minority groups: Jews, Quakers, Baptists, Catholics, immigrant groups, to name just some. Often, as this list suggests, these groups have been religious ones whose convictions were thought to stand in the way of their members' good citizenship. In the middle decades of the twentieth century, for example, the question of whether Roman Catholics could be good American citizens, committed to church–state separation, was elevated to national prominence by the rise of Franco in Spain and his commitment to a Catholic state, by the attempt to secure federal support for Catholic schools during the 1940s, and by the presidential candidacies of Catholics Al Smith and John Kennedy. The debate that followed turned, in part, on the empirical questions of whether Catholic Americans could demonstrate their loyalty and could participate in the common culture thought necessary for sustaining democratic institutions. But it also turned on deep philosophical questions about the nature of intellectual freedom, the moral and intellectual foundations of democracy, and the core commitments of a liberal state.[12] The course of that debate suggests two things that might be meant by asking whether participants of some group can be good citizens. Both ultimately raise just the questions about religious political argument with which I am concerned.

One thing someone might have in mind when asking whether members of a religious group can be good citizens is whether they can enter into the sort of relations that he thinks ought to hold among fellow citizens. Someone might wonder whether participants of that group can enter into a relationship of mutual respect, trust or civic friendship with other citizens, or whether they will always be alien and their loyalty in doubt. This question presupposes the availability of some criterion by which the relationship among citizens is to be assessed. As we saw in the discussion of what I called the "standard approach," good relations are sometimes thought to depend upon the generalized willingness to use reasons of the right kind in debating political questions. Clearly, then, the question of who can be a good citizen in this first sense turns on the question of what those reasons are.

Alternatively, in asking whether participants of a given group can be good citizens of a liberal democracy, someone might be asking whether they share the values, goals and norms that unite citizens of a country

---

[12] John McGreevy, "Thinking on One's Own: Catholicism in the American Intellectual Imagination, 1928–1960," *Journal of American History* 84 (1997): 97–131.

and make them a people. For someone who has this question in mind, it would be natural to ask whether participants of that group know how to participate in self-governance on the basis of those values and norms, whether they know how to honor them in practice and join with others in applying them to new conditions. It would be natural, that is, for her to ask whether they know how to conduct themselves properly in public deliberation.

The naturalness of this line of questioning receives some confirmation from the history of the debate about American Catholicism that I mentioned earlier. In the 1950s and early 1960s the Jesuit theologian John Courtney Murray argued, against neo-nativist sentiment, that Catholics *can* be good Americans. He defended this conclusion by showing that Catholics can participate in what he called the "public consensus." By this he meant that Catholics can accept the shared values and norms that justify American constitutional democracy. He was at pains to argue that among the norms American Catholics can accept are those norms of civility which ought to govern participation in "civil conversation."[13] Whether Murray was correct about this and whether he correctly identified the norms of civility are matters of scholarly controversy which are beside my present concern.[14] Murray's work illustrates a more general point. I am interested in a variant of the question that preoccupied Murray: how can religious believers be good liberal democratic citizens? As Murray recognized, good citizenship depends in part upon a willingness to participate in public debate in the right way. It therefore depends upon what "the right way" is. It depends, that is, upon what sorts of arguments citizens must offer or be prepared to offer each other.

The importance of who can be a good citizen, and how religious believers can be good citizens, thus lends significance to the questions I want to take up. But why is the question of who can be a good citizen such an important one? Liberal democracies publicly proclaim an ethics of equality. Many citizens of liberal democracies care deeply about being accepted as equals by others. They resent the suggestions that they are untrustworthy or disloyal, are free riders or are less worthy of citizenship than others. They are especially and understandably resentful when these suggestions are based on matters central to their identity, like their religion. Stigmata of this kind have profound effects on the way they

---

[13] John Courtney Murray, SJ, *We Hold These Truths* (New York: Sheed and Ward, 1960), especially pp. 97–124.

[14] See, for example, "Theology and Public Philosophy: A Symposium on John Courtney Murray's Unfinished Agenda," *Theological Studies* 40 (1979): 700–15.

think of themselves. They also have profound effects on their relations with others, especially when the stigmatizing claims are widely believed. Members of groups thought to be incapable of good citizenship are generally *not* accepted as equals. They may be subject to exclusion from opportunities, economically and politically if not legally; at least they may be treated with disdain or condescension. Thus the questions of who can be a good citizen and of how religious believers can be good citizens have implications for many people's self-respect and social status.

When I sketched the arguments for my own view, I said that it is important to be sensitive both to the contributions that religion can make to public debate and to the fact that liberal democratic citizenship is an achievement that churches and religious organizations help to bring about. To make good these claims I need to provide an analytical framework for locating and evaluating the contributions religion and churches make to democracy. Locating those contributions requires the use of categories that are not now part of the standard repertoire of democratic theory. In the next chapter I develop those categories and lay out the framework for presenting the empirical data that follow.

Participation, full participation and realized citizenship

Aristotle offered the most famous definition of citizenship when he defined a citizen as someone who takes part in ruling and being ruled. Since my target is the ethics of political participation, Aristotle's definition is the natural place to begin. Thus I use the term "citizen" to denote someone who is both affected by political outcomes and who is entitled to take part in bringing them about. In modern liberal democracies, the citizen's entitlement is a legal one.[1] That entitlement can exist *merely* in law. Alternatively, someone who is a citizen can have real opportunities to participate in political decision-making by affecting political outcomes. She need not have the opportunity to seek high office. But if she has the real opportunity to take part in decision-making, she must have real opportunities to vote, to inform herself about public affairs, to express her political opinions, to petition her representatives without reprisal, and to join with others in holding them accountable. The provision of these opportunities to all those who are legally entitled to take part in decision-making is a great achievement for a liberal democracy. But in calling citizenship an achievement, I have something more in mind. Citizenship is a social role. The achievement of citizenship requires that those who are entitled to play it be equipped to do so.

REALIZED CITIZENSHIP

All of us simultaneously occupy a variety of social roles associated with our places in our families, our occupations, our associations and our society – parent, child, spouse, physician, student, bureaucrat, cleric and so on. Learning to play a role involves learning to honor the obligations that one has in virtue of occupying that role, the role-specific duties. It

---

[1] On the emergence of citizenship as a legal status, see J. G. A. Pocock, "The Ideal of Citizenship Since Classical Times," in Ronald Beiner (ed.), *Theorizing Citizenship* (Albany: SUNY Press, 1995), pp. 29–52.

may also include learning to live up to various ideals, ideals realized by excellent performance of the activities normally associated with that role. The activities and duties associated with our roles are often not explicitly codified. What we acquire as we learn a role is not the explicit command of a systematically connected body of practical knowledge. It is more often an unsystematic welter of ideas, convictions, aspirations, entitlements, role models and rules of thumb. That as many people learn to play social roles as do is remarkable. Its remarkability should not blind us to a fact which stands in even greater need of explanation: that our occupancy of roles can be motivational. This is especially puzzling in the case of roles like citizenship, in which we find ourselves without any undertaking on our part, rather than roles like spouse, which we voluntarily and publicly assume, typically by acts of promising.

Though relatively few people assume the role of citizen by explicit consent, a great many people are moved by the ideals of citizenship and by the injunction to be a good citizen, hold themselves to the norms and obligations of citizenship. They feel entitled to its benefits and pride themselves on their status as citizens. In order for our citizenship to be motivational in these ways, we must think of ourselves as citizens. We must recognize the associated norms, ideals, benefits and opportunities as ours, as applying to us or as open to us. We must also think of ourselves, at least implicitly, as having the characteristic rights, interests, duties and powers of citizens. In sum we must, as I shall put it, *identify* with our citizenship. Acting on our identity as citizens to satisfy our obligations, assert our rights or take part in politics requires confidence that our actions will be effective. It may require courage in the face of dangers and obstacles. As a first approximation, let us say that someone who has a sense of herself, even an implicit sense of herself, as a citizen and the psychological resources to act on her identity as such *effectively identifies* with her citizenship.

Effective identification is one condition – the subjective condition – of what I shall call *realized citizenship*. Realized citizenship as I understand it has an objective condition as well. Someone who realizes her citizenship has the legally guaranteed opportunities to participate of which I spoke earlier. What makes those opportunities *real* opportunities – to employ the phrase I used above – is that she has the resources of information, skills, networks and influence to take advantage of them. The conjunction of opportunity and resources is the objective condition of realized citizenship. When I speak of citizenship as a social and political achievement, it is realized citizenship I have in mind. In this chapter I offer a preliminary argument for the claim that a commitment to liberal democracy provides grounds for valuing realized citizenship. That argument prepares the ground for chapter 2, where I suggest that churches contribute to democracy by promoting realized citizenship, and for chapter 3, where I vindicate the conclusions of this chapter and chapter 2 by appealing to various theories of democracy. Thus I shall have more to say about realized citizenship in the next two chapters. For now, I simply want to clarify the notion of realized citizenship somewhat by saying something more about the subjective and objective conditions of realized citizenship and by drawing some important distinctions.

I said that someone's identification with her citizenship is effective when she has the psychological resources to act on her sense of herself as a citizen. Let me try to make this more precise. There are some activities of citizenship – such as speaking up at a public meeting, protesting, confronting public officials – that draw on initiative, confidence or even courage, and a sense of efficacy or empowerment. Casting a vote requires the motivation to vote, which as we shall see in the next chapter is often connected with an effective sense of civic duty. Initiative, confidence, courage and the sense of empowerment, an effective sense of civic duty, are psychological resources on which citizens draw when they perform these activities of citizenship. These resources have a dispositional component. The presence and strength of the dispositions depends upon a number of highly complex factors. Some of these no doubt vary from individual to individual, so that identically placed individuals would develop the dispositions to different degrees. There are certain identifiable conditions which are normally conducive to the development of these dispositions. These include the regular exposure to the teaching that citizens can be efficacious if they act in concert and to the teaching that voting is a civic duty, and transmission of the collective memory of empowerment that came with a group's previous experiences of successful political action. These are the bases of the dispositions. When such bases of psychological resources are made available to someone, she has been provided with the *bases* of effective identification with her citizenship. She has therefore been provided with the bases for satisfying the subjective condition of realized citizenship.

The objective condition of realized citizenship is the conjunction of the legally guaranteed opportunity to participate in political decision-making and the resources to take advantage of opportunity. Democratic equality is sometimes said to require that citizens have equal chances to influence political outcomes. Since the realization of citizenship is supposed to be an accomplishment of liberal democracies, it might seem

that that achievement requires satisfaction or approximation of this condition of democratic equality. This, in turn, might be thought to suggest
an account of realized citizenship according to which citizens fully realize
their citizenship only if each enjoys an equal chance of influencing political outcomes and each individual realizes her citizenship to the extent
that her chance of influencing outcomes approaches what it would be
if all had equal chances. But this characterization ignores the subjective
condition and so ignores an important condition of realized citizenship
as I understand it. Moreover, it makes the extent to which someone realizes her citizenship dependent upon the extent to which others do. This
makes even gross, qualitative assessments of realized citizenship dependent upon information that would be very difficult to obtain. A more
usable characterization of realized citizenship is that it is a measure of
absolute access to resources. These include the psychological resources
of which I spoke above. They also include the other resources needed
to take advantage of legally guaranteed opportunities to participate
in political decision-making: information, skills, networks and financial
resources.

Realized citizenship is not the same as *active* citizenship. Someone may
satisfy the subjective and objective requirements of realized citizenship,
yet be politically inactive. But though realized citizenship and active
citizenship are different, they often have a common cause. This is because
the only or the best ways to provide someone with access to information
and political networks, for example, and to foster her sense of herself as a
citizen, may be to provide her with those resources and to encourage her
to participate. Thus it may be that the only or the best way to promote
realized citizenship is to promote active citizenship. Nonetheless I want
to maintain that realized citizenship is the more fundamental notion in
this sense. Part of what makes the encouragement of active citizenship
valuable is that it is the encouragement of realized citizenship.

Realized citizenship is not the same as *good* citizenship, if by "good
citizenship" is meant a disposition to promote the common good or to
advance justice. Clearly someone can have a vivid sense of herself as a
citizen but use her resources to advance self-, group- or class-interested
aims, even when these are contrary to the demands of justice. Nor is
realized citizenship to be explained in terms of good citizenship in the
sense in which I discussed it at the end of the introduction, as including a
disposition to participate in public discussion in the right way or to vote
on the right grounds. This is not simply because someone can realize her
citizenship while being mistaken about what norms of argument good

citizenship require. It is because norms of argument purport to express role-specific duties. What those duties are depends, I argue, upon the conditions of realized citizenship and not the other way around.

It might seem clear enough that realized citizenship as I have described it is valuable and that the achievement of realized citizenship by large numbers of citizens is a great accomplishment for a democracy. I do not, however, want to take its value for granted. Realized citizenship is one element of what I shall call *full participation* in one's society. Indeed in my own view it is the value of full participation which accounts for the value of realized citizenship. Once we see this and see why realized citizenship is valuable, we will be in a better position to see why realized citizenship is an achievement and what churches and religious organizations contribute to it. Introducing the notion of full participation, and the notion of participation *simpliciter*, also lays the groundwork for the argument that religion can make valuable contributions to public debate. Some of its most valuable contributions, I shall maintain, are arguments about who should be a full participant, and about what rights, privileges and entitlements participation and full participation in a society should confer. One difficulty with the line of thought I want to pursue is that the concepts of participation and full participation are not part of the standard conceptual repertoire of political theory. To show that, appearances notwithstanding, these concepts are politically important and theoretically illuminating, it is useful to distinguish the concepts of participation and full participation from various conceptions of them.[2]

PARTICIPATION AND FULL PARTICIPATION

It is sometimes said that a *concept* is given by the meaning of the term which denotes it, while *conceptions* are given by different standards for the term's application. Thus the concept of justice is said to be given by the meaning of the term *justice*, while different conceptions of justice are given by different normative principles for deciding whether states of affairs are just. Unfortunately, explaining the distinction between concepts and conceptions by appeal to linguistic meaning raises problems and questions in the philosophy of language that it is better to avoid. I shall therefore think of conceptions, in the usual way, as given by different standards for applying the term in question. In the case of participation and full participation, these standards are of two sorts. Because different

---

[2] The distinction between concepts and conceptions is found in John Rawls, *A Theory of Justice* (Cambridge, MA: Harvard University Press 1971), p. 5f.

categories of participant receive different benefits, these standards determine who is in each category, including the category of full participant, and what set of benefits, responsibilities, entitlements and recognition go with each. Different *conceptions* of participant are therefore given by different sets of these standards. The *concept* of participation, I shall assume, is what is presupposed by disagreements about which conception is the right one. As I suggest below, the fact that people adhere to different conceptions of full participation explains certain aspects of political history, and the presence and persistence of certain political controversies. These explanations presuppose that there is a shared concept about whose application contesting parties disagree. This is the concept of full participation.[3] In the remainder of this section, I shall give an initial characterization of its content by contrasting it with participation. I shall then defend three claims about it which will, I hope, make its content and importance more clear.

Any modern liberal democracy has a richly varied economic, cultural, political and associational life. I do not want to exaggerate the unity of liberal democracies, but I shall assume that these spheres of life hang together sufficiently within contemporary nation-states that there are societies which are picked out by national political divisions. Thus I assume that it makes sense to distinguish American society from French, British, German or Brazilian society. Society, as I am using the term here, is comprised of all the activities, institutions and practices which comprise national life. Thus it includes not only economic life and political life, but what is commonly called "civil society" as well. It is society in this broad sense, rather than political or economic life alone, that participants participate in. To get some sense of what it is to be a full participant, it is helpful to look at a couple of things that might be meant by calling someone a participant in his society.

(a) Participation of one sort is common to everyone, or very nearly everyone, in a society. Each society generates what is commonly called a "social product," the set of available goods which exceeds the sum individuals in a society could have produced on their own. Some of these goods are common goods and others are not. They include the material and economic goods which result from collective effort. They include political goods like rights, liberties, collective security, and the benefits which follow from solving assurance and coordination problems. They include goods of culture, leisure and association, including the goods

---

[3] Rawls explains the concept of justice by appeal to the social role of conceptions at *ibid.*, p. 6; he explains the concept by appeal to the meaning of justice at *Political Liberalism*, p. 14, note 15.

of friendship. Participation in the first sense has two conditions. First, someone who participates *contributes* to the social product. This contribution can and typically does assume a number of forms. Someone can contribute to the social product by joining and helping to sustain associations, by her economic activity, by even minimal political participation. Second, someone who participates in this sense *partakes* of the social product. She benefits from the goods made possible by social life. Thus to call someone a participant in this first sense is merely to say that he partakes of and contributes to the social product. Let us call what she does "mere participation."

Mere participation is a broader notion than cooperation in this sense: people can be mere participants in a society even if they are not engaged in social cooperation. Someone who cooperates with others consciously and voluntarily coordinates her plans with others, or acts from rules which coordinate her activities with those of others. Someone can participate even if she is incapable of cooperation, like children and the severely mentally disabled, or even if the voluntariness of her participation is in question, like a prisoner's. Children, the severely disabled and prisoners can contribute to the social product by entering into the relational life of their society. Those whose social position relative to others is so unequal that it is inappropriate to describe their efforts as cooperative can also participate in this sense.

(b) The term *participant* can also be used to ascribe a certain standing or social-cum-moral status to people in virtue of what I have called their "mere participation" in society. This status carries with it entitlements and responsibilities. When we say that someone is a participant in this sense, what we have in mind is that she is *entitled* to contribute to and partake of the social product in morally appropriate ways, and that she ought to be acknowledged by others as a person who enjoys that standing. Used this way, "participant" is a status term. Taking it as one adds a third condition – a recognition condition – to the two conditions of mere participation. It also adds an evaluative element, that of moral appropriateness, to the contribution and partaking conditions. Someone who has the status of participant should contribute to and is entitled to partake of the social product in morally appropriate ways. Thus in calling someone a participant, we can assert that she is entitled to certain rights and privileges, that she has certain responsibilities toward her society, and that she deserves certain forms of respect from government and in civil society. In what follows I shall use the term "participant" in this second sense.

Not all who have the status of participant are legally or politically equal. Some rights and privileges are reserved for adults, or for those who are legally citizens. A society's participants include those who are entitled to these rights and privileges, as well as children, refugees, stateless persons, prisoners, legal and illegal immigrants and those too severely mentally disabled or disturbed to exercise the rights and privileges of sane, competent adults. The status of participant may seem too inclusive. Yet this inclusiveness is why I begin with the category of participant rather than with the more commonly used categories of "free and equal citizens" or "persons capable of social cooperation." Since I regard citizenship as an achievement, it is important for my purposes to ask how people come effectively to identify with their citizenship. Beginning with the assumption that people are free and equal citizens or are capable of cooperation can prevent us from asking this question because these descriptions can presuppose that the requisite view of themselves is already in place. Furthermore, every society includes large numbers of people who lack the capacity for or status of citizenship, either temporarily or permanently. Their presence occasions political debate about what rights, resources and opportunities they are to be accorded. These are debates, I suggest, to which religion can make important contributions.

(c) Some participants in a society are *full* participants. Like "participant," the term "full participant" is a status term. Like the status ascribed by "participant," that ascribed by "full participant" has three conditions: a contribution condition, a partaking condition, and a recognition condition. There are duties to, and responsibilities and opportunities for, contributing to society which are appropriate to those who have the status of full participant. There are also rights, liberties, entitlements and privileges which are appropriate to full participants. For example, in a liberal democracy full participants are citizens in the Aristotelian sense. They are entitled to vote and to seek and hold political office. Thus the status of full participation is opposed to minority of age, to alienage, bondage, statelessness and disenfranchisement. But it is opposed to second-class citizenship as well. The term "full participant" is used to underline this, for I use the term "*full* participant" to emphasize that this is the highest status a democratic society can publicly bestow and that each person who has this status is as much a participant as anyone else who has it. Furthermore, according to some views, those who are entitled to full participation as I understand it are those who freely engage in, or are capable of freely engaging in, social cooperation. Full participants are therefore free and, by important measures, equals. Finally, this status ought to be acknowledged by others. Those who have the status of full participant are therefore entitled to be treated or respected as free equals by other full participants. This recognition should be accorded in political and economic life, and in important interactions within civil society as well.

When we ask about what benefits, burdens and conduct should be associated with a valued status, we can ask about what someone who enjoys that status has a right to or is entitled to, but our inquiry usually raises other questions as well. A valued status is typically thought to be a status with dignity. Indeed this is why those who hold the status should be recognized as holding it, for to accord someone recognition is to treat her as someone with dignity. Because a valued status confers dignity, some things are befitting persons of that status while others are beneath them. And so we can ask what privileges, burdens or standard of living are congruent with that dignity or befit someone who has that status. Because the status of participant in a liberal democracy is a valued status, it is natural to ask what rights, privileges or conditions of material life befit someone who is a participant of such a society or are worthy of someone who is a participant. And it is natural for us to criticize a democratic society in which many live in want for failing to address living conditions that are beneath the dignity of free and equal citizens. Questions about what benefits should accompany participation are therefore questions which typically require us to reason about a wide range of moral values – not only the values of liberty and equality, but also those of dignity, worth, and moral fittingness as well. I argue later that one of the ways religion can contribute to public deliberation is by bringing rich interpretations of those values to bear on questions about what is owed to participants.

My characterization of participation and full participation may seem worrisomely broad, for it is unclear who occupies them or what each status confers. The breadth is, however, essential, for participation and full participation are contested concepts.[4] Too much fixity would not allow for the range of positions taken in the contests.

I have distinguished full participation from other sorts of participation because the status of full participant is particularly important in democratic theory and practice. I now want to make plausible three claims about the status of full participant in liberal democratic societies.

---

[4] Whether they are "essentially contested concepts" in the sense of MacIntyre is a question I leave aside; see Alasdair MacIntyre, "On the Essential Contestability of Some Social Concepts," *Ethics* 89 (1973): 1–9.

(1.1) The concept of full participation is widely held in liberal democracies and being a full participant of society is highly valued by citizens.
(1.2) The standards of full participation are politically contested. That is, which conception of full participation is correct or is the most reasonable, is a subject of disagreements which are played out in politics.
(1.3) The extension of full participation to everyone who should enjoy it, so that they are and know they are full participants in their society, is a great social and political achievement.

Establishing the first and second of these claims shows how much political debate concerns participation and full participation, and raises questions about how such debates should be settled. This, in turn, makes it possible to show what churches contribute to the debate. Establishing the third makes it possible to show that churches make valuable contributions to liberal democracy by promoting an important element of full participation: realized citizenship.

THE ARGUMENT FOR (1.1)

Conclusively establishing (1.1) would take a great deal of historical, sociological and cross-cultural argument that I cannot offer here. I shall have to content myself with establishing its plausibility in a couple of important instances. (1.1) seems to me to be amply verified in the American case by the history of movement politics in the United States. The abolitionist movement, the movement for women's suffrage, the labor movement, the civil rights movement, the feminist movement, the gay rights movement, can all be seen as struggles by members of these groups for a fuller measure of inclusion and recognition in American life. Indeed the political assertiveness of the religious right, the activities of which did much to spark interest in questions about religion and political decision-making, may itself be part of a struggle for recognition.[5]

These movements may have been focused most immediately on obtaining freedom from slavery, the vote, better working conditions, a fuller range of civil and political rights, liberation from the perceived constraints of traditional gender roles and the range of benefits and rights sought by gay and lesbian Americans. Though these may have been the immediate goals, fully to understand these movements requires further reflection on why these goals were sought.

One reason for seeking them was surely that freedom, liberation, better working conditions, and the vote were all valued in their own right.

---

[5] See Justin Watson, *The Christian Coalition: Dreams of Restoration, Demands for Recognition* (New York: St. Martin's Press, 1997).

Another was that achieving these goals secured something of great instrumental value. In the case of suffrage movements for African-Americans and women, success meant obtaining the means for protecting and securing other goods through adequate political representation. But it is also plausible that those who joined in movement politics sought the goals they did because they believed that decent working conditions, freedom and the vote were things that befitted their dignity as individuals and as citizens. Groups deprived of them were relegated to second-class status and denied a badge of their dignity. Deprivation, they thought, indicated that second-class status was the status others thought members of their group deserved. Thus groups sought these things because without them they would not feel as if they were regarded as worthy of full inclusion in American life. The sense of being regarded as worthy of full inclusion is what the recognition condition of full participation is meant to capture. A condition of being a full participant is being recognized as an equal by those whom one regards as full participants. This is part of the aim of movement politics. Claiming that the notion of full participation is widely held and that the status of full participation is highly valued thus helps to explain important movements in American political history.[6]

To turn to a second case, T. H. Marshall famously outlined a developmental history of British citizenship according to which citizenship in Britain came to confer a greater array of rights and benefits from the seventeenth to the twentieth century and was extended to ever more British subjects.[7] What drove the development was, Marshall thought, political pressure to achieve what he called "full membership" for everyone. He did not distinguish the concept of full membership from various conceptions of it, nor did he distinguish full from partial membership in British society as I have distinguished participation from full participation. Still, I believe that what Marshall meant by "full membership" is roughly what I mean by "full participation." I also believe he thought that the notion of full membership was a contested one and that the political contests which resulted in the expansion of full membership were contests about what conception ought to determine the distribution of rights and privileges to British subjects. His history of the expansion of membership, though extremely sketchy, is interesting and not implausible. What

---

[6] In this paragraph I follow the guiding idea of Judith Shklar, *American Citizenship: the Quest for Inclusion* (Cambridge, MA: Harvard University Press, 1991).
[7] See the title chapter of T. H. Marshall, *Citizenship and Social Class and Other Essays* (Cambridge: Cambridge University Press, 1950), p. 8. For an introduction to Marshall's thought I am enormously indebted to Jeremy Waldron, "Social Rights and the Welfare Provision," in his *Liberal Rights*, pp. 271–308.

matters for present purposes is that the notion which answers to full participation can play the explanatory role it does in Marshall's history, as full participation can play the role I assigned it in American political history, only if the concept is widely shared and the status of full participation is highly valued. That is, it can play that role only if (1.1) is true.

The truth of (1.1) should not be surprising. In their public documents and in their political rhetoric, liberal democracies stress that they are societies in which everyone can participate on a footing of equality. They thus hold out the promise of full participation for all citizens and emphasize its value. They are surely right to emphasize the value of being a full participant, for being a full participant in one's society is a very great good. So, too, is having a well-founded sense of one's full participation, a sense of one's full participation that is not based on illusion, misperception or false consciousness. This is because all of us live, at least to some extent, in the eyes of others. How we think they view us affects how we think of ourselves. How we think of ourselves, in turn, conditions our ability to form, value and proceed with our plans. If others view us and treat us as full participants in society, as equals worthy of respect, this helps us to carry on with confidence, and without resentment of our society or alienation from it. It is especially important for citizens of liberal democracies to have a well-founded sense of their full participation. These, I have suggested, are societies which seem to promise full participation to all citizens. People who do not have a status they have been led to believe they would and should enjoy are likely to experience the sentiments that accompany frustrated expectations. These sentiments, if sufficiently intense, will deform their plans and their views of themselves.

THE ARGUMENT FOR (1.2)

That the standards of full participation are politically contested – that (1.2) is true – is borne out by the same evidence that shows the concept of full participation is widely shared: the history of movement politics. These movements encountered opposition, and indeed had to be pursued by movements in the first place, precisely because of deep disagreement about what the status of full participation should confer and about who should enjoy that status. That these movements were *political* movements as well as social ones shows that the disagreements about full participation were played out in politics.

The truth of (1.2) is also suggested by the fact that some contemporary political contests can helpfully be described as contests about what "full participant" ought to confer. I cannot show this in detail, but it seems plausible that the debate about abortion rights can be seen as a debate about whether women's full inclusion in society requires that they have the right to terminate their pregnancies. This seems especially apparent in debates about whether abortion is a requirement of women's political equality, rather than of their liberty or privacy. For the argument that reproductive rights are conditions of women's equality raises questions about just what is to be equalized. Pointing to the unequal burdens of child-bearing is not a sufficient answer, since it would still have to be shown exactly what these burdens impede or prevent women from doing. The answer offered by proponents of the equality argument – by, for example, Justices Souter, O'Connor and Kennedy in their opinion in *Planned Parenthood* v. *Casey*[8] – is that women need reproductive rights in order to participate in economic, political and social life as the equals of men. Since the men in question are full participants, their answer is that women need reproductive rights to be full participants in their society. Some debates about whether society should guarantee full employment can, I believe, be seen as debates about whether full participation requires that everyone has the opportunity to participate in the economy by having meaningful work. Debates about welfare reform can be seen, in part, as debates about whether the dignity of citizenship is compatible with dependence upon a welfare state on the one hand, or with lives of abject poverty on the other. They are, therefore, debates about what full participation ought to confer.

Political contests about what the status of full participant ought to confer and about who ought to enjoy that status are only to be expected. One obvious reason for this is that a claim to full participation is a claim upon resources. For example, the debate about whether citizens ought to be guaranteed some minimal economic support and what the minimum should be is a debate about scarce fiscal resources. When the allocation of scarce but valued resources is at stake, it is natural that people will disagree. Another obvious reason is that a group's demand for full participation for its members is a demand to be admitted to a status that may be jealously guarded by those who already enjoy it. They may be threatened by the prospect of extending that status to those they are accustomed to regarding as their social or political inferiors. There is still another reason why political contests about full participation are to be expected. I want to examine it at somewhat greater length. Doing so will bring to light the need for decision procedures which satisfy certain

[8] See 505 US 833, pp. 855–56.

conditions I shall identify in the next chapter. After identifying them, I shall argue that churches and religious organizations help to bring it about that some of these conditions are satisfied.

The questions of who should be admitted to the status of full participant and what benefits full participation ought to confer are moral questions. Attempts to answer them will be affected by all the diversity and disagreement that characterize any pressing moral debate in a pluralistic society. Some of these disagreements will be political disagreements, disagreements which are played out in politics. The presence of these disagreements has important consequences. To show what they are, I need to say something more about them and about how they are appropriately settled. Since these disagreements are often disagreements about what expectations of and demands on the state are to be satisfied, let me begin by saying something about the formation of expectations and their consequences for political disagreement.

A society can create expectations that its citizens will enjoy certain rights and privileges or a certain level of material well-being, and it can lead them to associate a certain level of well-being with the minimum necessary for living like a full participant. It can do so by publicly promulgating ideals of political and social equality. A society with a market economy can also form its citizens' expectations by the driving force of consumer capitalism: the continual creation and manipulation of needs, including basic needs. Furthermore, the processes by which a society forms expectations can *raise* them, so that people associate full participation in their society with continual access to the benefits of changing technology, with increasing liberty or with an ever higher level of material well-being.[9] A society's overall economic productivity may increase dramatically enough that people expect more than what was once an acceptable minimum income, both in absolute terms and as a percentage of what others earn.

The phenomenon of changing – and rising – expectations helps to show why *political* contests about the benefits of full participation are to be expected. It is natural for citizens who acquire new expectations about what the status of full participant ought to confer to expect the state to satisfy some of them. They can be expected to advance their claims in

---

9 See Robert H. Frank, "Why Living in a Rich Society Makes Us Feel Poor," *New York Times Magazine*, October 15, 2000. Frank's essay raises the very interesting question of whether material wellbeing, as measured in income and wealth, should be assessed in absolute or relative terms. On this, see Jeremy Waldron, "John Rawls and the Social Minimum", *Liberal Rights*, pp. 250–70 and Paul J. Weithman, "Waldron on Political Legitimacy and the Social Minimum," *Philosophical Quarterly* 45 (1995): 218–24.

politics, joining movements or pressing elected officials to satisfy them. But not everyone will accept those claims as worthy of satisfaction. Political conflict will be the result. The connection between rising expectations and political contests about full participation is especially clear when expectations change as a result of political debate itself. This can happen when claims about what the status of full participant ought to confer – universal health care, a decent minimum wage or guaranteed employment, for example – are advanced by a prominent political figure whose electoral fortunes are tied to the success of his proposals. Political disagreements about full participation can also be disagreements about who should enjoy the status of full participant. Immigrants, resident aliens or guest workers may come to believe that they should be extended all or many of the benefits of full participation. They may press their own case for political changes by demonstrating or striking, or their cause may be taken up by ordinary citizens, by secondary associations and by politicians who are sympathetic to their cause.

Thus political disagreements about full participation will be continual because of continually changing expectations. These changes can be brought about by new ideas about full participation which gain currency in civil society and which eventually make their way into political debate, by technological innovation which promises dramatic improvement in the quality of life, by changing demographic conditions such as a rapidly aging population or a large influx of immigrants, or by increasing familiarity with benefits provided by other welfare states. Once we appreciate the role of changing expectations in shaping the political agenda, the truth of (1.2) – the claim that standards of full participation are politically contested – should not be surprising.

How are these contests to be resolved? A politically legitimate solution to these contests requires those who are responsible for political decision-making to determine which expectations of the state are legitimate and how weighty a claim those who hold legitimate expectations is to their satisfaction. The problem is to make these determinations without giving too much weight to expectations that are based on either extravagant or adaptive preferences,[10] and to make them in such a way that those affected can be assured that neither sort of expectation was unduly weighted. At the minimum, this requires that the determinations be made on the basis of informed political debate in which the interests of citizens are adequately represented. In the next chapter, I lay down

---

[10] For the notion of adaptive preferences, see Jon Elster, *Sour Grapes: Studies in the Subversion of Rationality* (Cambridge: Cambridge University Press, 1983), pp. 109–40.

some conditions of political debate, conditions that must be satisfied if debate is to meet this minimum requirement.

When I introduced the notion of full participation, I said that the notion is important to liberal democratic theory and practice. In fact, it might be argued, the importance liberal democratic theories attach to full participation tells against my claim that religious arguments about the requirements of full participation are useful. Liberal democratic theories regard full participation as so important and have devoted so much attention to it, it might be said, that they have developed all the normative resources necessary to deliberate about fundamental political questions bearing on full participation. Appeals to religious reasons and arguments are unnecessary.

The plausibility of this claim is one of the reasons the standard approach to questions about religion and political decision-making seems so compelling. According to that approach, deliberations about fundamental political questions are to be conducted and settled by appeal to accessible reasons. What reasons are accessible is a philosophical question, one to be answered by liberal democratic theories. And, it might be said, it is one liberal democratic theorists have answered. Accessible reasons are identified in their extensive and nuanced discussions of autonomy, equality, rights, liberties, social cooperation and well-being. This set of reasons is sufficient for settling fundamental questions about full participation because full participants are properly regarded as free and equal bearers of rights, capable of autonomy and social cooperation. Thus John Rawls says that political conceptions of justice like justice as fairness should be "complete." "This means," he says, "that the values specified by that conception can be suitably balanced or combined or otherwise united, as the case may be, so that those values alone give a reasonable public answer to all, or to nearly all, questions involving the constitutional essentials and basic questions of justice."[11]

But even if this line of argument is correct, it is not clear that liberal democratic theories provide the resources needed to deliberate about those who either are not full participants in society or who never can be.[12] These are people who either temporarily or permanently lack the capacity for autonomy, or who face disabilities, whether legal or intellectual, which keep them from full participation. They include children and the

---

[11] Rawls, *Political Liberalism*, p. 225.
[12] See Allen Buchanan, "Justice as Reciprocity and Subject-Centered Justice," *Philosophy and Public Affairs* 19 (1990): 227–53.

severely disabled. They also include refugees, and legal and illegal immigrants, all of whose continued presence in liberal democracies is assured by the increasing ease of international travel, the increasing permeability of national borders and the political and economic instability of regimes around the world. I shall argue that religious political argument makes especially valuable contributions to public deliberations about those who are participants but not full participants.

THE ARGUMENT FOR (1.3)

The truth of (1.3) and the magnitude of the accomplishment it asserts can best be appreciated by looking at what the status of full participant in a liberal democracy ought to confer and at how someone's sense of her own full participant can be engendered. To be a full participant of a society, I said earlier, is to contribute to and to partake in its life and to be accorded a certain status in political life, economic life and in civil society. The attempt to specify full participation any further seems to face a problem. Full participation is a fluid and contested notion. It might therefore seem misguided to try pinning down what full participation requires with any precision. But though the requirements of full participation are subject to political contestation, something more specific can be said about them. Seeing what more can be said enables us to see that what I called "realized citizenship" is an especially important element of full participation. Establishing this, in turn, lays the groundwork for the argument that churches contribute to the achievement of full participation by promoting realized citizenship.

Any modern liberal society, I stressed, has a richly varied economic, educational, cultural, associational and political life. While these might not add up to a common project with a single end, they hang together sufficiently that they can be said to constitute a national form of life which can be marked off from those of other nation-states. Full participation in the society of a modern liberal nation-state, I want to suggest, is the full and secure integration into the national life. Despite deep disagreements, there are prerequisites for integration into that life that are valued as minimal requirements of full participation. At minimum, someone who can participate in the life of a liberal society securely must enjoy legal rights and protections, and must be able to seek redress in the legal and criminal court for wrongs done to her. She must be able exercise some measure of control over her society's political life by helping to hold public officials accountable. She must be able to receive an education.

If she is physically and mentally able to participate in economic life, she must be able to earn a living and contribute to economic life through meaningful work. If someone is to be integrated into her society's life, these opportunities cannot exist merely in theory or on paper. Rather, they must be *realistically available*. To have these goods realistically available – to have them, as it were, within one's reach – is required if one is to be a full participant of one's society.

This interpretation of full participation has the advantage of allowing us to distinguish two things which seem importantly different: *full* participation and *active* participation. As I mentioned when I introduced the term *full participant*, it refers to a status in one's society. There are appropriate and inappropriate ways for those who have that status to contribute to and partake of the social product. Still, it seems intuitively plausible that someone can have that status without being more than minimally active in her society's economic life or civil society, and without being at all active in its political life. Explaining full participation by reference to realistically available opportunities, rather than by reference to opportunities of which someone has availed herself or of which she has taken advantage, enables us to accommodate the intuition.

Being able to participate fully in the life of one's society is an important element of well-being. The *sense* that one can participate fully and that others recognize one as a person entitled to full participation is an important ingredient of *subjective* well-being, well-being as it seems from the inside. It can normally be expected to have psychological consequences. Thus when someone knows even implicitly that she can participate fully in her society's economic, political and educational life she will normally, as John Rawls has argued, reciprocate.[13] She will develop some sense of allegiance to the society that holds out those opportunities, give it her support and loyalty and affirm her membership in it. In this way she will come tacitly to identify with her status as full participant. Furthermore, the provision of full participation is not a matter on which a society can be neutral. If it does not take steps to insure that certain economic, educational and political opportunities are available to everyone, this will be well known. In the face of the obviously unredressed lack of realistically available opportunities, society will seem to prefer those who have the opportunities to those who do not. Its action – or rather, its inaction – will drive home and publicly sanction the fact that some are full participants and others are not. This, in turn, can be expected to engender a sense of alienation.

[13] See Rawls, *Theory*, pp. 472ff., 494ff.

The concept of full participation is, as I have stressed, a contested one. This way of understanding full participation is still incompletely specified, open to political contest and amenable to development through social and political debate and decision-making. It leaves open, for example, what economic, educational and social opportunities are requirements of full participation. Thus we can debate whether everyone should be guaranteed meaningful employment, whether employers should provide domestic partnership benefits to unmarried and homosexual couples, or whether a college education should now be an entitlement.[14] It leaves open questions about who is owed the status of full participant and about how to treat those who are temporarily or permanently incapable of enjoying it. Thus we can ask whether the public education of children should be education for autonomy, and how the developmentally disabled are to be treated. It leaves open what the criteria of realistic availability are. Thus we can debate whether preferential hiring and affirmative action programs are necessary if minorities and women are to be full participants. It leaves open the question of whether a society can be described as "democratic" when large numbers of people are not full participants or feel alienated from their society. Finally, it leaves open questions about what the role of the state is in extending full participation.

Some theorists of democracy and some political actors deny that a democratic society has any compelling interest in removing even great inequalities of political, economic or educational opportunity. Others have more demanding views of democracy. T. H. Marshall, for example, seems to have thought that the promise of democracy is the promise of full participation for everyone who has the legal status of citizen. He thought that there could be certain deep and enduring inequalities among full participants; inequalities of class are what interested him most. Nonetheless he intimates that the equality democracy promises is equality of a certain legal and social status. It is the equality that comes with full participation in, and having a sense of one's full participation in, one's society. In the face of the obstacles posed by economically differentiated, multiracial and multiethnic societies, making every citizen a full participant – according every citizen the realistic opportunity to participate in her society's economic, political, cultural, and educational life – would, as (1.3) asserts, be an enormous social and political achievement.[15]

---

[14] See Todd S. Purdum, "California enacts expensive college aid program," *New York Times*, September 12, 2000.

[15] Indeed Hannah Arendt seems to have thought it impossible. See Jean Cohen, "Rights, Citizenship and the Modern Form of the Social: Dilemmas of Arendtian Republicanism," *Constellations* 3 (1996): 164–89, at 167.

Given the power of the forces likely to be arrayed against it, it would be a precarious one as well. Yet it is one to which democratic societies have good reason to aspire, at least on moderately robust understandings of democracy.

For present purposes I shall assume such an understanding of democracy. I shall assume, that is, that liberal democratic societies have a strong interest in according all their sane, competent adult citizens the status of full participant. Furthermore, I assume that this is an interest they have by virtue of their commitment to liberal democracy. That commitment provides good reason to regard full participation by citizens, not just as highly valued by them – as (1.1) asserts – but also as valuable. Thus if a commitment to democracy provides good reason to regard full participation by citizens as valuable, it follows that their realized citizenship is as well. If this is so and if churches contribute to or promote realized citizenship, then they make valuable contributions to liberal democracy.

THE ACHIEVEMENT OF REALIZED CITIZENSHIP

Full participation, I have suggested, requires that the opportunity to participate in various spheres of life be realistically available. Of these opportunities, the opportunities to participate in political life – to exercise citizenship in the Aristotelian sense – have a special place. And of the opportunities associated with participation in political life, those opened by the right to vote are particularly important. In modern democracies it is those who have the right to vote who are eligible for full participation, whether or not they ever cast a ballot. This is because many educational and economic opportunities are legally open only to those who have this status, or who will have it automatically when they come of age. Possession of this legal status therefore makes it possible for them to gain access to other opportunities associated with the status of full participant. This status also helps people protect their access to these opportunities against government interference or unfavorable legislation. By voting or withholding their votes and by joining with others who take to the streets in protest, they can exercise their status as people whose voices must be heard by those in power. This requires that the opportunities to vote, to petition government officials and to protest are realistically available to them.

But the realistic availability of such opportunities for political participation, while necessary, is not sufficient to make someone a full participant. Full participation includes not just realistically available access to opportunities but also *secure* access. It requires someone to know that those opportunities are hers, that they are realistically available to her and will continue to be so. Thus the secure access to opportunities to participate in the life of one's society also requires that someone knows she can protect her opportunities by holding government officials accountable in these ways and that she has the confidence to do so. Those who can hold public officials accountable must have a sense of themselves, perhaps an implicit sense of themselves, as persons with this status. They must, that is, realize their citizenship.

The importance of realized citizenship is especially evident when we appreciate one of the conclusions I reached in the last section. There I argued that the legitimate resolution of political conflicts about the rights, privileges and entitlements of participation requires informed public debate. Whether public deliberation is conducted by citizens themselves or by elected officials, the interests of citizens must be adequately represented. Their interests will be adequately represented only if citizens, or a critical mass of them, either participate in politics themselves or hold officials accountable for taking due account of their views and legitimate expectations. Citizens will participate or hold officials accountable only if they have realistically available opportunities to take part in politics, to petition officials, to reelect them or vote them out of office and to make themselves heard. The legitimate solution of political conflicts about participation and full participation therefore requires that members of society realize their citizenship.

As I noted at the beginning of this chapter, realized citizenship requires that people effectively identify with their citizenship. Bringing about this mass self-identification is an important condition of extending the status of full participant to every citizen. It is often lamented that citizens of modern democracies embrace their rights but not their responsibilities. What truth there is to the lament should not blind us to an important fact. The extent to which people think of themselves as bearers of rights, worthy of being treated as such by a society and government which are in some sense theirs, is itself a signal accomplishment of modern society. It requires the regular transmission of a great deal of information about constitutionalism, democracy and citizenship. It also requires the transmission of attitudes toward symbols, icons and myths that are central to political culture.[16] When this transmission is successful, citizens acquire

---

[16] On this important point, see the sources cited at note 34 of Will Kymlicka and Wayne Norman, "Return of the Citizen: a Survey of Recent Work on Citizenship Theory," *Ethics* 104 (1994): 352–81.

a working knowledge of their society's commitment to honoring rights, liberties and democratic political outcomes. The successful transmission of this knowledge and culture, and the self-identification that results, are important parts of what I meant earlier when I said that citizenship is an achievement. The value of the achievement depends, I suggested, upon the value of being a full participant and of the opportunities and the recognition which come with possession of that status.

How is this achievement won? How are large numbers of people brought effectively to identify with their citizenship? I suggested earlier that a sense of full participation is an important component of subjective well-being. Liberal democratic government, I am supposing, has interests in providing some of the conditions of full participation and in insuring that social conditions are in place for knowing that those conditions are satisfied. Government certainly has interests in treating those who enjoy the legal status of citizenship as voters and constituents, in guaranteeing that their rights to vote are not infringed upon, that their votes are not unjustly diluted, and that they can petition officials with their grievances. When it is known that government acts on these interests, it affects the ways citizens think of themselves.

But government action is not the only mechanism by which people develop a sense of themselves as citizens. The formation of citizens takes place in civil society as well. In the contemporary United States, for example, much of the formation of citizens is effected through people's involvement in churches and religious organizations. There is ample empirical evidence to show that many people become interested in politics, informed about it and active in it through their churches. Churches convey political information to their congregants, and convey the sense that liberal democratic government is legitimate and is responsive to voters. They also convey the psychological concomitants of citizenship, including senses of empowerment and self-worth. This is especially so for the poor and for minorities. Churches can also foster attitudes toward the symbols and myths which are central to a nation's political culture. In these ways, churches make important contributions to many people's sense of themselves as citizens. They therefore make important contributions to many people's sense of themselves as full participants in their society.

As a consequence, there are often inferential and motivational links between people's political positions and their religious views. The political positions they adopt may be those favored by their churches. The arguments for those positions that come to them most readily may be those they have learned there. These may include religious or natural law arguments for policy positions on abortion, physician-assisted suicide, domestic partnership, the conduct of war, economic questions and the death penalty.[17] Citizens may come to regard voting as a religious duty and may develop religious reasons for being politically active. They may think of their citizenship and its duties in connection with their society's common good, a good they conceive in terms drawn from their religious tradition. Thus they may think of themselves as bearing part of a collective responsibility for attaining ends like the respect for God-given rights or for certain central precepts of the natural law. When they identify with their citizenship, the self-identification may be with a view to citizenship described in religious terms. At times when the proper place of religion in political decision-making is the subject of intense debate, as it is at present, they may also acquire views about the propriety of relying on their religious convictions in politics. All this is a natural consequence of the social mechanisms by which people realize their citizenship. Hence it is a consequence of the ways in which they come to realize one of the most important conditions of full participation in their society.

I assumed for purposes of argument that liberal democracy provides good reason to value full participation. This assumption made it possible for me to argue that realized citizenship is valuable. The next chapter presents empirical data on the contributions churches make to realized citizenship. If my assumption about the value of full participation is plausible, then those who are committed to liberal democracy would have reason to value the contributions churches make. In my view, the assumption is correct. Nonetheless, in the third chapter I will dispense with that assumption. There I will defend the conclusions of chapter 2 on the basis of weaker claims drawn from various theories of democracy. I have also tried to show that important political debates are debates about what particpation and full participation should confer. Seeing questions about participation and full participation as the subject matter of political debate helps us to see how churches contribute to that debate. Or so I shall argue.

---

[17] On abortion and assisted suicide, see for example Pope John Paul II and the American Catholic Bishops, *Life Issues and Political Responsibility* (New Hope, KY: Catholics United for Life, 2000). On the death penalty, see for example *Talking About the Death Penalty* (Indianapolis: Indiana Catholic Conference, 2000). I have chosen these two publications from many possible examples.

CHAPTER 2

Religion's role in promoting democracy

In the first chapter I introduced the notions of participation and full participation in liberal democratic society. These and the related concepts of participant and full participant are, I stressed, politically contested. Citizens of liberal democracies contest who should be accorded the status of full participant, what rights, privileges and responsibilities participation and full participation ought to confer, and which of these rights, privileges and responsibilities liberal democratic states should guarantee. I suggested a view of full participation according to which full participants should have and know they have certain realistically available opportunities for education, meaningful work, cultural enrichment and political participation. A particularly important element of full participation, I argued, is what I called "realized citizenship." Someone realizes her citizenship when she has realistically available opportunities to take part in the political life of her society and effectively identifies with her citizenship.

I introduced the notions of participation, full participation and realized citizenship to set the stage for the arguments of this chapter. Here I will look at what empirical investigation shows about the role religion and religious institutions actually play in democracy. Focusing on the example of the United States, I will argue that they make valuable contributions to democracy. These contributions, I shall suggest, help to produce the religious political argument and activity with which I am concerned. While I shall mention a number of contributions, there are two sorts I shall highlight. One is the contribution religion and religious institutions make to the realization of citizenship, especially by the poor and minorities. The other is the contribution they make to discussions and debates about participation, full participation, what they should confer and what the state should guarantee. I can be more precise about the empirical and philosophical claims for which I am arguing in this chapter, and their implications for the questions about religion and political decision-making, if I comment briefly on my use of empirical data and upon the conception of religion on which those data depend.

SOME REMARKS ON THE USE OF EMPIRICAL DATA

In this chapter I use the concepts of religion and church implicit in the educated common sense of most Americans. The paradigms of religion so understood are Judaism, Islam, Roman Catholicism, Eastern Orthodoxy, the native American religions and various forms of mainline, evangelical, pentecostal and fundamentalist Protestantism. A religion, for my purposes, is any system of beliefs and practices which significantly resembles the paradigms. Churches are, in most instances, the primary institutional bearers of religion. They include mosques and synagogues, but are generally to be distinguished from secondary institutional bearers like religious orders and religious schools. The boundaries of these concepts lack sharpness. Indeed they may be so vague that there may be no way of telling whether certain families of devotional or spiritual practice count as a religion or not: there may be no way of telling, or indeed no fact of the matter, about whether some candidate is close enough to these paradigms of religion to fall under the concept. But I am interested in the churches and forms of religion which made questions about religion's place in politics of interest in the first place. Clearly these fall under the concepts of church and religion as I understand them, regardless of whether these concepts can accommodate more difficult examples. In light of these restricted ambitions, reliance on these understandings of religion and church causes no difficulties.

My exclusive reliance upon data about the role of religion in American democracy might seem to severely limit the interest of my conclusions. Data exclusively about the United States may provide grounds for some conclusions about American citizenship. It might be objected, however, that they cannot warrant more general conclusions about liberal democratic citizenship. This is because it is far from obvious that what holds for the United States also holds for other liberal democracies.

I said in my introductory chapter that the duties of responsible voting and advocacy depend upon a society's circumstances. An argument for principles of responsible citizenship requires the provision of empirical data about one or more liberal democracies. The United States is an important test case for accounts of religion and democratic decision-making. It is the west's largest, oldest and most populous democracy.

It is also a liberal democracy in which the political role of organized religion has been much more intensely studied than in other countries.[1] At the very least, drawing together empirical data on the political role of American religion and drawing out their implications for outstanding philosophical questions suggest interesting lines of research to be done in other countries. Cross-cultural studies might well show that religion and religious organizations make some of the same contributions to democracy in other countries that they do in the United States. They may play some role in fostering realized citizenship. The contributions they make to public debate may be duplicated in other liberal democracies as well. Where this is so, (5.1) and (5.2) will be appropriate principles of responsible citizenship.

Perhaps researchers would find that while religion and religious organizations make contributions to American democracy, they do not contribute to democracy elsewhere. Then, perhaps, more stringent principles of responsible citizenship than (5.1) and (5.2) may be appropriate. Recall that churches are of interest for present purposes because they are the primary institutional bearers of views of the world which motivate political action. It could be that other societies include secondary associations such as Marxist or Christian Democratic political parties which, while not bearers of religion, are bearers of other sorts of comprehensive doctrine which raise questions analogous to those raised by religion. And it could be that those associations play a role analogous to that played by churches in the United States. If so, data about American churches are helpful because they suggest what parallels to look for and how those parallels bear on the place of comprehensive views in democratic decision-making.

There is another reason for using data from the United States, one which can be brought out by considering an objection to relying on empirical data at all. The objection is that sociological data do not merely limit the generality of conclusions. They are irrelevant to philosophical disputes. For it is always open to political philosophers to adopt a stance which is critical and revisionary of the existing practices social scientific inquiry reveals. Regardless of the roles that religion and religious institutions actually play in American democracy, it is always open to philosophers to argue that they *should* play different roles or that they *would* play different roles if the United States approximated the ideal of a well-ordered democracy. The arguments about what role they should

[1] I am grateful to Kraig Beyerlein for helpful correspondence on this point.

or would play do not depend at all upon the sort of data I shall marshal in this chapter. What they depend upon are the conceptual claims about freedom, equality and legitimacy which lie at the heart of liberal democratic theory.

The problem with this objection is that theoretical arguments often do depend upon intuitions and empirical conjectures. While philosophers working in liberal democratic theory may present their arguments as if they did not depend upon facts about any particular society, they often work with one or another society foremost in mind. The unacknowledged hold that that society has on their philosophical imagination affects the seemingly abstract intuitions and conjectures on which they rely. These intuitions and conjectures, in turn, depend upon sociological judgments about the causes of incivility and conjectures about what measures will remedy it under standard conditions. They depend on intuitions about reasonable and unreasonable behavior in the face of incivility. They also depend, I believe, upon unstated assumptions about the political positions religious citizens are likely to favor. One way to call those intuitions and assumptions into question, and to undermine the arguments that depend on them, is to adduce empirical evidence about the society in question that show it to be more complicated than the simplified picture which has philosophers in its grip. One way to correct our intuitions about what it is reasonable for people to believe and about what conditions are standard, for example, is to look at how people actually come to believe what they do and at what conditions actually obtain.

If this line of thought is correct, then arguments in political philosophy are much more intimately bound up with empirical claims than is usually recognized, and political philosophers should pay more attention to political sociology than they typically do. But whether or not sociology can contribute to political philosophy generally, it bears on the questions with which I am concerned. Most of the philosophical work now being done on religion and democratic decision-making is by American philosophers. It would be very difficult for American philosophers who write about this matter not to be influenced by the prominent role of religious conservatives in American politics. This influence betrays itself in assumptions underlying their arguments. Some philosophers who defend moral restrictions on the appeal to religious reasons in politics premise their arguments on the actual costs or the opportunity costs of failing to obey such restrictions. They claim that appealing to religion in public political argument or engaging in political action for exclusively religious reasons threatens civility, threatens the stability of democratic institutions, or impedes realization of the ideals of mutual respect or well-conducted public deliberation. Their arguments therefore depend upon claims about the current extent of incivility, the likelihood of incivility and instability under normal conditions, or the possibility of realizing those ideals. These claims derive much of their plausibility from an overly simplified view of religion's role in American politics. Data about the United States can make those claims seem less compelling and more questionable by complicating the view which lent them their plausibility.

My primary aim in this chapter, however, is not to balance an overly simplified or one-sided view of the role religion plays in liberal democratic politics. It is to lay the groundwork for the argument of chapter 5, by showing that churches make valuable contributions to democracy. There are, as I have said, two contributions that I want to document in some detail, though in the penultimate section of this chapter I shall mention another. The two on which I shall concentrate are the contribution churches make to realized citizenship and the contribution they make to debates about participation and full participation. To document the contribution churches make to realized citizenship, I want to begin with data presented in the landmark study *Voice and Equality* by Sydney Verba, Kay Lehman Schlozman and Henry Brady.[2]

RELIGION AND POLITICAL PARTICIPATION

Broadly speaking, Verba, Schlozman and Brady were interested in whether civic volunteerism and civil society contribute to political equality in the United States. To answer this question, they studied various factors which influence participation in activities that can be expected to have an impact on the outcome of elections and on what government does.[3] Thus political participation as they understand it includes making financial contributions to candidates or political campaigns, protesting, engaging in community activism aimed at securing the desired result from state, local or federal government, campaigning and voting. Political activism has at least three preconditions. It requires opportunities to

---

[2] Sydney Verba, Kay Lehman Schlozman, and Henry Brady, *Voice and Equality: Civic Voluntarism in American Politics* (Cambridge, MA: Harvard University Press, 1995). For alerting me to the importance of this work I am greatly indebted to David Hollenbach, SJ, "Politically Active Churches: Some Empirical Prolegomena to a Normative Approach," in Weithman (ed.), *Religion and Contemporary Liberalism*, pp. 291–306.

[3] Verba, Schlozman and Brady, *Voice and Equality*, p. 357.

participate. It requires motivation. Finally, it requires resources of time, money, confidence and the developed abilities Verba, Schlozman and Brady call "civic skills." Verba, Schlozman and Brady tried to isolate the mechanisms by which opportunities, motivation and resources are distributed and to determine whether the resulting distribution satisfies intuitively plausible norms of democratic equality.

Recall that I said people realize their citizenship when they have real opportunities to participate in politics and when they effectively identify with their citizenship, and that what makes opportunities real opportunities is access to the resources to take advantage of those opportunities such as information, networks and civic skills. Verba, Schlozman and Brady's research showed that churches promote realized citizenship by providing access to these resources and to the bases of effective identification with citizenship. This research also suggested that churches' contributions to realized citizenship are especially valuable because they promote realized citizenship among citizens who face serious political disadvantages. What evidence of these contributions did Verba, Schlozman and Brady find?

The evidence that churches promote realized citizenship can be gathered from the evidence that they promote active citizenship. Voting is the one form of political behavior in which the majority of Americans take part. It is also the form of political behavior with which religious affiliation is most highly correlated. The correlation is a direct one rather than an indirect one. It is not, for example, mediated by a correlation with the effects of church affiliation on personality or civic skills that *Voice and Equality* documented. More important for present purposes, no other form of institutional affiliation is nearly as highly correlated with voting as religious affiliation is.[4] Moreover, there is some evidence – in the form of inference to the best explanation – that religious affiliation plays a causal role in bringing about voter participation. For while there are a number of explanations on offer for the correlation between voting and religious affiliation,[5] the one that seems best to explain the direct correlation is one that assigns churches a causal role: churches teach the sacred character of civic obligations, including voting.[6] If this explanation is correct, then it seems that large numbers of American citizens regularly engage in one important form of political participation at least

---

[4] *ibid.*, p. 359.
[5] Kenneth D. Wald, *Religion and Politics in the United States* (Washington, DC: Congressional Quarterly Press, 1992), p. 35.
[6] Theodore F. Macaluso and John Wanat, "Voting Turnout and Religiosity," *Polity* 12 (1979): 158–69.

in part for religious reasons. Because of their churches, they see one of the characteristic activities of citizenship as theirs and have the motivation to engage in it. This identification and motivation are among the subjective conditions of realized citizenship.

For other kinds of political participation, the influence of religious affiliation is significant but indirect: it exercises an important influence on political participation by way of its effects on family life and by way of the skills and information it imparts. To take the former first, Verba, Schlozman and Brady claim that families which attend church regularly are less geographically mobile and pass along an attachment to the community which is correlated with participation in local politics.[7] A high school student from a family which attends religious services regularly is also more likely to be involved in high school activities[8] and participation in high school activity as an adolescent is correlated with participation in political activity as an adult.[9] Of those who attend services regularly or are members of religious congregations, 36 percent said they gave time to their church or synagogue in the previous year.[10] Furthermore, churches and synagogues function like other voluntary organizations in providing opportunities for people to gather. When they do, informal conversation can turn to politics. Of those associated with nonpolitical organizations like churches, 30 percent report political discussions at meetings and 10 percent report that politics sometimes appears on the agenda.[11] Eight percent of all those surveyed and 12 percent of those who attend services regularly or are members reported attending a church meeting on a political issue within the previous six months.[12] These meetings and conversations provide political information and can stimulate an interest in politics that carries over into political activity.[13] Religious services can also serve as sources of political cues and information: 16 percent of those surveyed and 25 percent of those who are religiously affiliated said that clergy sometimes or frequently discuss political issues from the pulpit.[14]

Political recruitment comes along with this exposure to political cues. Four percent of church affiliates whose clergy never discuss local or national issues from the pulpit said they were asked to vote in church and 11 percent were asked to engage in some other form of political activity, whereas 23 percent of those whose clergy sometimes or frequently discuss politics were asked to vote and half were encouraged to engage in some

7 Verba, Schlozman and Brady, *Voice and Equality*, pp. 457, 460.   8 *ibid.*, p. 432.
9 *ibid.*, p. 442.   10 *ibid.*, p. 75.   11 *ibid.*, p. 374.
12 *ibid.*, p. 373.   13 *ibid.*, p. 157.   14 *ibid.*, p. 373.

other political activity.[15] Of those who attended a meeting on a local or political issue at their church or synagogue, 30 percent were asked to vote and two-thirds were asked to participate in some other way.[16] Not only are religious organizations significant venues of political recruitment, but they are far more significant venues than other organizations. Requests to vote, requests to participate in some other form of political activity and requests to do either one or the other were almost twice as frequent in church as on the job and three to four times as frequent in church as in other organizations.[17]

Finally, voluntary associations including religious associations are places where citizens acquire and hone their civic skills.[18] They are venues where citizens learn to speak in public, write letters, chair meetings, organize activities, recruit others and approach authorities. While those who exercise these skills in voluntary associations often do not do so for political purposes – they do not exercise them with an eye toward influencing the outcome of a political campaign or obtaining government action – they do develop skills which can be exercised in politics by those recruited for political action. Verba, Schlozman and Brady observe that "[i]n this way the institutions of civil society operate, as de Tocqueville noted, as the school of democracy."[19]

In the US churches bulk particularly large among the institutions that operate in this way. Americans are more likely to develop civic skills at work than in church, particularly at higher income and educational levels; this is true even when the comparison is restricted to church members.[20] But among voluntary associations, nonpolitical organizations develop these skills as effectively as political ones.[21] Churches do as well as virtually any other nonpolitical organization at fostering civic skills and, interestingly, they do far better than labor unions. Thus 66 percent of church members surveyed practiced civic skills in church while only 39 percent of union members practiced civic skills in union activities.[22] In part, this is due to the fact that church members are almost twice as likely to attend services as union members are to attend meetings, even if the sample of church members is restricted to blue-collar workers.[23] Add to this the fact that Americans are more likely to be members of a church or synagogue than a union by 67 to 26 percent.[24] The result

[15] *ibid.*, p. 148.　　[16] *ibid.*　　[17] *ibid.*, p. 373.
[18] See also David C. Leege, "Catholics and the Civic Order: Parish Participation, Politics and Civic Participation," *Review of Politics* 50 (1988): 704–36, at 712.
[19] Verba, Schlozman and Brady, *Voice and Equality*, p. 366.　　[20] *ibid.*, p. 327.
[21] *ibid.*, p. 375.　　[22] *ibid.*, p. 378.　　[23] *ibid.*, p. 387.　　[24] *ibid.*

is that Americans are three to four times more likely to be mobilized in church as in a union and blue-collar workers are one and a half times as likely to develop their civic skills in church as in a union.[25]

The comparison with unions is particularly significant because of what it suggests about who gets taught in the "school of democracy" and about equality in the classroom where the learning takes place. Many of the data marshaled in *Voice and Equality* imply that opportunities to develop civic skills, access to networks of recruitment and to politically stimulating environments, access to political information, the ability to contribute financially to political campaigns, all are distributed in ways that favor the moneyed and the better educated at the expense of the poor and the working class. As Verba, Schlozman and Brady put it, "the effects of institutions in stimulating political involvement serve to reinforce initial advantage."[26] On the assumption that government officials respond to political participation and to financial contributions, it follows that those who have financial and educational advantages also enjoy greater political influence. This, Verba, Schlozman and Brady conclude, is at odds with the requirements of political equality and democratic government.[27]

Religious institutions provide the only counterweight to this institutional tendency to reinforce educational and financial advantage, particularly in the way they foster the development of civic skills.[28] For one thing, religious institutions provide what might be called "formal equality of opportunity" to develop civic skills, since many of the church-related opportunities to develop them are open to all. More important is that they provide real equality of opportunity. Church membership does not vary significantly across income levels and only slightly along racial lines, so those with incomes under $15,000 are as likely to belong to a church as are those with incomes over $125,000.[29] Those with lower incomes are as likely as those with higher ones actually to develop civic skills: as Verba, Schlozman and Brady remark, "there is no systematic relationship between family income and the exercise of civic skills in church."[30] They conclude:

The domain of equal access to opportunities to learn civic skills is the church. Not only is religious affiliation not stratified by income, race or ethnicity, but

---

[25] *ibid.*, p. 388.   [26] *ibid.*, p. 18.   [27] See *ibid.*, pp. 526–28, 531–33.   [28] *ibid.*, p. 18.
[29] *ibid.*, pp. 315, 317. The racial difference results from the facts that almost three-quarters of African-Americans belong to a church, while roughly two-thirds of Latinos and Anglo-Whites do.
[30] *ibid.*, p. 318.

churches apportion opportunities for skill development relatively equally among members. Among church members, the less well off are at less of a disadvantage, and African-Americans are at an actual advantage, when it comes to opportunities to practice civic skills in church.[31]

Other data might seem to suggest that while churches foster skills equally, they are not venues of equal recruitment. Those with higher incomes and greater educations are more likely to be recruited into political activity than are those with less income and education, even in church.[32] But even though this is so, churches are more egalitarian venues for recruitment than workplaces or nonpolitical associations. Someone with no high school diploma is five times as likely to be recruited for political activity in church as on the job, and three times as likely in church as in a nonpolitical organization. Furthermore, the disparities in recruitment are significantly narrower in church than elsewhere.[33] Someone with no high school diploma is only one-tenth as likely to be recruited for political activity on the job as is someone with a graduate education, whereas he is only 3.25 percent less likely to be recruited in church.[34]

Thus the data amassed in *Voice and Equality* suggest that religious institutions and religious affiliation play very important roles in the realization of American citizenship. As we have seen, they are important in the distribution of civic skills, political information and opportunities for recruitment into political activity. As we have also seen, they are important in overcoming other sources of participatory inequality by increasing the ability to participate of citizens who would otherwise be "resource poor."[35] This conclusion raises the very important question of what institutions would counterbalance the sources of participatory inequality if religious ones withdrew from politics in the name of liberal democracy. It raises the possibility that, far from being inimical to liberal democracy, churches are crucial to making American politics as democratic as it is.

The argument that religion and religious organizations play an important role in overcoming political inequality is made even more compelling by data on the political role of African-American churches. Religiosity among African-Americans is positively correlated with racial consciousness which, in turn, promotes political involvement.[36] What

---

[31] *ibid.*, p. 320.   [32] *ibid.*, p. 376.   [33] *ibid.*, p. 376.   [34] *ibid.*, p. 376.   [35] *ibid.*, p. 320.
[36] See Clyde Wilcox and Leopold Gomez, "Religion, Group Identification and Politics Among American Blacks," *Sociological Analysis* 51 (1990): 271–85, at 283 for the correlation between religiosity and racial consciousness and at 272–73 for the claim that racial consciousness promotes political involvement.

Frederick Harris calls "internal religiosity" – personal religious commitment and a feeling of closeness to God – is positively correlated among African-Americans with an interest in politics and with a sense of political efficacy.[37] This sense of political efficacy is one element of effective identification with one's citizenship.

The role of churches in fostering civic skills helps to overcome the manifest political inequality of African-Americans, particularly those in jobs Verba, Schlozman and Brady characterize as "low status." African-Americans in these jobs have almost no opportunities to plan meetings at work and a negligible chance of giving presentations; by contrast, 45 percent of the same group have given presentations at church and a third have planned meetings there. Historically, of course, black churches played an important role in the American civil rights movement[38] and a study conducted in 1970 found a positive correlation between black militancy and orthodox religiosity.[39] As Harris remarks:

> Religious institutions within African-American communities are important resources for black political mobilization. These resources include clerical appeals, candidate contacts at religious services, church-sponsored political forums and rallies, group endorsements by ministers and religious groups, and fund-raising for political candidates. These sources of information and activism have deep historical roots.[40]

Note too that African-American churches are more effective than white churches in educating and mobilizing their members. African-Americans who are church members exercise slightly more civic skills at church than do Anglo whites who also belong to a church.[41] This slight edge, together with the fact that African-Americans are more likely to belong to a church in the first place,[42] helps to compensate for the fact that

---

[37] Frederick C. Harris, "Something Within: Religion as a Mobilizer of African-American Political Activism," *Journal of Politics* 56 (1994): 42–68, at 62.

[38] See Aldon D. Morris, *The Origins of the Civil Rights Movement: Black Communities Organizing for Change* (New York: Free Press, 1984), p. 4: "The black church functioned as the institutional center of the modern civil rights movement."

[39] Thomas W. Madron, Hart M. Nelson and Raytha L. Yokley, "Religion as a Determinant of Militancy and Political Participation Among Black Americans," *American Behavioral Scientist* 17 (1974): 783–96.

[40] Frederick C. Harris, "Religious Institutions and African-American Political Mobilization," in Paul E. Peterson (ed.), *Classifying by Race* (Princeton: Princeton University Press, 1995), pp. 278–310, pp. 306–07.; also see C. Eric Lincoln and Lawrence H. Mamiya, *The Black Church in the African-American Experience* (Durham, NC: Duke University Press, 1990), chapter 8.

[41] Verba, Schlozman and Brady, *Voice and Equality*, p. 319.

[42] *ibid.*, p. 317; also Robert Joseph Taylor, Michael C. Thornton and Linda M. Chatters, "Black Americans' Perceptions of the Sociohistorical Role of the Church," *Journal of Black Studies* 18 (1987): 123–38, at 124.

African-Americans lag significantly behind Anglo whites in the civic skills exercised at work.[43] Furthermore, African-American churches provide more exposure to political stimuli and to requests for recruitment than do white churches. According to *Voice and Equality*, 28 percent of Anglo white Protestants and 24 percent of Anglo white Catholics reported exposure to political stimuli at church; for African-Americans the figures are 50 and 52 percent respectively.[44] African-American Protestants were slightly more likely to be recruited for political activity in church than were Anglo white Catholics or Protestants, and African-American Catholics were significantly more likely to meet requests for political activity in church.[45] A survey conducted in Chicago found that 65 percent of black church members reported that they were encouraged to vote in church while only 30 percent of white church members said that they were. Visits paid to African-American churches by candidates for office receive a great deal of media attention, at least during presidential elections. These visits are, as the quote from Harris suggests, important sources of political information; visits by prominent politicians may also bolster the self-esteem and feelings of political efficacy of the congregants. Black churches were more than four times as likely as white churches to host candidate visits "sometimes" and *seven times* as likely to do so "frequently."[46] While church attendance is a less reliable predictor of voter turnout among African-Americans than it is among Anglo whites, church activism is a much stronger predictor among the former than among the latter.[47]

The black Christian churches of today were founded in the second half of nineteenth century, as it became clear that free African-Americans were not welcome in white Protestant churches.[48] They have from the beginning seen opposition to political and social inequality as integral to their mission. They continue to fulfill a political function which Verba, Schlozman and Brady claim is played by churches in the United States generally: that of promoting the political effectiveness of citizens who would otherwise be "resource poor." Indeed they seem to be more activist in this regard than white churches, no doubt to compensate for the even greater poverty of resources endured by those they serve. Thus if Verba, Schlozman and Brady are correct that American churches provide counterbalances to the participatory inequalities reinforced by other institutions, African-American churches provide an especially weighty one.

---

[43] Verba, Schlozman and Brady, *Voice and Equality*, p. 319; also above note 29.   [44] *ibid.*, p. 382.
[45] *ibid.*   [46] Harris, "Religious Institutions," p. 302.   [47] Harris, "Something Within," p. 63.
[48] John Hope Franklin, *From Slavery to Freedom* (New York: Alfred A. Knopf, 1947), p. 164.

The data marshaled by Verba, Schlozman, Brady and by other so-cial scientists suggest that American churches play an important role in achieving the realization of American citizenship. Their provision of re-alistically available opportunities to participate in politics is shown by the fact that they encourage participation. By fostering civic skills and self-confidence, they encourage citizens' effective identification with their citizenship. It is safe to assume that when churches mobilize or give po-litical cues to citizens, churches also give them religious reasons for action and arm them with religious political arguments. They may also encour-age them to conceive of political norms in explicitly religious terms or in terms drawn from their religion's tradition of moral reflection. They may come to believe that norms of justice are ultimately religious norms or are part of the natural law, and that political duties are duties owed to God. In sum, congregants may conceive of the role of citizen in religious terms, associating it with religious norms, duties and ideals.

As the data suggest, some of these are citizens who would either be left out of political processes altogether or would participate at a significant disadvantage. Therefore the role played by churches in achieving the re-alization of citizenship should also give pause to those who think that, in the name of liberal democracy, citizens should refrain from acting in pol-itics for religious reasons or from offering religious political arguments in public. The weight of the counterbalance black churches provide to offset other sources of African-American political inequality presses the ques-tion of what other institution would play this function if churches ceased to play a prominent political role. They thereby make the problems with these restrictive views especially clear. For if no other institutions served African-Americans in this way, then the consequences for American democracy would be particularly troublesome. The political inactivity of black churches would leave immobilized and vulnerable a group of citizens that is particularly marginalized and ill-treated to begin with.

RELIGION, CIVIC ARGUMENT, AND PUBLIC POLITICAL DEBATE

Another way that churches contribute to liberal democracy is by con-tributing to civic argument and public political debate about political questions. Public political debate is the discussion of electoral, legislative and policy questions which takes place in the public forum, especially governmental fora. It is the discussion on which a government's political decisions are supposed to be based. As we shall see in chapter 4, where I discuss public argument in more detail, it includes but is not limited to arguments and testimony in court proceedings, legislative sessions and hearings, in administrative hearings and in town meetings. The reason for isolating public political debate is its connection with political decision-making. This, I shall suggest, imposes certain conditions on public political debate that takes place in governmental fora, conditions which churches can help it meet. By "civic argument" I mean discussion of political questions in civil society. Civic argument is a broadly inclusive category of political exchange. The category may seem so broad as to be uninteresting. Yet it is in civic argument that many participants and full participants in society arrive at their political opinions and acquire their political motives. Using the Catholic Church as my example, I shall point out ways in which churches contribute to the formation of motives and opinions by contributing to these forms of political discussion.

American churches provide a wide range of social services which help to mitigate some of the grosser material inequalities engendered by the American economy. These social services include running soup kitchens, temporary and permanent shelters for the homeless, homes for single women and their children, homes for unmarried pregnant women and for victims of domestic violence, medical and dental clinics, hospitals and schools, including hospitals and schools which serve the poor. Insofar as democracy takes equal access to education, housing and health care as requirements or ideals, churches go some small way toward bringing about the material conditions associated with democratic equality.

It might seem that the provision of these services, valuable as they are, has little to do with the issues at hand. Running hospitals, educational systems, soup kitchens and homeless shelters seems unconnected with argument or activity in support of legislation and public policy, especially the legislation and policy restricting human conduct with which those who defend restrictions on argument are most concerned. This conclusion is mistaken. It is mistaken because much of the charitable and service work in which churches engage depends upon the work of volunteers. Those who engage in religious volunteerism are often exposed to the views about the social good and political responsibility that motivated churches to engage in the activities which require their help. Exactly what these views are and how systematically volunteers are exposed to them varies from church to church and, perhaps, from activity to activity. What is important for present purposes is that through religious voluntarism citizens can and often do acquire views of the social good and of their own responsibilities to bring it about. It may also contribute to their identification with their own citizenship, though they may conceive of their citizenship in religious terms. This is suggested by empirical study

of religiously based and affiliated volunteer organizations. As one executive of Habitat for Humanity told an interviewer: "I am looking at the
way I carry out my Christianity as a way of expressing my citizenship."
A Habitat volunteer said: "I tend to think of myself living my life as a
disciple and that being also how I am a citizen [*sic*]."[49]

Volunteers' collective reflection on their experience can solidify the
impressions that political issues are moral ones and that religious morality has implications for the social good. It can encourage them to think of
those implications using the set of moral concepts in which their church
has developed its political views, particularly if reflection is conducted in
the company of someone with formal theological or ministerial training.
If a church has developed its political views in secular as well as religious moral terms, then it is natural that those who are thus exposed
to its views will be encouraged to think of issues in both ways. Thus
religious volunteerism may not only vivify volunteers' commitment to
the social good by giving them an opportunity to live it out. It may also
serve as a channel through which a church's tradition of moral thought
gets transmitted to its adherents, with the result that their arguments in
civic argument may well become more sophisticated than they would
otherwise be.

Still another way churches contribute to civic argument is connected
with the way some church leaders see their role and responsibilities.
The Catholic bishops think of themselves in the first instance as moral
teachers and pastors who have inherited a long tradition of moral and political thought. They have a duty to transmit this patrimony to American
Catholics, to bring that tradition of thought to bear on public issues as
concerned citizens, and to bring it to bear on their collective experience
as the titular operators of a vast network of institutions providing a varied
array of social services. They do all this in the occasional teachings and
statements they make in the course of their ordinary work. They do so
less frequently but more visibly in the statements and pastoral letters they
issue as a corporate body.

One of the best known of these pastoral letters was that on the
American economy, published in the 1980s.[50] The bishops explicitly

---

[49] The quotes are taken from pp. 264 and 265 of John Coleman, SJ, "Deprivatizing Religion and
Revitalizing Citizenship," in Weithman (ed.), *Religion and Contemporary Liberalism*, pp. 264–90.

[50] *Economic Justice for All: Pastoral Letter on Catholic Social Teaching and the US Economy* (Washington,
DC: National Conference of Catholic Bishops [NCCB], 1986). The pastoral letters issued by
the Catholic bishops of the United States between 1792 and 1983 are collected in *Pastoral Letters*,
volumes I–IV (Washington, DC: United States Catholic Conference [USCC]/NCCB, 1983); a
fifth volume, updating the collection through 1988, was issued in that year.

issued the letter as teachers, as bearers of a tradition of moral thought, as citizens concerned with pressing public affairs and persistent economic injustice, and as the overseers of social service agencies.[51] The letter was intended for Catholics and for the American public more generally, including American public officials.[52] It was intended at once to inform, provoke and persuade. The authors of the letter on the economy attempted to inform their readers by mustering a wealth of empirical data on food and agriculture, poverty, employment, the distribution of wealth in the United States, and the economic relationship of the United States with the developing world. They attempted to provoke discussion by putting forward principles of economic justice and specific economic policies. The reflection that led to these principles and policies drew heavily on the tradition of Catholic moral and social thought. Indeed the composition of the pastoral was itself an important episode in the tradition's development. It advanced that tradition by bringing it into contact with contemporary secular political philosophy[53] and by drawing out its implications for a large, mature market economy. Once issued, the document acquired precedential value. It provided a basis for the bishops' subsequent analyses of and documents on the American economy and social justice.[54] The result was work which is neither liberal nor communitarian but shows the impress of both,[55] and which supports its conclusions by a variety of arguments both religious and secular. It is because the arguments of the pastoral letter are both religious and secular that its authors hoped to persuade so many audiences. The letter was widely discussed by American Catholics and by the public, provoking a preemptive response coauthored by a former secretary of the US Treasury.[56]

One of the reasons *Economic Justice for All* was so timely a contribution was that it appeared during a period of rising prosperity from which the bishops' congregants were benefitting. The bishops used their moral and religious authority to raise pointed moral questions about the distribution of wealth in the United States. The letter called attention to the many poor in the US and to the presence of those left behind by

---

[51] See *ibid.*, "Why We Write," paragraphs 7–11.   [52] *ibid.*, preface, paragraph 3.

[53] For example, *ibid.*, chapter 2, paragraphs 86 and 90 advances a principle of economic justice that sounds remarkably like Rawls's difference principle. Rawls was cited in the first draft of the letter, though not the final one; see *Origins* 14 (1984): 378, note 23.

[54] See, for example, "Everyday Christianity: to Hunger and Thirst for Justice" (Washington, DC: USCC/NCCB, 1998); "A Fair and Just Work Place" (Washington, DC: USCC/NCCB, 1999).

[55] David Hollenbach, SJ, "Liberalism, Communitarianism and the Bishops' Pastoral Letter on the Economy," *Annual of the Society of Christian Ethics* (1987): 21–39.

[56] William E. Simon and Michael Novak, *Liberty and Justice for All* (Notre Dame, IN: Brownson Institute, 1986).

economic recovery. Like other documents the bishops issue, it presented
a sophisticated reflection on the moral implications of public policy. It
did so at a time when the increased use of fax and electronic mail by political pressure groups, the advent of sound-bite political journalism and
the gradual eclipse of the printed word as the medium of mass political
communication make sustained public reflection on political questions
increasingly rare. This made it an especially valuable contribution to
civic argument.

The fact that the pastoral letter on the economy can convey information and represent points of view that might otherwise be unheard
reflects the fact the most audible religious contributions to American
civic argument are often oppositional. They are critical of what are seen
to be powerful trends toward, for example, abortion, assisted suicide
or the coarsening of human sexuality. Sometimes these contributions
are the most audible because the contributions of churches are selec-
tively amplified by public media of communication. A statement by the
Catholic Church opposing abortion is more likely to be widely reported
and discussed than one opposing the increased concentration of wealth
in the hands of a small percentage of Americans, in part because the
former plays into prejudices that the latter does not. At other times, of
course, these statements are the most audible because they are made
most loudly and persistently. Oppositional advocacy, at least when it
is put in the form of argument, contributes to the intellectual vitality
of civic argument in a democratic society. Sometimes it contributes by
mustering information that it would otherwise be convenient to ignore.
Sometimes it contributes by forcefully putting forward alternative and
unpopular interpretations of values that democracy professes to advance,
interpretations intended to challenge the complacency of the majority
or the received understandings of what participation or full participation
should confer. The Catholic bishops put forward such a reinterpretation
in *Economic Justice for All*, arguing that "the American promise of liberty
and justice for all give the poor and the vulnerable a special claim on
the nation's concern."[57] So too did Martin Luther King, when he implied that relationships among fellow citizens in a democracy ought to
go beyond civic friendship to what he called "total interrelatedness."[58]
These alternatives may be put forward in moral language that might not
otherwise be employed to discuss politics.

[57] *Economic Justice for All*, chapter 1, paragraph 19.
[58] Cited by Robert M. Franklin, "'With Liberty and Justice for All': the Public Mission of Black
Churches," in W. Clark Gilpin (ed.), *Public Faith: Reflections on the Political Role of American Churches*
(St. Louis: CBP Press, 1990), p. 56.

Sometimes the language is biblical in its resonances; this was notably true of Martin Luther King, who tapped collective acquaintance with the Hebrew and Christian scriptures to persuade the United States to make African-Americans full participants in American society. As King's biblical allusions showed, the imagery and stories of the Bible could be used to express the aspirations for freedom that fueled the civil rights movement. Religion can also provide the concepts and narratives which some groups believe most accurately convey their experiences and aspirations. For some African-American theologians, the exodus illustrates God's role as the liberator of the oppressed. The oppression from which God wants humanity liberated, they argue, includes racial discrimination and injustice.[59] African-American women who want to narrate their experiences of oppression and alienation may invoke the biblical story of Hagar, the slave woman cast out of the house of Abraham.[60]

Like Martin Luther King, the Catholic bishops sometimes use biblical language or language with biblical resonances. Their arguments on a range of questions more commonly rely on the premise that human beings have an inviolable dignity because they are made in God's image. For example, in *Economic Justice for All* they write:

The basis for all that the Church believes about the moral dimensions of economic life is its vision of the transcendent worth – the sacredness – of human beings . . . Human personhood must be respected with a reverence that is religious. When we deal with each other, we should do so with the sense of awe that arises in the presence of something holy and sacred. For that is what human beings are: we are created in the image of God (Gen. 1.27). Similarly, all economic institutions must support the bonds of community and solidarity that are essential to the dignity of persons.[61]

Their arguments draw out the implications of this inviolable dignity for participation and full participation. Premises about human dignity are natural claims with which to begin these arguments since, as I remarked when I introduced the notion of participation in chapter 1, "participant" and "full participant" are status terms. A valued status carries dignity

59 Peter J. Paris, "Comparing the Public Theologies of James H. Cone and Martin Luther King," in Hopkins (ed.), *Black Faith and Public Talk* (Maryknoll: Orbis, 1999), pp. 218–31, especially p. 222.
60 Delores Williams, *Sisters in the Wilderness* (Maryknoll: Orbis, 1993). For the importance of narrative in political discussion, see Iris Marion Young, *Inclusion and Democracy* (Oxford: Oxford University Press, 2000), pp. 70ff.
61 *Economic Justice for All*, paragraph 28. For connections among dignity, participation, and full participation in other spheres of American life, see "From Alien to American: Acceptance Through Citizenship" (Washington, DC: USCC/NCCB, 1998) and "Human Dignity Through Naturalization" (Washington, DC: USCC/NCCB, 1994).

with it. A natural way to determine what rights and privileges that status should confer is to ask what rights and privileges befit the dignity of someone who has it.

It is tempting for those who take part in civic argument to rely largely or exclusively on terms and premises which have become familiar because they are used in public political debate by public officials who are trying to build consensus or appeal to a number of constituencies. Thus when we reason about poverty, it is tempting to claim that it is unjust or restricts the autonomy of the poor. These claims are true. But exclusive reliance on claims about fairness and autonomy keeps us from seeing this truth in a different light. Reading that the institutions which create poverty are "forms of social sin" can provoke or offend.[62] The shock value of the provocation can itself have a moral pay-off since we can be shaken from our complacency by offensive speech. Alternative moral concepts can also expand the imagination and challenge us simply by their novelty.

Perhaps talk of human dignity can be recast in more familiar moral vocabulary or its conclusions supported in other terms. But if these other arguments were employed exclusively, the opportunity to see issues in a new light or from a different point of view would be lost. Providing these opportunities is part of what the exchange of ideas in democratic deliberation is for. These opportunities, especially the opportunities to rethink issues which bear on the worst-off, are particularly valuable in societies characterized by great differences of power and wealth. These are societies in which the poor have especially powerful incentives to develop adaptive preferences, and in which it is especially tempting for the better off to ignore the poor or to deceive themselves about their deprivation and subjective well-being.

SOME CONDITIONS ON DEBATE ABOUT PARTICIPATION AND FULL PARTICIPATION

In the first chapter I said that political conflicts about participation and full participation should be settled by informed public political debate in which the interests of all citizens are adequately represented. Since legislative and policy questions are settled in governmental fora, I want to lay down some plausible conditions on public political debate in governmental fora about participation and full participation. Satisfaction of these conditions, which churches help to bring about, helps make that debate better informed and more representative than it would otherwise be.

---

[62] *Economic Justice for All*, paragraph 77.

(2.1) *The minimally democratic agenda condition.* The agenda of public political debate in governmental fora should not be set entirely by political elites or public officials; ordinary citizens should be able to affect it. This is necessary if the political issues of concern to ordinary citizens are to be adequately aired and addressed.

(2.2) *The adequate representation condition.* Some philosophers who argue that political questions should be settled by public deliberation mean that they should be settled by deliberation in which large segments of the public take part. But while this may be desirable for some purposes, it is not clear that this is necessary if debate is to be adequately informed or representative. For the purposes that concern me, what is required is that diverse segments of the public be represented in public deliberations. Representation might be by elected representatives, nongovernmental organizations and private associations.

(2.3) *The deliberative basis condition.* Discussion that takes place in government fora should be the basis for political decisions which are ultimately reached. It should not simply precede decision-making without affecting it. Still less should it camouflage the real basis for decisions. This ensures that points of view which are represented when (2.2) is satisfied are actually taken into account.

(2.4) *The publicity condition.* The public political debate with which I am concerned now takes place in governmental fora. It therefore takes place in fora the proceedings of which should be open in some way to public view. This enables citizens to assure themselves that they can affect the political agenda, that their points of view are adequately represented and taken into account, and that decision-makers act knowing citizens can assure themselves of these things.

Churches can do relatively little to bring about satisfaction of the last two conditions. They can, however, help bring it about that public political debate in governmental fora satisfies the *minimally democratic agenda* and *adequate representation conditions*.

They can help to satisfy the *minimally democratic agenda condition* by way of their contributions to civic argument because the discussion that takes place outside governmental fora influences debate inside them. The salience of issues in civic argument can force them on to the state's agenda or ensure their continued presence and prominence there. For example, in 1995 Pope John Paul II declared the Catholic Church opposed to the death penalty in all but the most exceptional circumstances.[63] Since then the American Catholic bishops have been more active in asserting their own long-standing opposition to it. They have taken advantage of the annual observance of Christ's execution on Good Friday to draw increased

[63] Pope John Paul II, *Evangelium Vitae*, paragraph 56.

attention to their position.[64] The increased awareness of this position among Catholics has, in turn, led large numbers of them to join with people of other faiths in petitioning state governments for a moratorium on the death penalty.[65]

What of the *adequate representation condition?* As a result of engaging in charitable activities and establishing institutions that provide social services, churches acquire a stake in legislation that affects those institutions and the segments of the population they serve. Furthermore, churches provide the services they do from a concern for charity and justice and the associated interest in bettering the lives of those who need them. These same concerns and interests give churches an interest in the legislation and policy that could also better their lives. Churches' experience gives them insight into the social conditions to which their efforts are a response, and, in some cases, into the political decisions that helped to create those conditions.

Some of the political activity in which churches engage is a natural consequence of their having acquired stakes and expertise through their involvement in charitable and service work. This is especially clear in the case of church lobbying, Congressional testimony by church representatives and in some major public statements by churches themselves. These forms of ecclesiastical political activity are far less discussed or attended to than the mass mail campaigns and grass-roots political activity of highly visible conservative groups like the Moral Majority or, more recently, the Christian Coalition. These latter activities are the forms of religious political activity most salient in both the popular and philosophical imaginations. Strong reservations about these latter activities explain the sympathy many feel for moral restrictions on religious political activity. Their salience obscures other forms of activity which might support different or more carefully qualified conclusions about the value of appealing to religion in the public forum. I therefore want to look more closely at these other forms of political activity.

The proliferation of lobbying and interest groups in recent decades has been accompanied by an increase in religious organizations devoted to lobbying and to public policy research.[66] These organizations vary in their relationship to churches. Some base their legislative agenda on their

[64] "A Good Friday Appeal to End the Death Penalty" (Washington, DC: USCC/NCCB, 1999).

[65] "Diocese Observing 'Moratorium Sunday' Oct. 29," *NC Catholic*, October 22, 2000, p. 3. See also the Tennessee entry on the "State News" page of the "Catholics Against Capital Punishment" website; at the time of writing news about the interfaith petition to the Tennessee state government can be found at http://www.igc.org/cacp/news_06.html

[66] Allen D. Hertzke, *Representing God in Washington* (Knoxville: University of Tennessee Press, 1988), pp. 213–16 for a partial list.

own interpretation of a church's teaching; some base it on an authoritative interpretation but have no official connection with the church itself. Still others have been separately incorporated by a church or group of churches in order to conduct research and to advance the church or churches' public policy agenda. The United States Catholic Conference (USCC), for example, has an official connection to the Catholic Church since it was incorporated by the National Conference of Catholic Bishops (NCCB) of the United States. When the USCC issues a statement on a matter of public policy, undertakes lobbying efforts or files an *amicus* brief, it does so on behalf of the American bishops.[67] The USCC's Office of Government Liaison tracks and lobbies for or against legislation and public policy that has an impact on churches and on religious liberty. It does the same with a wide range of legislation and policy touching on social, economic, cultural and global issues for which the teachings of the Catholic Church have implications. Because the Catholic Church has historically been a force in American politics, especially American urban politics, because it continues to wield some political influence among voters, because the propriety of political activity by churches is itself an important philosophical issue and because the work of the USCC *is* the work of the American Catholic bishops, the political efforts of the USCC provide an example that is worth pursuing.

As would be expected, the legislative agenda of the Office of Government Liaison for the 105th Congress attaches importance to pro-life legislation and to legislation concerned with religious freedom, religious education and with the voluntary support of religion.[68] In that agenda,

---

[67] For a brief history of the USCC and the NCCB, see Thomas Reese, SJ, *A Flock of Shepherds* (New York: Sheed and Ward, 1992).

[68] The Office of Government Liaison sorts legislation in which it is interested into four categories: Lobbying, Tracking/Lobbying, General Advocacy, and Monitoring. Legislation is put into the first when a "Substantively important issue [is] addressed <u>which is likely to be enacted by Congress. The USCC expects to commit all appropriate lobbying efforts to amend, pass or defeat specific legislation</u>. If Congressional action favorable to the USCC position is uncertain, the USCC intends to commit the necessary resources at the 'grassroots' level to insure the Congress takes action" (underline original). It falls into the second if a "Substantively important issue [is] addressed in legislation <u>which is likely to be seriously considered</u> by Congress on which <u>the USCC expects to take a formal position and may or may not commit additional efforts to influence its disposition by Congress</u>" (underline original). It falls into the third if a "Substantively important issue [is] addressed in legislation <u>which is likely to be seriously considered</u> by Congress on which the <u>USCC expects to take a formal position but does not anticipate committing additional lobbying efforts to influence</u> its disposition by Congress" (underline original). The agenda mentioned in the text fall into one of these three categories. I reserve the word "lobby" for the first, while using "track" for the second and "advocate" for the third. The descriptions of these categories and all information about the USCC Office of Government Liaison's agenda comes from the "Legislative Agenda for the 105th Congress," on file with the USCC. I am grateful to the staff of the office for making this document available to me.

the office indicated that it would lobby for a ban on so-called "partial-birth abortions" and for legislation maintaining a federal ban on funding for experiments that destroy human embryos. It indicated that it would lobby for legislation that prohibits the use of federal monies to pay for physician-assisted suicide, an effort consistent with the Catholic Church's efforts to prevent both the legalization of this practice and the constitutional recognition of a "right to die."[69] It indicated that office staff would track legislation protecting existing provisions for the participation of religious students and teachers in federal programs, legislation that includes religious school administrators, instructors, drug and guidance counselors in professional development programs, and legislation which includes religious school students in services provided by the "'America Reads' Challenge." It indicated that the USCC would lobby for legislation to increase existing incentives for charitable giving.

The USCC takes an especially strong interest in what rights, liberties and protections should come with participation and full participation in American society. The agenda signaled the intent to lobby for according special protection to children's health in the Clean Air and Clean Water Act. It shows that the USCC's interest in the protection of refugees and immigrants is particularly intense. The Office of Government Liaison indicated it would lobby against efforts to cap the number of refugees that can be admitted to the US and in favor of protecting, enhancing and financing the settlement of refugees in this country. It also indicated that it would track and oppose "legislation to create new limits on legal immigration," "efforts to legislatively increase draconian border enforcement methods" and legislation that would "further diminish the safety net available to legal immigrants." It indicated that it would track and support efforts to restore due process protections in immigration proceedings and legislation to "mitigate the damage" done by welfare reform, "which virtually eliminated most immigrants' eligibility for public benefits." The USCC also takes a strong interest in what it calls "Domestic Social Development." The legislative agenda indicated that the Office of Government Liaison would advocate campaign finance reform to promote wider political participation "especially for the poor and vulnerable" and track legislation attempting to dismantle affirmative action. It indicated that it would lobby for "redress of provisions in new

[69] For the bishops' argument against according constitutional protection to the "right to die," see the *amicus* brief filed with the US Supreme Court by the USCC in the cases of *Quill* and *Glucksberg*. The brief can be found in *Origins* 26, December 12, 1996, pp. 421, 423–30. These cases were also the subject of a letter written to the justices of the Court by the late Cardinal Joseph Bernardin of Chicago. The letter is reprinted in Joseph Bernardin, *A Moral Vision for America*, ed. John Langan, SJ (Washington: Georgetown University Press, 1998), pp. 129–30.

welfare law eliminating food stamps for adults 18–50 without dependents," that it would assume "a leadership role in developing legislative proposals to address the current lack of health care for children and pregnant women not eligible for Medicaid or covered by employer-provided private insurance" and that it would lobby against "efforts to lessen the role of the federal government as a partner in providing low income housing."

The bishops' interest in the legislation which their Office of Government Liaison indicated it would track, support or oppose in the 105th Congress stems from the same conviction that led them to put forward specific economic policies in *Economic Justice for All*: the conviction that legislation and public policy are means by which to build an economic and social world they regard as more just. As I indicated, in writing the pastoral letter the bishops arrived at their conclusions about the demands of justice in part by reflecting on the American Catholic Church's experience in providing social services. They reflected on these experiences in light of a long tradition of moral thought and the publication of the results was an important moment in the development of that tradition. Much the same can be said about the formulation of their legislative agenda. The experience of running far-flung missionary and development efforts gives them access to information about conditions in many parts of the developing world. This no doubt influenced their decision to press for humanitarian aid for central Africa. The experience of running large schools and hospitals systems that increasingly serve the poor influenced their conclusions about legislation affecting education and health care.[70] Their views on how the law should treat legal and illegal immigrants and refugees reflect their experience of ministering to these groups.[71] Transmission of these views helps public political debate satisfy the *adequate representation condition.*

Lobbying for legislation, especially when lobbying is accompanied by testimony before the relevant committees, is a way of sharing these experiences and showing how the information they provide supports the legislation in question. A typical example is the testimony given on immigration reform to the Immigration Sub-Committee of the House Judiciary Committee by John Swenson, Executive Director of Migration and Refugee Services of the USCC.

[70] On the experience of running schools systems and its influence on the bishops' public policy stance, see "Principles for Educational Reform in the United States," *Origins* 25, February 22, 1996, pp. 588–91.
[71] See, for example, Bishop Robert Lynch, "The Human Story Behind an INS Round-Up," *Origins* 26, October 3, 1996, pp. 245, 247; also Nine Georgia Priests, "The Essentials in Reforming Immigration Law and Practice," *Origins* 25, August 10, 1995, pp. 155–56.

The Roman Catholic Church in the United States has a special sensitivity to the newcomers in our midst. Since the founding of this nation, the Catholic Church has been assisting immigrants and these immigrants have, in turn, profoundly shaped the character of the Church in the United States. As a result, the Church . . . has also developed a special knowledge of human migration, both in its effects on human beings involved and in its legal technicalities. I will draw on that experience in my testimony today. As part of a global Church, the US Catholic Conference hopes to bring to this discussion a more transnational perspective on immigration. This broader viewpoint is concerned with the common good of all peoples.[72]

Lobbying and testimony can be among the most important ways that information is transmitted to lawmakers in a representative democracy. Lobbying and testimony by churches can be one of the most important ways of pointing out the moral implications of the legislation being considered. It can be especially important when those who work with the poor and the marginalized transmit information and make moral arguments that might not otherwise be voiced or heard. Of the nineteen witnesses who testified before the House Immigration Sub-Committee on this occasion only two, including Swenson, represented organizations which provide social (as opposed to legal) services for refugees and immigrants. Swenson was one of only two witnesses who criticized the bill for its potential to break up the families of immigrants and refugees.[73] The hearings at which Swenson testified were called at short notice. Relatively few witnesses were called for so important a piece of legislation, and so the hearings no doubt fell short of what is required by the *adequate representation condition*. Swenson's testimony illustrates how churches can make such hearings more representative – and thus more democratic – than they would otherwise be.

Ecclesiastical lobbying also affects wider civic argument by affecting the political behavior and opinions of the church's members. This is so because the arguments by which a church defends its political position presumably have some impact on the arguments by which its members

---

[72] Swenson testified on June 29, 1995. His testimony concerned HR 1915, the "Immigration in the National Interest Act" of 1995. At the time of writing the official record of his testimony can be found at http://www.house.gov/judiciary/609.htm

[73] Other witnesses were less bothered by this possibility. Robert Rector, Senior Policy Analyst for the Heritage Foundation, said near the end of his testimony that "US immigration policy should also dramatically reduce the number of low skilled, poorly educated immigrants and should increase the relative share of high skilled immigrants. *This can be accomplished by dramatically reducing the high number of relatives entering by way of family preference under current law*" (emphasis added). He opened his testimony by remarking that "The United States welfare system is rapidly becoming a deluxe retirement home for the elderly of other countries." Rector's testimony can be found at http://www.house.gov/judiciary/605.htm

defend theirs and on the reasons they have for voting as they do. Exactly what that impact is is hard to specify. It may be that some religious believers examine their own political positions in light of the arguments and principles their churches put forward. Often, particularly when those arguments and principles are quite detailed, a church's engagement with political issues is more likely to have an impressionistic effect. Church members may get the impression that their churches have positions on issues of economic justice or foreign aid and that those issues are to be thought of as issues on which moral considerations as well as self-interested or strategic ones have some bearing. Whether they conceive of those moral considerations as exclusively religious and whether they come to think of the social good in largely religious terms depends upon the arguments the church teaches its members to deploy, on the impressions it creates and on the kind of citizens it encourages them to be. This, in turn, depends upon what church members hear discussed in church meetings and from the pulpit, and upon what memories they retain of the church's more systematic attempt to educate them in the social and political implications of their faith.[74] If a church develops a wide range of moral arguments in defense of its positions, it is to be expected that its members will retain at least the impressions that a wide range of moral considerations bear on public issues and that public issues bear on the social good as well as on their own. Creating these impressions is itself an important contribution.[75]

The Catholic Church may or may not be atypical of American churches in the amount of research and lobbying it undertakes, in the wide range of issues that it confronts and in the sophistication of the secular political analysis that it employs.[76] Even if it is, some examination of its political activities is useful for a number of reasons. One is that that examination reveals a neglected part of the behavior to which norms of public political argument and activity would apply. It is useful to have the example before us to test the plausibility of those norms. Another is

---

[74] See Anthony Bryk, Valerie Lee, and Peter Holland, *Catholic Schools and the Common Good* (Cambridge, MA: Harvard University Press, 1993), p. 289 for some discussion of the citizenship encouraged by Catholic schools and a passing contrast with "fundamentalist academ[ies]."

[75] *ibid.*, pp. 340–41.

[76] It might seem that denominations without their own traditions of systematic theological inquiry or with a tradition of scripturally based ethics would be limited in the secular arguments they can muster. Where this is so, it might also seem that the pronouncements on public issues which representatives of these churches are invited to make would reflect this and reinforce the tradition. In fact matters are more complicated. See Gilbert Meilander's remarks on cloning, made to the National Bioethics Advisory Council on March 13, 1997 and published as Gilbert Meilander, "Begetting and Cloning," *First Things* (June/July 1997): 41–43. I am grateful to Maura Ryan for this reference.

that the example of the Catholic Church illustrates how the provision of social services can be linked to a church's public political activity and argument. Still another is that it illustrates the consequences such argument and activity can have for the intellectual life of the church in question: the felt imperative to put forward arguments in the form of public statements and Congressional testimony can lead the church to further refinement and development of its moral positions and arguments, including the secular arguments it offers for those positions. Examination of the Catholic Church's political activity therefore goes some way to dispelling the stereotype of religious lobbying according to which it advances conservative positions on a handful of issues through the use of political pressure or crude religious argument. In doing so, it provides an example of religiously inspired political activity and argument that makes valuable contributions to civic argument and public political debate about participation and full participation in American society.

As I noted in the last section, these contributions are sometimes oppositional or contestational. It is important, however, that churches do not contest political outcomes on the grounds that democratic institutions should be replaced by undemocratic ones or that liberal and democratic values should give way to values of some other kind. Rather they oppose some arguments about what participation and full participation in liberal democracy require with others. They offer alternative accounts of the authority of liberal and democratic values, and of why full participation in democratic society is important. This is especially clear in the cases of Martin Luther King and the Catholic bishops, discussed at the end of the last section. If these arguments and accounts have even an impressionistic effect, the impression will be that political questions bearing on participation and full participation in a liberal democracy like the United States must be settled on the basis of liberal and democratic values such as freedom and equality, somehow understood. And if this is so, then it adds an important qualification to my argument that churches encourage their members' effective identification with their citizenship. Churches encourage their members' effective identification with their *democratic* citizenship. This draws further confirmation from one last contribution that churches make to liberal democracy.

RELIGION AND POLITICAL LEGITIMACY

Contemporary philosophical discussions of institutional legitimacy, support and stability typically focus on the reasons citizens have to support and to regard as legitimate institutions which comply with principles of justice.[77] This focus is largely due to the fact that Rawls has devoted so much attention to these questions. Yet citizens' support of any existing democracy, including the United States, arguably depends upon their acknowledging the legitimacy of institutions which fall well short of the demands of justice. Distinguishing and measuring the various sources of political support in modern democracies is a notoriously complicated business; indeed the meanings of "political support" and "political legitimacy" are themselves highly controverted.[78] I cannot hope to settle these matters here. I simply note that the support many citizens actually render to the institutions under which they live depends upon at least two things. First, it depends upon citizens' positive affect for their country, the corporate entity governed by those institutions. This, in turn, may depend upon reverence for its origins and for the great figures of their country's past, upon attachment to the moral and political ideals for which they believe their country stands, and upon their inarticulate sense that patriotism is a virtue. Their support for institutions also depends upon their belief that those institutions enjoy some political legitimacy. Belief in institutional legitimacy itself may depend upon the factors that engender positive affect. In a democracy, it also depends upon citizens' belief that those institutions are responsive: upon the widely shared beliefs that political outcomes depend in some way upon the preferences of the people, that those outcomes are satisfactory even if suboptimal, and that justice can be approximated, changes brought about and institutions themselves reformed through established political processes if that is what the people wish.

I want to suggest that organized religion contributes to American democracy by helping to build up these sources of support for democratic institutions. The fact that churches engage in the various forms of political activity discussed earlier – teaching that there is a religious obligation to vote, disseminating political information, serving as venues for political recruitment, hosting candidate visits, lobbying – can be explained only by their belief that American political institutions are responsive. This is a belief which will be transmitted to their members and, to the extent that it is, will contribute to their support for American

---

[77] See Thomas Nagel, *Equality and Partiality* (Oxford: Oxford University Press, 1991), pp. 33ff. For a nuanced alternative, see A. John Simmons, "Justification and Legitimacy," *Ethics* 109 (1999): 739–71.

[78] See, for example, David Easton, "A Reassessment of the Concept of Political Support," *British Journal of Political Science* 5 (1975): 435–57; also M. Stephen Weatherford, "Measuring Political Legitimacy," *American Political Science Review* 86 (1992): 149–66.

political institutions. Indeed black churches have worked to transmit this belief despite great disparities between political outcomes which affect their congregants and the national ideals which they teach their congregants to support.[79] It would be more difficult to document ways in which churches foster positive affect for country and the dispositions on which that affection depends. Some churches may explicitly teach their members to revere those who have played important roles in American political history.[80] Some may teach that their church owes its existence or well-being to religious liberty and the institutions that sustain it. Some churches, in efforts to demonstrate that their members can be good citizens, have consistently taught their congregants that the United States is worth dying for.[81] Where these teachings have taken root, churches can claim to have fostered a belief in institutional legitimacy and to have sown the seeds of political support, to have taught that the citizenship with which their members should identify is democratic citizenship.

The rapid changes characteristic of large industrial democracies, the increased social and geographic mobility they demand, the moral pluralism they encourage and the erosion of traditional communities and ways of life that they bring about, can all engender a profound sense of dislocation if not alienation. It is inevitable that these will be felt and that they will find expression. In the United States citizens have often turned to religion for the concepts they need to articulate their frustrations and to describe what they think has been lost as a result of the changes in their social world. They have also turned to organized religion as a foundation for political reactions against some of the forces of change. This is connected with the fact that religious political argument is often oppositional. It is also why so many liberal thinkers are disturbed by the prominence of religion in American public political debate. Because American religion has historically supplied some of the conceptual and political resources citizens have used to react against their felt dislocation, religious support for basic American political institutions is all the more important. Elsewhere in the world, citizens turn to nationalism, tribalism, fascism or extreme forms of fundamentalism for the resources they need and reject liberal democracy as a result. The fact that American

---

[79] Peter J. Paris, *The Social Teaching of the Black Churches* (Philadelphia: Fortress Press, 1985), pp. 30–31.

[80] In a pastoral letter issued by the Third Plenary Council of Baltimore, December 7, 1884, the American Catholic Bishops wrote: "We believe that our country's heroes were the instruments of the God of nations in establishing this home of freedom; to both the Almighty and to His instruments in this work, we look with grateful reverence[.]" *Pastoral Letters*, volume 1, p. 216.

[81] *ibid.*, volume 1, pp. 295, 321; for black churches, see Paris, *Social Teaching*, p. 31.

religions support American constitutionalism[82] may be important in explaining why what American reactions there are against modernity are relatively well contained.

CONCLUSION

In this chapter I have argued that churches make valuable contributions to American liberal democracy. The value of the contributions churches make to democracy should, I believe, lead us to reconsider intuitions according to which this argument and activity violate the expectations it is reasonable for citizens to have of one another. To determine whether someone does something wrong when she votes against an assisted suicide referendum for religious reasons or weighs her religiously based opposition to capital punishment heavily when deciding whether to vote against a candidate who favors it, we need to see how she was brought to her convictions. The fact that she was brought to them by mechanisms by which she realized her citizenship ought, I believe, to undermine the intuition that she has done something wrong by voting on her convictions. For since some citizens have realistically available opportunities to participate in politics only because their engagement has been facilitated by a religious organization, it is possible that the only reasons they have for getting involved at all or for getting involved in controversy over a particular issue are religious ones. To maintain that citizens should not engage in political action solely for religious reasons is to require these citizens to withdraw from democratic politics, or at least from political involvement on the issue in question. To maintain that churches should not be engaged in politics is, in effect, to require that they not facilitate the realized citizenship of large numbers of Americans. A properly democratic view would, I believe, preserve the valuable contributions that religion makes. Or so I shall argue.

The arguments of this section and of this chapter presuppose that churches contribute to democracy when they educate and recruit citizens who otherwise would not take part in the process of self-government, when they help to equalize the resources needed for effective political

---

[82] I make this claim with an important caveat. The role of religion in the ideology of the American militia movement requires much more study than it has received. So, too, does the relationship between that ideology and American constitutionalism, since many militias oppose the United States government precisely because they claim it has overstepped its constitutional bounds. For a recent and accessible study of American militias which touches on the role of religion, see Kenneth Stern, *A Force Upon the Plain: the American Militia Movement and the Politics of Hate* (New York: Simon and Schuster, 1996).

participation and when they contribute to public political debate and to civic argument. Implicit in these assumptions, and in the chapter, is a conception of democracy according to which political processes become more democratic as more information is transmitted to elected representatives, as more citizens develop a vivid attachment to the public good, as more citizens have realistically available opportunities to take part in politics on a more equal footing, and as civic argument and public political debate become more representative, informed and diverse. So far I have relied on the concepts of participation and full participation to make this view of democracy plausible. I believe that the concepts of participation and full participation are useful both for locating important functions churches fulfill and for arguing that their doing so contributes to the democracy of American politics or helps to make American politics as democratic as it is. But these concepts are not part of mainline democratic theory, as I noted when I introduced them. The assumptions of the chapter may go beyond what many liberal democratic theorists are prepared to grant. In the next chapter I therefore support the conclusions of this one by appealing to different assumptions about democracy than those I have relied on so far.

CHAPTER 3

Conceptions of the democratic citizen

In the previous chapter I adduced evidence that churches perform a number of activities which contribute to the democratic character of American politics. These activities foster or consist in just the forms of religiously motivated political behavior and religious political argument which some philosophers think should be subject to moral restrictions. The observance of such restrictions is typically said to promote liberal democratic values. I suggested that this claim needs to be rethought in light of the conditions that produce this behavior and argument, and the contributions churches make to democracy. This suggestion can be made good only by identifying the features of political processes that make them democratic. The suggestion also seems to depend upon the claim that political processes can be more or less democratic in character. In what follows I shall assume that this is so. I shall assume, that is, that "democratic" is a degree concept and that political processes can be more or less democratic. The degree to which they are so will then depend in some way upon how they exhibit and combine what might be called their "democracy-conducing" features.

This last conclusion points to a host of complex and intriguing philosophical questions. It could be, at least in theory, that there is no limit to the degree to which political processes can be or become democratic. On the other hand, one natural way to ground judgments about the degree to which a subject possesses some morally desirable property is by tacit reference to maximal, perfect or ideal possession. It is therefore natural to ask whether there is some one way that political processes could combine democracy-conducing features so as to be maximally democratic and, if there is, whether processes which are maximally democratic are also ideally or perfectly so.

Alternatively, it may be incoherent to speak of a unitary ideal of democratic practice. Perhaps democracy is best understood pluralistically. Perhaps there are a number of different and optimal ways of combining the various features which make political processes democratic, and perhaps each of these ways of doing so merits the honorific "ideal." If it is assumed for the sake of argument that ideals carry with them prima facie reasons to attempt to realize them, then this pluralistic conception of democracy raises two further questions: whether a society could have ultima facie reasons to pursue one ideal of democracy rather than another and, if so, upon what possession of such ultima facie reasons depends. Any conception of a democratic ideal, whether unitary or pluralistic, depends upon assumptions about the circumstances in which that ideal could be realized. Distinguishing those circumstances which are constitutive of the ideal from those which are prerequisites of its realization is itself a complicated philosophical task. So too is the comparative study of moral and political ideals which presuppose circumstances that can rarely if ever be realized and those which can be realized under circumstances that are highly favorable but realistic.

Further questions arise once attention is shifted from ideal democracies to actual ones. One such question is how societies which balance democracy-conducing features in different ways are to be compared and ranked if, indeed, they can be ranked at all. Another concerns what it would be rational for a society to do if faced with the necessity of trading off one of these features against another. A full treatment of these matters would also take up the sentiments appropriate to recognizing that we have conformed or failed to conform to an ideal. It would discuss aspiration, which I take to be a distinctive form of moral motivation with special connections to ideals. It would take account of important distinctions among the genres of political literature in which social and political ideals have been presented, distinctions blurred by the regrettable use of "utopian" as a catch-all.[1] And it would tie these discussions to the fact that human beings seem capable of only episodic commitment to social ideals.[2] The morality of ideals is ill-understood. It is also remarkably understudied, given the perennial appeal of perfectionism in moral philosophy. Unfortunately I cannot pursue these issues in a systematic way. But because restrictions on religious political argument and activity are often presented in tandem with certain democratic ideals, I will have to touch on some of these issues in this and subsequent chapters.

---

[1] For a nuanced discussion, see Judith Shklar, "The Political Theory of Utopia: From Melancholy to Nostalgia," *Daedelus* 94 (1965): 367–81.

[2] On this point, see Arthur M. Schlesinger, Jr., *The Cycles of American History* (New York: Houghton Mifflin, 1986), pp. 25ff.

In the second chapter I argued that churches make American politics more democratic by providing citizens with opportunities to participate in political life, by encouraging them to identify with their citizenship, and by contributing to civic argument and public political debate. I relied on the notions of participation and full participation to explain why promoting realized citizenship and contributing to debate and discussion count as contributions to democracy. But my claims about participation and full participation may go beyond what some democratic theorists are willing to grant. Having used these concepts to describe what churches do, I now want to vindicate the claims of the last chapter by appealing to assumptions about liberal democracy that may seem less controversial, assumptions drawn from liberal democratic theories. Because those who defend restrictions on religious political argument and activity do so in the name of different views of liberal democracy, I do not want my argument to depend on any one view. I shall therefore look at various theoretical accounts of democracy. The data of the last chapter should, I argue, lead those who defend such restrictions to rethink the intuitions on which their arguments rely.

In the first chapter I distinguished the concept of full participation from various conceptions of it. There are also different conceptions of citizenship that can be distinguished from the concept of citizenship. This is important because each of the views of democracy I shall look at is associated with a distinctive conception of citizenship. Because these theories are associated with different conceptions of citizenship, they make different claims about why it is good for citizens as they conceive them to realize their citizenship, different claims about how their doing so makes political processes democratic, and different claims about the value of discussion and debate. I shall argue that proponents of each of the views of democracy I examine have reasons to value the political contributions of churches and to regard those contributions as contributions to democracy, though the reasons vary in strength. Proponents of some views of democracy have stronger reasons to value religion than proponents of others. In order to make these arguments, I must first say something more about conceptions of citizenship.

SPECIFICATIONS OF CITIZENSHIP

The concept of citizenship I introduced in chapter 1 is that of someone who is legally entitled to participate in political affairs. This rough understanding of citizenship leaves much unspecified. It leaves open how citizens should be able to participate in politics or hold officials account-able. It also leaves unstipulated the role-specific capacities and interests of citizens. It leaves open what capacities occupants of that role are presumed to have, what interests are served by cooperating, and what interests are protected when officials know they can be held accountable. Finally, it leaves unspecified what nonobligatory activities are normally associated with the role of citizenship and what obligations citizens have as occupants of it. Thus the concept of citizenship can be elaborated in various ways to yield diverse *conceptions* of democratic citizenship or, as I say, diverse *specifications* of that social role.

Some specifications of citizenship are implicit in the political practices of diverse democratic polities, which accord their citizens somewhat different sets of rights, privileges and responsibilities. These specifications can be teased out by systematic reflection on the political culture of the society in question. Others are consciously elaborated by theories of democratic politics. Different democratic theories specify the role of citizenship in different ways, associating different interests, capacities, duties and characteristic activities with the role and drawing out different normative political implications.

The specifications of citizenship associated with diverse theories can be described in qualitative terms which highlight their differences. Pluralist theories of democracy, for example, are sometimes said to conceive of citizens as "judges" or "referees" of political contests among competing groups. Their primary task is to register their verdicts at the polls.[3] Elitist theories are said to conceive of citizens as consumers of the programs marketed by political elites, consumers whose tastes and preferences, like those of retail customers, are shaped by the individuals and firms whose products are on offer. This seems to have been Joseph Schumpeter's view, for example.[4] A quite different specification of citizenship is associated with theories according to which citizens are participants in public debate who help to set the political agenda and who exercise some control over the political processes which shape their preferences. These gross qual-itative differences among the specifications of citizenship gain further

---

[3] Ronald Dworkin, "The Curse of American Politics," *New York Review of Books*, October 17, 1996, pp. 19–24, at p. 23.

[4] Joseph Schumpeter, *Capitalism, Socialism and Democracy* (New York: Harper and Row, 1976), p. 282. For the lasting impact of Schumpeter's economic conception of citizenship, see Gabriel Almond, "Rational Choice Theory and the Social Sciences," in Kristin Monroe (ed.), *The Economic Approach to Politics* (New York: Harper Collins, 1991), pp. 32–52, especially pp. 34–35. For the need to take account of Schumpeter's view, I am indebted to Joshua Cohen's "Money, Politics, Political Equality" (unpublished manuscript on file with author).

content from different elaborations of citizens' characteristic activities, interests, privileges and role-specific duties.

To see why proponents of different theories of democracy should recognize and value the contributions churches make to liberal democratic politics, it is necessary to look at the different ways they specify the social role of citizenship. Specifications according to which citizens are thought of as participants in public deliberation will presumably have different implications for churches' contributions to civic argument and public political debate than specifications according to which citizens are passive consumers of products offered by political elites. Furthermore, proponents of most specifications presumably think that citizens should identify with that specification or with specifications that are relevantly similar. Those who think of citizens as participants in public deliberation also think, as I shall show, that citizens should come to see themselves that way. Their reasons for valuing the ways churches promote people's effective identification with their citizenship will differ from the reasons other democratic theorists have for valuing this. Reasons for valuing the provision of realistically available opportunities to participate in politics differ as well.

THREE MODERATELY DEMANDING CONCEPTIONS OF DEMOCRACY

(a) Consider a conception of democracy according to which political outcomes are arrived at democratically only if they meet one of two conditions. Either they are the decisions of representatives elected by the people after open and fair elections in which votes are weighted equally and in which public issues are freely debated, or else they are the decisions of public officials accountable to representatives elected in this way. On this view, citizens have various unspecified interests they want government to protect, advance or respect. They can most effectively insure that that happens by holding officials accountable in periodic elections. Thus on this view citizens are thought of primarily as *voters*; voting is the characteristic activity of citizenship. Citizens are not conceived of as having an interest in maintaining substantive political equality or in having that guaranteed or publicly proclaimed by their political institutions. The only requirement of political equality this view imposes is "one person, one vote." It is compatible with the existence of political elites who control the choice of candidates, platforms and policies and who shape public opinion. It is also compatible with the existence of powerful private interests who significantly affect public policy and the choice of alternatives among whom citizens are expected to choose.

Someone who thinks it desirable that political outcomes be democratic even in this weak sense presumably thinks it important that political institutions be responsive to the preferences of citizens, even among restricted alternatives, and that citizens have a well-founded belief that institutions are responsive to preferences. It is natural that someone who endorses this view would also think it desirable that a number of conditions hold which make this responsiveness possible. She will think it desirable that citizens be sufficiently interested to take part in politics at least by voting, that the results of elections reflect the votes of more of the eligible citizens rather than less, and that voters be informed about the positions leading candidates take on the major issues of the campaign. As I have shown, churches help to bring about these conditions by promoting realized citizenship. They provide opportunities for volunteerism that heighten citizens' attachment to the social good, by exposing them to conceptions of it according to which public policy has moral implications, by encouraging voting, by disseminating information about issues and candidates, and by transmitting the view that institutions are responsive. The proponent of this weak conception of representative democracy is therefore bound to recognize that churches make important contributions to American politics by bringing about conditions that she naturally regards as valuable in light of the commitments of her democratic theory.

(b) Votes are very imperfect ways for citizens to inform representatives of their preferences. Consider therefore a somewhat stronger, though still quite weak, variant on the weak conception of democracy. According to this variant, elected officials should not function as an insulated elite who gather their own information and decide on policies themselves. Neither should they rely exclusively on information and incentives provided by economic and social elites or by nonelected political ones. Rather, it is desirable that many citizens have the skills, motivation and confidence necessary to make their concerns known to their representatives between elections. This view takes citizens to be, not merely voters, but *constituents*. They do not only protect their interests merely by electing their representatives; they may also give them periodic instruction.[5] As I have shown, churches foster civic skills and help at least some citizens form the senses of self-worth and political efficacy they need to approach

---

[5] The need to distinguish this view from the previous one is evident from Carlos Santiago Nino's discussion of Schumpeter's theory; see his *The Constitution of Deliberative Democracy* (New Haven: Yale University Press, 1996), pp. 79–82, especially p. 81.

public officials. Proponents of this conception of democracy should value the contributions churches make.

(c) Now strengthen the modified weak conception of democracy so that political outcomes are arrived at democratically only if, in addition to satisfying the requirements of that view, citizens have and believe they have realistically available opportunities to participate in elections and campaigns on a footing of political equality. Let us understand political equality as requiring that citizens' access to political information, their ability to influence the outcomes of elections and their ability to influence their elected representatives are independent of their race, economic status and educational attainment, and that citizens understand themselves as politically equal in this sense. On this view, citizens are thought of as *equal constituents* who reflect on their status as such, who want their status guaranteed and affirmed by their political institutions, and whose political participation is affected by the outcome of their reflections. Clearly the politics of many democracies, including the United States, is far from satisfying the conditions of this stronger view. Indeed the conception of political equality associated with this form of democracy might be presented as part of an ideal theory which we should strive to realize. What matters for present purposes, however, is not the failure of contemporary politics to live up to that ideal or to the norms of political equality, but the role churches play in bringing it about that the conditions of this ideal are realized to the extent that they are.

Here the fact that churches and religious organizations counteract other sources of participatory inequality is crucial. As I have stated already, Verba, Schlozman and Brady argue that "only religious institutions provide a counterbalance" to the tendency of political resources to accrue to the financially and educationally advantaged.[6] They are venues where civic skills are imparted regardless of income and education and they are venues of more egalitarian political recruitment than the job. They provide the encouragement to vote and to organize politically. This is particularly important for African-Americans. In the US the role of black churches in mobilizing their congregants and promoting effective identification with their citizenship is crucial to giving many African-Americans what political power they enjoy. Finally, many churches may foster a sense of equality by making equality of decision-making power manifest in their own internal structures. Or at least this may be so of churches which serve those whose experiences outside

---

[6] Verba, Schlozman and Brady, *Voice and Equality*, p. 18.

the church foster a sense, if not of powerlessness, then of relative political disadvantage. Thus the Catholic Church is more hierarchical than many Protestant churches and it attaches greater emphasis to complementarity of function and division of decision-making labor. Protestant churches, by contrast, are more egalitarian in their internal governance. This is suggested, not only by comparing the structures of ecclesiastical government, but also by the role of women in the Catholic Church and by the fact that the American Catholic Church gives its members fewer opportunities to develop civic skills than do American Protestant churches.[7] The governance of Protestant churches therefore makes one form of equality evident to its members: the equality of power and competence to make decisions affecting this important form of collective life.[8]

It may be that this sense of equality lays the basis for a sense of political equality as well. That is, it may be that citizens who have learned to regard others as their equals in church governance regardless of social and economic status have thereby learned to discount social status and wealth as qualifications for political governance. If so, then since the membership of the Catholic Church in the United States, at least, is relatively affluent, this provides another example of a phenomenon noted earlier in the discussion of black churches. Not only do churches generally go some way toward overcoming the political inequalities created and reinforced by other institutions, but churches which serve the relatively disadvantaged are more effective at doing so than are churches which serve the relatively advantaged. Proponents of the stronger conception of democracy should therefore value the contribution churches make to the realization of citizenship.

TWO VERSIONS OF DELIBERATIVE DEMOCRACY

Now consider the view that has come to be called "deliberative democracy." This is a more demanding conception of democracy than any of those discussed in the previous section. It is premised on an even richer specification of the duties and characteristic activities of citizenship.

---

[7] *ibid.*, pp. 320–25.

[8] It is sometimes said, however, that mainline Protestant churches are more democratic in name than in fact, particularly with respect to the church's stand on public issues; see Hertzke, *Representing God*, p. 203. On criteria of democracy for private associations generally, see James Q. Wilson, *Political Organizations* (Princeton: Princeton University Press, 1995), pp. 235ff. For an argument that the hierarchical structure of Catholic parishes facilitates community organizing and helps parishes contribute to democratic politics, see Mark Warren, *Dry Bones Rattling: Community Building to Revitalize American Democracy* (Princeton: Princeton University Press, 2001). I am grateful to John McGreevy for this reference.

While proponents of deliberative democracy have less compelling reason to value contributions of the sort I have discussed than proponents of other democratic theories, they still have some reason to do so.

As I mentioned earlier, deliberative democracy conceives of citizens as *equal participants* in public debate who help to set political agendas and who control the political processes in which they participate. According to one version of this view, deliberative democracy is a political ideal. In a society which realizes that ideal, political outcomes are democratically arrived at only if they are the outcomes of reasoned deliberations among citizens which are focused on the common good and in which citizens participate as free equals.[9] In a fully deliberative democracy, citizens' deliberation would not be bound by antecedently given norms except those which must be observed for the continuity of free deliberation itself. Political deliberations would be transformative: citizens would not bring preferences to political processes which were antecedently fixed and which they would try to satisfy by strategic voting or by exploiting their power. Rather their preferences would be subject to change through their engagement in public deliberation. Thus political outcomes would be determined only by the persuasiveness of the reasons that are adduced for the outcome by citizens engaged in public deliberation. They would not be determined by the power, wealth or status of those putting forward the arguments or by norms fixed prior to deliberation except for those norms the observance of which is necessary for deliberation itself. Finally, some versions of deliberative democracy include a theory of reasons. Good political reasons – the sort of reasons the force of which should determine the outcome of democratic deliberations – are reasons that would or could be persuasive to every other participant in public deliberation. In a democracy which was fully deliberative, citizens would look for and offer one another reasons of that sort.

Most contemporary democracies clearly fall far short of being ideally deliberative. Quite apart from the shrillness and incivility of contemporary public political debate, some democracies like the United States allow money to play far too large a role in determining the viability of candidacies and the outcome of elections. This violates the deliberative demand of political equality. Furthermore deliberative democracy may well require political and economic structures which are currently

---

[9] The literature on deliberative democracy is very extensive. For the view on which I draw in this paragraph, see Cohen, "Deliberation and Democratic Legitimacy"; also Henry Richardson, "Beyond Good and Right: Toward a Constructive Ethical Pragmatism," *Philosophy and Public Affairs* 24 (1995): 108–41.

lacking, including far greater workplace democracy to effect greater economic equality and to foster deliberative skills,[10] more and stronger political parties, and more fora in which public deliberation can take place. These may be conditions for realizing the ideal of deliberative democracy. Yet, as with the weak and modified conceptions of democracy so with the deliberative one, what is primarily at issue is whether churches play a role in bringing it about that American politics satisfies the requirements of this conception to the extent that it does and thus whether proponents of the view have reason to think that churches help to make democracy as deliberative as it is.

Those who value what deliberative elements there are in American politics have some powerful reasons to value the contributions of churches. What political deliberation American citizens now engage in clearly depends upon their realized citizenship. It depends upon realistically available opportunities for political participation, and hence upon access to political information and to networks of recruitment. We have seen what role churches play in providing such access. Citizens who engage in collective deliberation about politics can do so effectively only if they have the skills and confidence needed to speak out in meetings and political discussions and to get items on the agenda. These skills are fostered by churches. As I have also shown, churches help to foster these skills among those who would otherwise have the fewest opportunities to develop them. They counterbalance inequalities in access to deliberative skills and foster the sense that political competence is independent of wealth and status. They therefore contribute to what might be called "deliberative equality,"[11] the ability to participate in public deliberation on an equal footing. As I argued in the last chapter, religious volunteerism may provide citizens with an opportunity to think about what the social good requires by exposing them to their church's teaching about it. It may also enliven their commitments to it by giving volunteers an opportunity to act on that commitment. This, as we saw, can heighten their sense of their own citizenship and so promote their effective identification with it.

Deliberative democrats are divided about just what civic argument constitutes public deliberation. Some have argued that in a society which

---

[10] For one view of the economic structures that deliberative democracy presupposes, see Joshua Cohen, "The Economic Basis of Deliberative Democracy," *Social Philosophy and Policy* 6 (1988): 25–50.

[11] Jack Knight and James Johnson, "What Sort of Equality Does Deliberative Democracy Require?," in *Deliberative Democracy: Essays on Reason and Politics* (Cambridge, MA: MIT Press, 1997), pp. 279–319, especially pp. 306–07.

realizes the deliberative ideal or approximates it closely, deliberation would take place primarily in "governmental processes" rather than in the fora provided by churches, religious organizations and other voluntary associations.[12] For these thinkers, public deliberation consists in, or primarily in, what I called "public political debate." Others have a more expansive view of public deliberation, thinking it includes political discussion in civil society or in what Jürgen Habermas calls "the public sphere." According to these thinkers, public deliberation includes what I have called "civic argument." I am less concerned with the issues that divide these two positions – though I will touch on them – than I am with showing that those who hold each should value the contributions churches make to public deliberation as they conceive it.

(a) Consider first those who think that public deliberation consists in public political debate, in the discussion of political issues in the public forum. I argued in the last chapter that their provision of social services gives churches a measure of expertise on certain policy issues. Public political debate must surely be informed by expert information.[13] Deliberative democrats should therefore value the role churches play in transmitting information to which they have access in virtue of their social and charitable work. They should value the fact that churches sometimes represent the poor and the marginalized in public political debate, thus helping public political debate satisfy (2.2), the *adequate representation condition*. They should also value the fact that, as we saw in the last chapter, churches sometimes call for the political reforms necessary for the poor and marginalized to represent themselves. Furthermore, there may be some moral considerations bearing on the public good which would not be introduced into public deliberations if churches and their representatives did not introduce them. Even deliberative democrats who do not ultimately find these considerations compelling should recognize the importance of their being publicly articulated and examined.

As I also suggested, the charitable and social work of churches gives them a stake in legislation and public policy affecting their work and those they serve. Their reflection on the experience of doing such work and their interest in legislation provides the motivation to put forward political arguments which, at least in some cases, are addressed to a number of audiences, both religious and nonreligious. Crafting arguments that might be expected to persuade these audiences requires the

---

[12] Sunstein, "Republican Revival," pp. 1541–42.
[13] See Mark Warren, "Deliberative Democracy and Authority," *American Political Science Review* 90 (1996): 46–60.

churches offering them to expand and refine their traditions of moral thought. This, as we have seen in the case of the American Catholic Church, can include the careful analysis of policy issues and the development of secular arguments for their positions. The arguments that result constitute valuable contributions to public political debate in part because of the information and experience that are transmitted. They are also valuable because religious believers who follow the lead of their churches will make more sophisticated contributions to public debate in their own right. Finally, they are the results of practices which deliberative democrats should value: the practices of analyzing policy by using sophisticated intellectual tools, of reasoned political engagement and of accumulating a reservoir of expertise. I noted in the last chapter that these enable churches to issue responsible rather than spasmodic pronouncements when political stakes are especially high and when political deliberation is especially important.

On some accounts, citizens' participation in public deliberation requires that they develop an attachment to the public good and an ability to reason about its requirements. Proponents of deliberative democracy typically think that the content of the public good is to be determined by the on-going deliberations of free and equal citizens.[14] Since the outcome of those deliberations obviously cannot be known before they take place, it is impossible to show that churches foster a commitment to the detailed contents of the public good. Still, if citizens are to be committed to the public good as proponents of deliberative democracy understand it, they must have what John Stuart Mill famously called "enlarged sentiments" that extend beyond their self-interests and group interests. Reliable attachment to the public good, a settled willingness to reason sincerely about what it requires and a readiness to act on the outcome of deliberations even at one's own cost, all require that citizens not be too attached to their own good. The well off, for example, must be able seriously to entertain parting with their material wealth. They must therefore have a temperate disposition to material goods.[15] Certainly many religions teach an enlargement of the sentiments by teaching that the well-being of each depends upon the well-being of all, discouraging greed and encouraging moderation in the accumulation and enjoyment of wealth. This teaching

---

[14] See, for example, Cass Sunstein, *The Partial Constitution* (Cambridge, MA: Harvard University Press, 1993), p. 137.
[15] I take this up at greater length in "Perfectionist Republicanism and Neo-Republicanism" (unpublished manuscript presented at the American Philosophical Association Eastern Division meeting, December 2000).

may not be as successful as we might hope, but in the absence of evidence that it is counterproductive, proponents of deliberative democracy have reason to value it.

Under current conditions, at least in the United States, relatively few ordinary citizens take part in public political debate. Governmental institutions and party structures would have to be significantly reformed to permit or encourage their participation, as deliberative democrats recognize. Thus if American politics became more deliberative, this would be in part because new political institutions were created, but it would also require the reform of the governmental institutions which already exist. It might be that these latter institutions and the political outcomes they produce would then be regarded as legitimate because they were reformed. It might be that citizens would regard these as legitimate because they have come to exhibit the features deliberative democrats prize. Among these is institutional responsiveness. As I argued in the last chapter, politically active churches encourage the expectation that institutions be responsive and the belief that they are. Those arguments therefore show that churches would contribute to citizens' support for deliberative political institutions.

But it seems unlikely that possession of these democracy-conducing features would be the *only* reason citizens will regard reformed institutions and their outcomes as legitimate, or that citizens would take it as a *sufficient* reason to do so. In the absence of very powerful arguments to the contrary drawn from moral and empirical psychology, it seems more likely that the perceived legitimacy of these institutions will also depend crucially upon citizens' recalling the reasons those institutions were regarded as legitimate and enjoyed support even before their reform. Insofar as churches contributed to the support and perceived legitimacy of unreformed institutions, they also contribute to the support and perceived legitimacy of the reformed ones.

It is important to see that the need for institutional reform does not provide reasons for deliberative democrats to deny the value of the contributions churches now make to democracy. Thus it may be that according to the most compelling elaboration of the deliberative view, a fully deliberative democracy would provide ample political fora for public deliberation in the form of strengthened political parties, more frequent public meetings and more accessible media of public communication. It may also be that these fora would supplant voluntary associations as the primary venues of political deliberation and opinion formation. It surely does not follow from *this* claim that political deliberations ought not to take place in voluntary associations under current conditions when these public fora are either relatively inaccessible to ordinary citizens or are altogether absent. These associations provide their members the opportunity to be active and engaged citizens. It may therefore be that what political deliberations now take place in voluntary associations are necessary to move politics closer to a deliberative ideal in which, *ex hypothesi*, far more political deliberation takes place outside voluntary associations than in them.

It may also be that even in an ideally deliberative democracy, characterized by greater economic and political equality, churches would still engage in charitable, educational and social service work. These activities, as I have shown, give churches information and experience of which their representatives could remain valuable conduits. Finally, it could be that churches would continue to play an important role as institutions which foster the skills citizens would employ in public fora when they engage in political deliberations. If such a society would value democracy in the workplace because it fosters civic skills,[16] then it could also rely on and value the demonstrated capacity of churches to do the same thing. Indeed it could do so even if in an ideally deliberative democracy there would be fewer sources of participatory inequality for churches to counterbalance than there are under current conditions.

(b) Now consider deliberative democrats who think that public deliberation should be understood to include discussion and debate outside governmental processes as well as in them. Let us call their view the "broad view of public deliberation." According to the broad view, public deliberation should be understood to include discussions and debates in the associations and communications media of civil society. Associations and the media of public communication identify problems which demand political solutions, help people identify and articulate their interests in political outcomes and their expectations of the state. They are the means by which ordinary citizens, singly and collectively, can put pressure on the state to achieve the outcomes they want. In modern mass societies, the exertion of pressure originating in the debates of civil society is one of the ways ordinary citizens have to express their will. Since democratic theory concerns the expression of the public will on political questions, restricting attention to governmental processes or to public political debate excludes from view some of the proper subject matter of democratic theory. State action that responds to rightly conducted deliberation in civil society is, according to some proponents

---

[16] See Cohen, "Economic Basis of Deliberative Democracy," p. 46.

of the broad view, democratically legitimate. Restricting public deliberation to what takes place in governmental processes and claiming that public deliberation legitimates political outcomes yield a faulty view of political legitimacy.[17]

Proponents of the broad view, like those who restrict public deliberation to what takes place in governmental processes, should value the contributions churches make to public political debate, to the perceived legitimacy of governmental processes, to the enlargement of sentiments and to realized citizenship. They should value the ways in which churches help to get or keep items like the death penalty on the political agenda, thus helping public political debate satisfy (2.1), the *minimally democratic agenda condition*. They should also value the contributions churches make to civic argument. In the last chapter, I showed how churches encourage sustained reflection on the moral dimensions of public policy. They make available arguments that might otherwise be unheard and gather information that might otherwise be ignored. They contest dominant understandings of democratic values. They sometimes do so using theological concepts that can challenge and provoke. Some deliberative democrats think that public deliberation in civil society includes other forms of discourse than argument. They should value the fact that the religious traditions churches bear make narratives and images available that can be used to articulate experiences of oppression and hopes for liberation.[18]

Those who take the broad view must make clear exactly what the relationship is between deliberation broadly conceived and political legitimacy. Surely rightly conducted deliberation about some political outcome cannot be a sufficient condition of political legitimacy, regardless of the form such deliberation takes. It is surely possible that the outcome is illegitimate because it was enacted by a state agent who exceeded her authority by enacting it. But it is hard to see how rightly conducted deliberation can be necessary either. That would make the legitimacy of rational, effective, duly enacted legislation hostage to the proper conduct of deliberation in associations whose connections to the outcome were quite remote. Surely a piece of legislation enacted after public hearings should not be deemed illegitimate simply because of undemocratic deliberations in one of the associations which first identified the problem to which the legislation is a solution. Perhaps adequate deliberation in civil society is neither a necessary nor a sufficient condition of legitimacy, but a contributing one. This could be so if legitimacy is a degree concept and if deliberations in civil society enhance or diminish an outcome's

---

[17] In this paragraph I draw on Young, *Inclusion and Democracy*, pp. 177ff.

[18] See Young, *Inclusion and Democracy*, pp. 70ff. for a discussion of narrative.

degree of legitimacy. Or it could be so if legitimacy, like some perceptual concepts, is a threshold concept – if legitimacy, like smoothness, seems to vary by degrees until it reaches a critical point beyond which all differences are imperceptible – and if deliberations in civil society can help push outcomes across the threshold.

A more pressing question for the broad view grows out of considerations which led other deliberative democrats to restrict public deliberation to governmental processes in the first place. Some proponents of deliberative democracy have reservations about the political role of secondary associations because those associations can encourage political preferences which they regard as undemocratic, illiberal, or unjust. What they think holds true of secondary associations generally may seem especially true of churches and religious organizations: some churches and religious organizations may be thought to encourage preferences for undemocratic, illiberal or unjust political outcomes when abortion rights, physician-assisted suicide, education and the relationship between church and state are at issue. But if the charge against churches is correct, it does not just raise questions for the broad view of public deliberation. It raises very serious questions about the argument I have put forward in this chapter and chapter 2. For if churches really do encourage undemocratic, illiberal or unjust preferences, then the fact that they provide opportunities and skills needed to act on those preferences is not something *any* liberal democratic theorists should value.

ADDRESSING THE OBJECTION THAT RELIGION FOSTERS ILLIBERAL PREFERENCES

Before addressing the claim that churches foster undemocratic or illiberal preferences, I want to pin down the conclusion that that claim is supposed to support. Undesirable preferences can pose a filtering problem for democratic theories of preference aggregation. This is the problem of reliably identifying such preferences so that they can be excluded from purportedly democratic mechanisms of preference aggregation like voting. The claim that churches foster undemocratic or illiberal preferences might be used to support the conclusion that political preferences formed by churches may properly be excluded when preferences are aggregated. Or the claim that churches form undemocratic preferences, plus the claim that religious political preferences are formed by churches, might be used to support the conclusion that citizens ought not express such preferences in political argument or that they ought to be prepared to qualify their expression of those preferences in some way. The claim that churches foster undemocratic preferences might, that is, be used to support just the kind of moral restrictions on public political argument that interest me.

Though the claim might be used to support these conclusions, that is not the way it is being used in the objection I am now imagining. It is being used to make the point that, because of the undemocratic preferences their churches have formed, it would be better if religious citizens were less rather than more engaged in politics. It would be better, for example, if they had fewer opportunities to participate, less access to networks of political recruitment and less effective identification with their citizenship. This, in turn, is supposed to support the conclusion that the political contributions of churches I identified in chapter 2 are not *valuable* contributions to liberal *democracy* at all.

To see how the claim about undemocratic preferences is supposed to support this conclusion, it is useful to distinguish two ways in which a preference can be undemocratic. Preferences can be undemocratic *in content* and they can be *held undemocratically*.

Consider first the claim that churches encourage preferences which are undemocratic in content. This is a claim about the political outcomes churches encourage their members to favor. The objection that begins from this claim says that because churches encourage their members to favor outcomes which are undemocratic, it would be better from the point of view of democratic theory if these citizens were less involved in politics. Because it would be better if they were less involved in politics, churches do not make valuable contributions to democracy by providing them the opportunity and the skills to become involved.

Liberal democracy is a substantive and demanding moral-cum-political view. Surely some political outcomes are incompatible with it. It is natural to describe preferences for those outcomes as undemocratic in content. The problem with the objection now under consideration is not that it asserts that some preferences are undemocratic in content. The problem is that the possibility of preferences which are undemocratic in content cannot be exploited to show that churches do not make valuable contributions to democracy. For if the objection is to work, criteria of undemocratic content must be strong enough that they exclude preferences held by people whose participation is unobjectionable, but weak enough that they include the objectionable preferences which are said to result when citizens acquire political preferences in their churches. These criteria will not be easy to specify.

Suppose, for example, that a preference on some issue is undemocratic in content if it is a preference for an outcome at odds with the outcome a just liberal democracy would reach. And suppose it is possible to specify the outcomes a just liberal democracy would reach. It is overwhelmingly likely that many citizens hold preferences for outcomes that differ from the specified ones on gun control, the appropriate level of the minimum wage, immigration restrictions, agricultural price supports, the regulation of campaign financing, the availability of pornography on the Internet, and trade policy. Yet it would surely be a mistake to conclude that it would be better for liberal democracy if those who hold these preferences were not involved in politics. A stronger criterion of democratic content is necessary, perhaps one which takes account of the importance of the question on which the preference is held.

Suppose instead that a preference is undemocratic in content if it is a preference for an outcome that is at odds with the preconditions of liberal democracy. And suppose that the preconditions of liberal democracy can be identified, perhaps as the preconditions of public deliberation or perhaps as the preconditions for full participation as I discussed it in chapter 1. It is far from clear that most of the preferences which are held to be objectionable – preferences fostered by churches concerning late-term abortion and assisted suicide, for example – are in fact undemocratic in this sense. This is because it is far from clear that the preconditions of public deliberation or full participation are violated by, for example, the prohibition of late-term abortions, the prohibition of physician-assisted suicide, or the requirement that students in public schools be allowed a moment of silence at the beginning of their school day. Proponents of some views of democracy would claim they are not. Others would disagree, arguing that these political outcomes are wrong, undesirable or even unjust. But even if they are, it is far from clear that they are wrong, undesirable or unjust in the way they would have to be if preferences for them are to be undemocratic in content according to the criterion at issue.

Even if a tenable criterion for undemocratic content could be found, it would not obviously be better that citizens with undemocratic preferences be uninvolved or less involved in politics. Truth may be strengthened by contest with error, as John Stuart Mill famously pointed out. Therefore even the advocacy of erroneous positions can contribute to public deliberation. Furthermore, it may also be that in some cases, the right political outcomes are arrived at only as the result of a contest between extreme positions. Thus those who favor the legalization of physician-assisted suicide, for example, surely recognize that the practice would be liable to abuse if not properly regulated. It is surely possible that the regulations many moderate advocates regard as proper would gain popular support only as a compromise between those who favor relatively few restrictions and those who favor absolute prohibition. In that case, citizens who have been encouraged by their churches to hold conservative preferences would serve a valuable political function by pushing political outcomes toward the desirable middle.

Those who hold undemocratic preferences on some issues may hold preferences which are, in the view of the objector I am imagining, unexceptionable or even exemplary on others. As I was at pains to show in the last chapter, some of the churches most prominently associated with the preferences said to be undemocratic in content defend political outcomes on immigration, the death penalty and economic justice that might meet with a different assessment. If these churches are successful in shaping the preferences of their members, then these religious citizens will have some political preferences which are undemocratic in content and others which are not. The claim that it would be better if they were not politically engaged would have to rest on an all-things-considered judgment about the desirability of their acting on both their unobjectionable and their objectionable preferences, a judgment that would be difficult to defend. Finally, not all churches favor the political outcomes which are said to be undemocratic, nor do those that do favor them succeed in imparting them to all their members. Some, perhaps many, religious believers pick and choose. They may acquire their views about economic justice from their churches, but not their views on abortion. The blanket claim that citizens whose preferences were formed in church hold the preferences which are said to be undemocratic in content is too sweeping to be defensible. It therefore cannot be used to support the conclusion that churches do not make valuable contributions to democratic politics.

The argument from undemocratic content was supposed to show that citizens whose political preferences are formed by their churches are unsuited for participation in democratic politics. The argument foundered on the difficulty of showing that citizens in this group have preferences with objectionable contents. But perhaps the problem with these citizens lies, not in what they prefer, but in how they hold their preferences. Perhaps their political preferences are undemocratic because they are undemocratically held.

Some democratic theorists argue that citizens in a democracy should be committed to making political decisions together, on the basis of collective reasoning and discussion. If citizens really are to reason together about political problems or to be properly affected by the collective reasoning of their representatives, they must be committed to listening to others and open to revising their preferences in light of what they hear. Someone holds her preferences undemocratically, it might be said, if she is unwilling to change them as a result of civic argument and public political debate.

According to the argument from undemocratically held preferences, citizens whose political preferences are formed by their churches have the preferences they do because they have acquired views about correct and incorrect political outcomes under the influence of a source they regard as authoritative. Because of the reliability and authority they attribute to that source, they are not open to revising their views. For example, many citizens who have religious reasons for being staunchly opposed to the legality of abortion are convinced that their view is right and the opposing view is wrong. They are not open to revising their positions as a consequence of civic argument or public political debate with others. According to the objection I am imagining, they therefore hold their political preferences undemocratically. They hold their preferences this way because their churches have influenced the content of their preferences and because they regard their churches as authoritative. Moreover, it might be argued, churches encourage them to hold their preferences undemocratically by emphasizing their own authority to speak on matters like abortion. Because churches are responsible for the fact that their members participate in democratic politics in the wrong way, in a way that is at odds with the spirit of democracy, the value of their contribution to democracy is questionable.

The objection from undemocratically held preferences is an objection deliberative democrats will be especially inclined to make. Consistent with their stress on the transformative potential of public deliberation, they claim that citizens engaged in deliberation should "attempt to understand points of view different from their own"[19] and that they should be prepared to "reconsider [their] ends and commitments."[20] Political deliberation is not political bargaining from entrenched positions. Willingness to reconsider one's preferences is what genuine deliberation requires.

Deliberative democrats make claims like these because of commitments at the heart of their theory. At least some prominent views of deliberative democracy are committed to the view that citizens should regard collective deliberation as the basis of or as a sufficient condition

---

[19] Sunstein, "Republican Revival," p. 1555.
[20] Frank Michelman, "Law's Republic," *Yale Law Journal* 97 (1988): 1493–1538, at 1528.

of political legitimacy.[21] Thus, to be legitimate, political outcomes need not conform to a moral code the authority of which is independent of collective deliberation. This view of legitimacy goes hand in hand with a deliberative specification of citizenship. As we saw, some deliberative democrats think citizens as such are not bound by such a code. This is an important part of citizens' political freedom. The specification of citizenship that includes freedom of this kind is, moreover, a specification with which deliberative democrats think citizens should effectively identify. Joshua Cohen says, for example, that participants in public deliberation "are to regard themselves as bound only by the results of their deliberation and by the preconditions for that deliberation. Their consideration of proposals is not constrained by the authority of prior norms or requirements."[22] It is because citizens of a deliberative democracy have this view of themselves that they are ready to revise their political preferences as a result of collective deliberation. Thus the deliberative democrat's insistence that citizens hold their political preferences democratically is ultimately rooted in their views of political legitimacy and in the view they think citizens should have of themselves.

When I argued that churches contribute to democracy by promoting realized citizenship, I mentioned that they encourage their members effectively to identify with their democratic citizenship. The specification of democratic citizenship with which churches encourage identification might, however, be quite different from the deliberative one. They may encourage their members to think of themselves, singly and collectively, as bound by natural law or divine commands when they form their political preferences, defend those preferences in civic argument and public political debate, make political decisions and vote.[23] And they may encourage a correspondingly nondeliberative conception of democratic legitimacy, one according to which outcomes are legitimate only if they

---

[21] Cohen, "Deliberation and Democratic Legitimacy," p. 21: "For [members of a deliberative democracy] free deliberation among equals is the basis of legitimacy"; also p. 22: "participants [in ideal deliberation] suppose that they can act from the results, taking the fact that a certain decision was arrived at through their deliberation as a sufficient reason for complying with it."

[22] *ibid.*, p. 22.

[23] Bishop Joseph Gossman of Raleigh, NC wrote a letter to his diocese in anticipation of the 2000 election. He wrote: "we recognize that we must exercise our civic responsibilities, such as voting, in ways that are consistent with how our consciences have been formed. Relying on the teaching of the Church, the witness of Scripture, and diligent personal spiritual devotion will enable us to have well formed consciences on which we can depend to lead us to the Truth." He hastened to add "I would not presume, nor should any person claiming to represent the Catholic church presume, to tell you for whom to vote or not to vote. But I do want to urge you to vote. And I invite you to consider your options in light of the Gospel." The letter is quoted in John Strange, "Bishop Gossman urges Catholics to make the tough call on Nov. 7," *NC Catholic* 56.1 October 22, 2000, p. 14.

are consistent with these norms. This, in turn, may lead citizens who have formed political preferences in their churches to hold their preferences undemocratically. They may be unwilling to revise some of their political preferences because they view themselves as bound by norms of which they think their churches are the authoritative expositors. Churches may become what Cass Sunstein and other deliberative democrats warn that secondary associations can be; the "exclusive determinants of political participation," at least on some issues.[24] Thus what I argued is a major contribution to democracy – the promotion of realized democratic citizenship – appears from the deliberative democrat's point of view to be the real problem at the root of undemocratic preferences.

I identified the argument from undemocratically held preferences as an objection deliberative democrats would be especially inclined to make. In fact the other theories that I have discussed in this chapter say little about the attitudes citizens should adopt to their political preferences. Pluralist democratic theories are premised on the assumption that citizens' political preferences are exogenous and *not* altered through public deliberation. Proponents of these views presumably would not offer the argument from undemocratically held preferences. They could not exploit that objection to make the further argument that churches encourage identification with an objectionable specification of citizenship. The argument from undemocratically held preferences may not be available only to deliberative democrats, but there are democratic theories which either do not or cannot make it.

Perhaps their views about preference formation, about the alterability of preferences in public deliberation and about the basis of political legitimacy all give deliberative democrats some reasons for thinking that churches impede genuine public deliberation in contemporary politics. But the view that legitimate political outcomes must be consistent with antecedently given moral norms is not incompatible with the claim that public deliberation also plays a role in legitimating them. Churches could encourage the view that an outcome's appropriate connection to public deliberation is a necessary but not a sufficient condition of its legitimacy. They could also, I have suggested, encourage their members to participate in public deliberation. The deliberation in which they urge their members to take part will be deliberation constrained by antecedently fixed moral norms, but these could still allow a great deal of scope for public deliberation.

[24] Sunstein, "Beyond the Republican Revival," p. 1575.

It could be that these norms are very specific, that few deliberative outcomes would run afoul of them and that the constraints they impose on citizens' on-going deliberations are therefore easily satisfied. Alternatively, these norms could be very general or abstract, with the task of working out their implications left to public deliberation. Thus it might be argued that no society should permit the killing of innocent persons and that political decisions to the contrary are illegitimate. But it might also be argued that the tenability of a distinction between killing and letting die, the relevant notion of innocence and the appropriate criteria of personhood are all matters for citizens to decide through public deliberation. If this is so, then the fact that churches encourage citizens to think of themselves as bound by antecedently given moral norms tells much less forcefully against the claim that churches make valuable contributions than first appears.

The deliberative democrat might grant these replies but object that the real problem with constraining public deliberation by antecedently given norms lies elsewhere. It lies, she might say, not in the consequences for political outcomes, but in the psychological consequences for how citizens are encouraged to think of themselves. A view according to which citizens are seen as collectively unconstrained in their deliberations (or as constrained only by principles which must be honored to safeguard deliberation itself) encourages citizens to think of themselves as politically autonomous. By contrast, it might be objected, a view according to which public deliberations are constrained is one which teaches the deliberative democrat that their political autonomy is constrained.

Perhaps some churches present these antecedently given norms as precepts of natural law or as divine commands. But it could be that the moral norms in question can be presented in some other way as well. Perhaps they can be presented as the objects of citizens' general, free and informed agreement. But then on some views, those norms are not antecedently given at all, since they are not given prior to citizens' possible or ideal deliberations. If this is so, then the constraint they impose on citizens' deliberation would, at least on some views, be far less morally objectionable. Indeed it is open to question whether such a constraint would be a constraint on citizens' autonomy at all. And if it is not, then a view which endorses these constraints cannot be one which *ipso facto* compromises citizens' self-conception as politically autonomous.

The real problem with the objection, however, is that the claims about citizenship on which it relies are presented as part of an ideal of deliberative democracy. They are presented, more specifically, as part of a sketch of how liberal democracies could or should be in order to realize certain political excellences. Perhaps in societies which realize those excellences, citizens would have to identify with a deliberative specification of citizenship according to which they are politically autonomous. It is not at all obvious, however, what bearing this has on how citizens should think of themselves under nonideal conditions. Under nonideal conditions the votes and political preferences of many citizens are determined by their private economic interests and their prejudices, rather than by their views about the common good. Perhaps under these conditions religiously formed preferences are an important counterweight. A great deal needs to be said about why it is so important that citizens conceive of themselves as autonomous in the sense that would be compromised were they to view themselves as bound by antecedently given norms.

I argued in the last chapter that many citizens refine their political views and develop their civic skills, not by engaging in politics, but at work and through their involvement in nonpolitical voluntary organizations. Furthermore, many citizens act on their commitments as citizens – they contribute to the social good as they conceive it, and try to help those they think of as their fellow citizens – in religiously inspired, nonpolitical voluntary organizations like Habitat for Humanity or through volunteer opportunities provided by churches and community organizations.[25] These activities presumably play large roles in maintaining the vitality of their commitments to the social good and in providing them opportunities to think further about what those commitments entail. Churches therefore play an important role in facilitating political engagement and deliberation. They promote some democracy-conducing features at the expense of a feature which would be found in an ideal deliberative democracy. The importance of political autonomy would have to be very great indeed if the fact that some churches teach their members they are not autonomous in the relevant sense is to support the claim that churches do not contribute to democracy under current conditions.

CONCLUSION

I suggested in the introduction that debates about ordinary citizens' reliance on religion in their political decision-making turn on what ordinary citizens can reasonably expect of one another. More precisely, they turn on what sorts of arguments ordinary citizens can reasonably

---

[25] See Coleman, "Deprivatizing Religion and Revitalizing Citizenship."

expect others to offer them, the grounds on which they can reasonably expect others to vote, and how they can reasonably expect others to regard them in political life. The contents of reasonable expectations depend, in turn, on the view that it is appropriate for ordinary citizens to have of themselves. This line of thought is confirmed by what I called "the standard approach" to questions about religion's role in democratic decision-making. At crucial junctures in the argument for accessible reasons, the standard approach appeals to the need to maintain mutual trust, mutual respect and civic friendship. Whether people believe they have been respected, and whether or not trust and friendship obtain among them, depend upon whether they have been treated as they think they should be. This depends upon the view they have of their own citizenship or, in terms I have used, upon the specification of their citizenship with which they effectively identify.

I argued that churches contribute to democracy in the United States by fostering realized democratic citizenship. They encourage their members to accept democratic values as the basis for important political decisions and to accept democratic political institutions as legitimate. The means by which they make their contributions, including their own interventions in civic argument and public political debate, affect the political arguments their members may be inclined to use, the bases on which they vote, and the specification of their citizenship with which they identify. They may encourage their members to think of themselves as bound by antecedently given moral norms with which political outcomes must be consistent. The realization of citizenship by those who are legally entitled to take part in political decision-making is an enormous achievement for a liberal democracy, one in which the institutions of civil society play a crucial role.

In this chapter I have contended that proponents of various democratic theories should regard churches' promotion of realized democratic citizenship and their contributions to civic argument as valuable, despite the reservations they may have about these consequences. Moreover, if churches did not make these contributions, it is not clear what other organizations would. This seems to leave two alternatives. One is that nonpolitical voluntary associations will play important roles in the political engagement of many of those who do get involved in politics. Thus those who have political and social commitments will live them out through these associations, will be recruited through them in the service of causes associated with them, will acquire their political information and civic skills there, will form their political preferences there, and will vote the preferences they form in nonpolitical associations. The other alternative is that involvement in voluntary associations, though historically important in eliciting political engagement, will drop off and citizens will become increasingly politically quiescent.

If, as I believe, quiescence is undesirable and realized citizenship is unlikely without the help of voluntary associations, then it is important to make different assumptions and raise different questions about religious associations than some contemporary political philosophers do. It is a mistake to begin by defining the obligations of citizenship and then ask whether religious organizations should take stands on political issues, whether they should play crucial roles in forming citizens' political preferences, or how political processes might be reformed so that citizens' participation is increased and their preferences are properly filtered. Instead we should work in reverse. We should begin by noting that voluntary, nonpolitical organizations, including religious organizations, play a role in eliciting citizens' political engagement. We should accept the fact that, as a consequence, some citizens will participate in politics for religious reasons and some will offer religious political arguments in public. We should then ask what expectations it is reasonable for citizens to have of one another in a liberal democracy in which this is so. In the next two chapters I begin doing this by clarifying and defending the principles laid out in the introductory chapter.

CHAPTER 4

Public argument

It is time to take stock. I have introduced the notions of participation and full participation, argued that the status of full participation is highly valued and that the conditions of both participation and full participation are politically contested. I have used these notions to locate the contributions churches make to democracy. Churches contribute to their members' realization of citizenship, which is an important part of full participation. They also contribute to public political debate and public civic argument about the conditions of participation and full participation. Having used the notions of participation and full participation to locate the contributions of churches, I dropped the assumption of their importance. I argued that the contributions churches make to democracy should be valued by proponents of a number of democratic theories, none of which makes use of the concepts of participation, full participation or realized citizenship.

In chapter 5 I shall use the conclusion that churches contribute to democracy to argue for the claims about religion and democratic decision-making which I laid out in the introduction. Those claims are:

(5.1) Citizens of a liberal democracy may base their votes on reasons drawn from their comprehensive moral views, including their religious views, without having other reasons which are sufficient for their vote – provided they sincerely believe that their government would be justified in adopting the measures they vote for.

(5.2) Citizens of a liberal democracy may offer arguments in public political debate which depend upon reasons drawn from their comprehensive moral views, including their religious views, without making them good by appeal to other arguments – provided they believe that their government would be justified in adopting the measures they favor and are prepared to indicate what they think would justify the adoption of the measures.

WHERE THE PRINCIPLES APPLY AND WHY: THE SIMPLE STORY

The principles I shall defend apply to some of the votes citizens cast and to the contributions citizens make to public political debate when their most important interests are at stake. In presupposing that principles about religion and democratic decision-making apply to these forms of speech and conduct, I have followed other philosophers writing about this matter, including proponents of the standard approach. One reason I have done so is that this makes my differences with others clear: we defend different principles to cover at least some of the same cases. Another reason why I have followed them is that their treatments of religion and political decision-making presuppose a number of assumptions which I share. Those assumptions are that actions to which these principles apply seem to comprise categories of behavior which it is natural to distinguish from other speech and conduct, that behavior in these categories should be engaged in responsibly, that responsible behavior is to be spelled out in terms of reason-giving and that the obligations to engage in these behaviors responsibly are role-specific duties of citizenship. The principles which apply to these forms of behavior state how those duties are satisfied.

Though I have said that I accept widely held assumptions about the scope of these principles, I have not yet said much about either of the categories of behavior to which they apply and why they apply there. There may not seem to be much that needs saying. Voting is a common form of political behavior. While there are some philosophical puzzles about it, what behavior is picked out by the term *voting* seems clear enough. Given the role of voting in the determination of political outcomes, it also seems clear enough that citizens are obligated to vote responsibly by basing their votes on what they take to be good reasons. Whenever citizens advocate an outcome, their advocacy suggests that they intend to vote for it and that they intend to do so on the basis of the reasons they bring forward in its favor. Sincerity therefore demands that whenever they advocate a political outcome, the reasons they offer for it include the ones on which they do in fact intend to base their votes. "Otherwise," as Rawls says, "public discourse runs the risk of being hypocritical: citizens talk one way before one another and vote another."[1] The norm of sincerity, which requires advocates to reveal the bases of their vote, plus the norm of responsibility, which requires citizens to base their votes on what they take to be good reasons, imply that citizens should offer what they take to be good reasons when they advocate political outcomes.

[1] Rawls, *Political Liberalism*, p. 215.

Furthermore, advocacy is typically an exercise in persuasion. It is an attempt to get others to support and vote for the outcome one advocates. If citizens must vote responsibly, surely they should not encourage others to vote irresponsibly by offering them what they take to be bad reasons to vote. So citizens' obligation to advocate responsibly depends upon the general norm of responsibility plus the obligation not to encourage others to violate their duties. Call this "the simple story" of where the principles apply and why.

The simple story is too simple. It needs qualification. (5.2) and other advocacy principles do not apply to all political advocacy. The attempt to qualify it precisely leads to complication and difficulty. Advocacy principles are commonly said to apply only when fundamental questions are at issue or when important interests are at stake. The need for this qualification raises the question of what questions are fundamental and which of citizens' interests are most important – questions I defer until the third section. Furthermore, such principles are commonly said to apply only to "public political argument," to "public deliberation" or to political arguments offered in the "public forum," the "public square" or in some other configuration of "public space." The need for qualification to the simple story therefore raises the question of what "public political argument," "public deliberation," the "public forum," the "public square" and "public space" are. Unfortunately these crucial notions are often either assumed to be self-explanatory or are defined in ways that exclude examples of political speech which seem as though they should be subject to advocacy principles. As a result, the principles are vulnerable to counterexamples or raise puzzles which their proponents fail satisfactorily to explain.

Some of these puzzles are of special interest because of the way I have said citizens learn to vote and argue on the basis of their comprehensive doctrines. They are puzzles posed by the political argument of religious leaders, arguments which will affect the political behavior of those they lead. For example, on Sunday, May 24, 1998 John Cardinal O'Connor, the late Roman Catholic archbishop of New York, delivered a homily critical of a domestic partnership act under consideration by the New York City Council. As part of a homily delivered in a church during a religious service, the argument might seem to fall outside the scope of principles like (5.2). Because of the circumstances, however, the homily raises many of the same questions raised by political argument which seems to take place in public.

Reporting on the homily, the *New York Times* wrote: "Cardinal O'Connor . . . is perhaps the only person in New York with a platform to rival that of the mayor." The story went on to say of the cardinal: "he seems to revel in the role: his plan to discuss the domestic partnership bill had been announced. The cathedral has a platform for television news cameras with jacks for them to plug into the sound system, and the Cardinal's staff distributed the seven-page text of his homily – with the most newsworthy passages in bold type."[2] I believe that the homily is best regarded as a piece of public political debate despite the setting in which it was delivered. O'Connor acted as if his homily took place in the public forum and tried to provide accessible reasons for his position.[3] Those who advocate principles governing speech in the public forum must, I believe, characterize the public forum so that this intuition can be accommodated.

My own (5.2) is no exception to the generalization that principles governing political argument often refer to the "public forum." That principle applies to public political debate when important interests are at stake, a category of political speech I distinguished from civic argument in chapter 2. There I said that public political debate is "the discussion of electoral, legislative and policy questions which takes place in the public forum, especially governmental fora." It is clear enough what governmental fora are. In order to say more precisely what other forms of political advocacy are covered by (5.2), and to show that it covers the homily, it seems necessary to say something about what other fora are public.

What makes a forum "public" is, however, very difficult to pin down with any precision. The forensic metaphor suggests that the publicity of advocacy in the public forum depends on the fact that the advocate espouses her position openly before the public. But who is the public? And if the openness of someone's espousal of a position does make her advocacy of it public, what is it that makes her espousal open? This second question is one the other metaphors I mentioned are often pressed into service to answer. Unfortunately they mislead rather than illuminate. Metaphors which evoke collectively owned municipal locales, such as "public space" and "the public square," suggest that the public forum is, like monuments and parks, a permanent feature of our shared world. Because these metaphors imply permanence, they suggest that the public square is a feature of our world which persists even when political debate

---

[2] *New York Times*, May 25, 1998, pp. A1 and B5.

[3] As *The Times* reported: "Cardinal O'Connor . . . acknowledged that the church 'has no right to impose specifically Catholic teaching on others,' and said it had no desire to do so. Instead, he couched his criticism in nonsectarian terms that seemed intended to resonate beyond the Gothic cathedral on Fifth Avenue."

is not being conducted there but in which audiences of the requisite sort can periodically assemble. These metaphors can also suggest that publicity and privacy are properties which attach, derivatively, to what is said within one or other forum because of the inherently public or private character of the forum itself. This last suggestion, in turn, can make public speech in private space – like the homily to which I referred – seem needlessly puzzling.

Such puzzles are examples of a more general problem. The views that public space is an enduring feature of our social world and that the public character of activity depends entirely on the space in which it occurs can suggest that the only activities which count as *political* are those that occur within public space. This, in turn, can lead the political theorist to ignore or misdescribe actions with which politics and political theory should be concerned, such as some actions and deliberations in the family, in the workplace and in civil society. It is not surprising that Hannah Arendt – one of the twentieth-century thinkers most strongly associated with a clear line between the political and the nonpolitical – extends the metaphor of public space in a way that makes its permanence explicit. Speaking of "the worldly in-between space by which men are mutually related," she says:

binding and promising, combining and covenanting are the means by which power is kept in existence; where and when men succeed in keeping intact the power which sprang up between them during the course of any particular action or deed, they are already in the process of foundation, of constituting a stable worldly structure to house, as it were, their combined power of action.[4]

Not only is there public space, according to Arendt, but people build on it. As I shall show, Arendt is correct to suggest that publicity depends upon commitment – upon something akin to the "binding and promising, combining and covenanting" of which she speaks in this passage. Her remarks mislead because they suggest that by making those commitments, citizens construct "a stable worldly structure" that houses public advocacy. In fact, to vary the metaphor, public advocacy is a floating enterprise which takes place wherever citizens make commitments of the right sort.

What began as an attempt to qualify the simple story of where the principles apply and why, has led to troubling questions with implications for the subject matter of political philosophy. Why was it so tempting to suppose that the publicity of advocacy depends upon the public character

---

[4] See Hannah Arendt, *On Revolution* (Harmondsworth: Penguin, 1990), p. 175.

of the space in which it takes place? The sources of this temptation, I believe, are the assumptions that a sufficient condition of public advocacy is its actual or intended availability to the public and that there are spaces which are inherently available. The second of these assumptions is highly questionable given the diversity of uses to which churches, for example, can be put. Rather than pressing this objection, however, I want to turn to the problems with the first assumption. Seeing what those problems are will help us see what else besides availability is required for publicity.

The claim that actual availability is sufficient seems subject to obvious counterexamples involving spies, eavesdroppers and hidden microphones. Surely we would not want to say that some instance of advocacy takes place in the public forum because, though we would intuitively regard it as part of a private conversation, it was clandestinely taped and broadcast. The claim that intended availability is sufficient for publicity seems unpromising because an advocate might intend to argue before an audience that never materializes. Without some further explanation, it is hard to see why an instance of advocacy no one hears should be thought to take place in the public forum. It is even harder to see why if the circumstances in which the advocacy was uttered were those in which a reasonable person would not expect an audience even if the person actually doing the advocating does.

If neither the actual nor the intended availability of advocacy is sufficient to make advocacy public, then the usual strategy for identifying public advocacy may be misconceived. That strategy begins by saying what makes a forum public. It then identifies public advocacy by reference to the forum in which it takes place. But perhaps it would be better to proceed in reverse. Perhaps we should begin by saying what makes advocacy public and then explain the public forum by reference to the advocacy which takes place within it. This makes it possible to retain talk of a public forum without taking it as a fundamental idea or as an enduring feature of our world, like a town center. Instead we can think of it as *instantiated* whenever citizens engage in advocacy which satisfies the requisite conditions.

An important feature of public advocacy can be brought to light by looking at how constructions such as "I will publicly advocate his resignation" can function. Imagine that a prominent legislator switches his party affiliation. A high functionary of the political party the legislator left encounters a group of journalists at an airport. He tells them that he will publicly call upon the legislator to resign his office.[5] We may

---

[5] The example is adapted from Paul Zielbauer, "Possibility of defection is met with anger and delight," *New York Times*, Thursday, May 24, 2001, p. A21.

imagine that the party functionary intended his remark to be reported by the journalists. The audience to which the remark was addressed was therefore the public, or the voting public. Furthermore, the remark makes it clear that the functionary thinks the legislator should resign and that he wants him to do so. Yet the functionary's remark does not constitute the public advocacy of the resignation that it promised. To say "I will publicly call for his resignation," even in these circumstances, is not publicly to call for a resignation any more than "I will promise to uphold the laws" or "I will vow to avenge my sister's dishonor" are performative even if uttered before the same people before whom the speaker will subsequently make the promise or the vow. In this way, all three locutions differ from "I will let you know that I dislike you," which conveys the speaker's dislike immediately when addressed to the object of the animus.

If we can see why "I will publicly advocate his resignation" is more like "I will vow to avenge my sister's dishonor" than it is like the performative "I will let you know that I dislike you," we will be able to see what conditions besides availability are required for advocacy to be public. This, in turn, will help us to identify the public forum and provide the needed qualification to the simple story.

Note first that "I will vow to avenge my sister's dishonor" does not express a commitment to avenge my sister's dishonor; at most it expresses a commitment to make that commitment on a later occasion. Similarly, I want to suggest, "I will publicly advocate his resignation" does not commit the speaker to the resignation. It implies only such a commitment will subsequently be made. This similarity between "I will vow to avenge my sister's dishonor" and "I will publicly advocate his resignation" provides a promising clue to the distinctive features of political advocacy in the public forum. To advocate an outcome publicly, in the public forum, is not only to engage in advocacy which is in some way available. It is also to commit oneself to that outcome. Of course people change their minds about their publicly stated political positions, often in response to the arguments others present in the public forum. The commitment made when one publicly advocates a political position need not be irrevocable. But it is, I suggest, a commitment nonetheless. The presence of this commitment is necessary for advocacy to be public. It helps explain why public advocacy, or some of it, is subject to advocacy principles. But what is it to be committed to a political outcome? And how does that commitment subject advocacy to principles which express obligations?

The basic idea is that when someone makes a commitment before others, he creates legitimate expectations about his subsequent behavior in those before whom the commitment is made. Literature on commitment typically focuses on how the expectations of others encourage those who make commitments to honor them. But those expectations have other consequences as well. They affect one's relationship with those before whom the commitment is made, particularly if they will be affected by the conduct they have been led to expect. Because commitments have consequences, we can ask whether they have been made responsibly, for what can reasonably be regarded as good reasons. Thus someone who commits himself to avenging his sister's dishonor creates the expectation that he will seek out and punish those who have dishonored his sister. This affects his relationship with others, particularly those who expect to be affected by his actions. Because there are consequences to this commitment, we can ask whether it is made for good reasons, whether such commitments have a place in the modern world, and so on.

I have suggested that the public advocacy of a political outcome implies a commitment to it that other political advocacy does not. When someone makes such a commitment, she evinces her intention to vote for it and otherwise support the outcome she advocates, and engenders expectations that she will do so. This has consequences for those who will be affected by the outcome and her support of it can affect her relationship with them. Because of these consequences, we can ask whether the commitment is one she has made responsibly or irresponsibly. But responsible behavior is not always obligatory. There are times when it is *permissible* to behave irresponsibly even if it is not *good* or *ideal* to do so. And so people may not always be obligated to advocate political outcomes responsibly. When the consequences of political outcomes are important enough, however, responsible commitment to political outcomes becomes obligatory. Moreover, that obligation is an obligation of citizenship. Advocacy principles such as (5.2) are, in my view, principles which state how citizens are obligated to behave when they have a *duty* to advocate responsibly.

As I said at the beginning of this section, I am interested in which activities of ordinary citizens are subject to principles like (5.1) and (5.2) and why those activities are subject to the principles. The attraction of the simple story was that it explained where and why (5.2) applies by appeal to an intuitively plausible account of why (5.1) applies where it does and a supposedly self-explanatory notion of the public forum. Unfortunately the simple story proved too simple. To identify the advocacy governed by (5.2), it is necessary to say more than the simple story does about what makes political advocacy public. The argument so far has not yielded an answer. It has, however, brought to light some conditions that the answer must satisfy. One condition is availability: the account must somehow accommodate our intuition that advocacy in the public forum is available to the public. In this I agree with those who rely on metaphors of public space to locate the advocacy which falls within the scope of principles. But the account must also pick out advocacy which entails the right sort of commitment to the political outcomes advocated. It should explain the entailment by showing what it is about this advocacy that gives rise to the commitment. It must show why other sorts of advocacy do not entail such a commitment. Finally, it should show why it is subject to principles which express role-specific duties of citizenship.

The centrality of commitment to the account of public advocacy hints at a more complicated connection between public advocacy and voting than the simple story implies. In order to arrive at the right account of where the principles apply and why, and of what the connections are between them, it is necessary to rethink the simple story from the beginning. I therefore want to rethink the simple story, return to (5.1), ask why the conduct it covers is singled out, and see what this tells us about the scope of (5.2).

COMPLICATING THE SIMPLE STORY: WHAT MAKES ADVOCACY PUBLIC

Just as advocacy principles answer the question: how must citizens behave when they are obligated to advocate responsibly?, so principles like (5.1), which apply to voting, address the question: on what basis may citizens vote when they are obligated to vote responsibly? Unfortunately it is not easy as the simple story suggests to say exactly what the connection is between voting and advocacy. This is because it is not immediately clear what a vote *is*. According to some theories, votes are expressions of preferences.[6] If this were the description of votes that was relevant for present purposes, then once we knew what features of voting raise the questions (5.1) answers we would be well on our way to knowing what features of advocacy raise the questions (5.2) answers. This is because advocating a political outcome surely is (or entails) expressing a preference for that outcome if voting for it is an expression of a preference.

---

[6] See David M. Estlund, "Democracy Without Preference," *Philosophical Review* 99 (1990): 397–423. Estlund (p. 399) argues powerfully for the need to give an account of "what kind of action is referred to . . . by the term 'vote.'" Estlund himself argues against the view that votes are expressions of preferences.

Thus the view that votes are expressions of preference promises a unified account of why (5.1) and (5.2) single out the conduct that they do.

But the description of votes as expressions of preferences is a false start. However useful that description may be for other purposes, it is clearly not helpful for present ones. Votes differ from other expressions of preference in that they are counted and the count determines political outcomes. The connections between votes and political outcomes seems crucial to the explanation of why citizens should vote responsibly. Thus it is the *difference* between votes and other expressions of preference, rather than the alleged fact that votes *are* expressions of preference, that does the explanatory work. Once it is clear that describing votes as expressions of preference does not shed light on (5.1), there is less reason to try exploiting the description to illuminate the scope of (5.2). Furthermore, an explanation of why (5.2) singles out the conduct it does would need to show how the political advocacy to which it applies differs from the political advocacy to which it does not. As with voting so with advocacy, it seems more helpful to begin with what distinguishes the phenomena from other expressions of preference than to fix on the fact that they are such expressions.

A more promising start interprets votes, not as expressions of preference, but as exercises of power.[7] According to this view, voting is an exercise of citizens' role-specific power to determine political outcomes. The importance of political outcomes, and the very great interest citizens have in how political questions are decided, explains why that power should be exercised responsibly. The fact that advocacy must be engaged in responsibly can then be explained by the connections among advocacy, voting and political outcomes. When someone advocates a political outcome, she adduces certain considerations as reasons for others to exercise their own power to produce the political outcomes she advocates. This, it seems, is something that it is good to do responsibly, with due attention to the sorts of reasons she offers. When the stakes are sufficiently high, it is plausible to conclude that advocacy *must* be responsible. Advocacy principles spell out how this obligation can be satisfied.

The problem with this line of thought is that while votes determine political outcomes when taken together, the chance that any one person's vote will be decisive is negligible, at least in elections of any significance. Since any one individual's vote is overwhelmingly likely to be inconsequential, it seems paradoxical to call her vote an exercise of *power*. While

---

[7] See Rawls, *Political Liberalism*, p. 217.

it is true that citizens have a great interest in political outcomes, this is an interest in the effect of votes taken together. It does not follow that they have an interest in the effect of any one person's vote. Indeed if individual votes really are inconsequential, then there is not a consequence for citizens to have an interest in. But then the case that citizens should vote responsibly – and hence the case that (5.1) provides an answer to a pressing question – looks much less compelling. Finally, the resulting account of why citizens must advocate responsibly is clearly too simplistic. It fails to distinguish the advocacy that seems to take place in the public forum, and is therefore subject to (5.2), from advocacy that does not.

To avoid the paradox of describing inconsequential individual votes as exercises of power, it is better to think of someone who votes as voluntarily doing his part in a role-specific collective undertaking: citizens' collective undertaking of determining political outcomes. I take it that participating in this collective undertaking responsibly requires that one vote on the basis of reasons that meet certain conditions. Those conditions, when fully spelled out, would say whether and under what circumstances someone may cast self-interested votes, what ends other than self-interest someone may or must intend to advance when he votes, what evidence he may rely on to determine whether the measures he votes for advance those ends, how much time and energy should be devoted to the investigation of alternative policies and, crucially, what someone must do to assure others that her vote satisfies the other conditions. Let us say that someone who satisfies these conditions votes on the basis of "adequate reasons" and that someone who fails one of the conditions votes on the basis of "inadequate reasons."

At the moment I am not concerned to lay down principles expressing all such conditions, though (5.1) does lay down one. For now I simply want to show the need for such principles by noting the plausibility of the claim that responsible voting requires voting for what one takes to be adequate reasons. I also take it that voting responsibly, on the basis of what one takes to be adequate reasons, is a good thing for citizens to do. It is a good or an excellence or an ideal of citizenship. But when the consequences of the collective choice are especially important – when the questions at stake have especially important consequences for citizens' interests – then responsible voting seems not merely to be good or excellent. In that case it is arguable that citizens are obligated to vote responsibly.

To see this, note that the question "Why can't I vote irresponsibly?" can be met with the response "What if everyone did that?" If everyone

voted and was known to vote for reasons she knew to be inadequate –
if, for example, everyone voted and was known to vote on the basis
of self-interested reasons when she knew she should not – then those
whose interests were adversely affected by the outcome would know
that their political opponents had consulted only their own interests in
deciding how to vote. But if my interests were adversely affected by
some political outcome, I would want to know that my interests have
been properly taken into account in arriving at it. Irresponsible voting
therefore seems to fail the universalizability test. This, I suggest, accounts
for our intuition that irresponsible voting is wrong. Thus the obligation
expressed by (5.1) does not get its grip from the consequences or potential
consequences of an individual citizen's irresponsible vote. It gets its grip
on us from our sense that when someone voluntarily participates in
a collective undertaking which has important consequences, he has a
responsibility to do his part in ways that pass a universalizability test.

Public political debate should also be seen as a collective undertaking:
citizens' undertaking to debate what binding choice they should make
from among the political outcomes open to them. I want to suggest
that what distinguishes advocacy in public political debate is that when
citizens advocate outcomes in public political debate, they advocate or
can reasonably be taken to advocate as citizens addressing either other
citizens or public officials in their official capacity. It is clear enough
what is meant by saying that some public political debate is addressed to
public officials in their official capacities. What might seem less clear is
the claim that in other public political debate, citizens advocate or are
reasonably taken to advocate as citizens addressing other citizens. Let me
put this claim somewhat more technically, putting aside the "reasonably
taken" qualification for a moment.

I have stressed that citizenship is a social role with which people can
identify. The central element of this social role is what I called the Aristotelian description of citizenship: the description of citizens as those who
are affected by, and who are entitled to take part in, political decision-
making. When someone participates in public political debate by addressing her fellow citizens, she identifies with this core element of her citizenship, acting as someone to whom the Aristotelian description applies
and addressing others as persons who also satisfy that description. In a
democracy, she acts as someone with the entitlements and status of a
voter and addresses others as persons with the same entitlements and
status. That is, she acts as someone whose fundamental interests will be
affected by political outcomes and who can join with others in affecting

those outcomes and holding officials accountable. She addresses others as persons whose interests will also be affected by those outcomes and who can join her in affecting political outcomes and holding officials accountable by voting.

One of the ways in which exchange among citizens differs from other exchange, even some other exchange about politics, is in its subject matter. When citizens address others as citizens, they discuss political questions as questions which they are entitled to influence by political means – by voting, by demonstrating, by making their views known to officials who are accountable to them. Such exchange differs from exchange among fellow members of a religious group who share a concern about what political outcome would best accord with the moral demands of their religion. It differs as well from exchange among those in the same sector of the economy about what outcome would best advance their interests. Both of these latter two forms of exchange about what outcome would be good differ from exchange about the outcome they should try to effect by exercising their authority as citizens. When someone addresses others as citizens, one of the things she may do is offer others reasons for favoring an outcome and for joining her in bringing it about. She advocates responsibly if the reasons she has and offers, or is ready to offer, are adequate ones.

Identifying with and acting from one or another of one's social roles is a common phenomenon. So, too, is slipping from one to another role even in the course of a conversation. In the same discussion I may speak to someone else as friend, member of the same university faculty or colleague in the same profession. In saying that citizens identify with their citizenship when they engage in public political debate, I mean to refer to an instance of something which is no less ordinary than speaking from one of these other social roles. Identification with one role does not preclude simultaneous identification with another. I may think that my acquaintance with the demands of parenting gives me some insight into what flexi-time policy should be adopted by my childless employers. I may therefore advocate a policy as an employee who is also a parent. Similarly, someone may think that various experiences and insights suit him to judge what political outcome would best serve citizens' interests. He may therefore speak as both cleric and citizen or as both a parent and citizen.

At this point it is tempting to press for more, asking what interests someone takes as fundamental when she identifies with the Aristotelian description of her citizenship and what reasons should be taken as adequate ones when she addresses them as persons who satisfy that description. The temptation should be resisted, for asking these questions is asking too much. The role of citizenship can be specified in various ways by providing different accounts of the interests, rights, responsibilities and obligations had by those who occupy the role, or of the norms and ideals that apply to them. In a pluralistic society, different citizens accept different but overlapping specifications of citizenship. They may agree on some set of fundamental rights, for example, but have different views about what interests those rights serve or protect, what responsibilities citizens have, what nonfundamental rights they enjoy or how basic or nonbasic rights are properly exercised. They may think of citizens as utility maximizers, or as Rawlsian free and equal persons, as having God-given natural rights or as standing under the natural law. Two people can argue for a piece of legislation or a candidate for office, identifying with their citizenship and addressing others as citizens, yet offer arguments that presuppose very different accounts of what interests are fundamental. One may think that it important that laws encourage and protect traditional family life because she thinks all citizens' real interests are furthered in a society which does this. Her interlocutor may disagree. Just what arguments people may or must be prepared to offer is the question advocacy principles like (5.2) are supposed to answer. I am not trying to answer that question now. Rather, I am trying to zero in on the political arguments that raise it, the arguments to which advocacy principles apply. What matters for that purpose is that citizenship is a shared concept despite the different specifications of it on offer, that those who live in a democratic society can identify with the Aristotelian core of their citizenship, can speak and address others as decision-makers whose interests will be affected by the decision they make, and can judge – though quite imperfectly – when they are being addressed that way by others.

Thus whether political advocacy is an instance of public political debate depends upon the role the advocate adopts when speaking, the description under which she addresses her interlocutors, how her advocacy in that role suggests that she will act and what effect she intends her advocacy to produce in her interlocutors. It also depends upon what role her interlocutors take her to have adopted, the description under which they take her to be addressing them, and the effect they take her to be trying to produce. These are matters of conversational pragmatics: of the expectations, illocutionary force and perlocutionary force that attach to verbal behavior. These pragmatic features of advocacy can be affected by the setting or space in which the advocacy takes place. Someone's advocacy may satisfy the conditions of publicity because it takes place in a town meeting. But it – like the commitment to avenge the dishonor of one's sister[8] – can also depend entirely upon unspoken conventions and uncodified practices. What matters for my purposes is that it is the pragmatic features rather than the setting which make advocacy public and which subject it, or some subset of it, to advocacy principles like (5.2).

So far I have spoken about public political debate as debate in which people advocate political outcomes having adopted the role of the citizen. But I said earlier that in public political debate, citizens advocate or *are reasonably expected to advocate* as citizens addressing other citizens. I then put aside the clause about reasonable expectations. I now want to return to it briefly. There are some situations which carry with them or have built into them the collective expectation that those who speak or write in them will speak or write as citizens addressing other citizens or office-holders in their official capacities. Town meetings, hearings, open council sessions and other gatherings convened explicitly for public deliberation are the clearest examples. Those who come together on such occasions are expected to participate as decision-makers addressing other decision-makers who will be affected by the outcome that is reached.

Someone may flout the expectation by failing to participate in the ways legitimately expected – by bringing irrelevant concerns to bear or by speaking off the topic, for example. By doing so, he may seem to violate the duty to participate responsibly in public political debate. In that case the participant cannot excuse his behavior by claiming that, since he did not adopt the role of citizen, he was not engaged in such debate in the first place. The presuppositions of the context in which he spoke, its built-in conversational pragmatics, establish the reasonable expectation that participants speak as citizens. If he flouts the expectation he is participating irresponsibly in public political debate, not failing to participate in it.

I said that one of the conditions that must be satisfied by an account of public political debate is an availability condition. Public political debate – or that part of it which is not addressed to public officials – must be available to the public. The public is comprised of citizens considered in their public role. It is comprised, that is, of citizens considered as persons whose interests are affected by political outcomes and who are entitled to take part in political decision-making. In sum, it is comprised of citizens as such. Public political debate as I have characterized it is

---

[8] As in Gabriel Garcia Marquez, *Chronicle of a Death Foretold* (New York: Alfred A. Knopf, 1983).

therefore debate which is addressed, or can reasonably be taken to be addressed, to members of the public. But does this make it *available* to the public?

Advocacy that is addressed to citizens as such is intended to be available to them. The intention is part of what is meant by saying that the advocacy is "addressed" to citizens. Substituting the requirement that the advocacy actually be available is a mistake for the reason I mentioned when I first introduced the availability condition. An actual availability requirement would be subject to counterexamples involving clandestine broadcasts. Conjoining a requirement of actual availability with the requirement that advocacy be addressed to citizens makes publicity too demanding. As I have already suggested, advocacy is subject to principles that express role-specific duties because of the commitment the advocate makes. If it happens that no one is aware of the commitment because, for example, all the copies of the pamphlet in which the advocacy takes place are accidentally burned in a house fire, it is hard to see why this should free the author from an obligation to which she would otherwise be subject. Commitments should be undertaken responsibly regardless of whether the advocacy which entails the commitment is actually available.

What might seem more troubling about the availability condition as I have construed it is that advocacy satisfies it even if addressed only to a very small number of citizens. Someone who advocates as a citizen addressing only a couple of other citizens seems still to have made her advocacy available. Indeed if only one person addresses another, citizen-to-citizen, it follows from what I have said that that advocacy is publicly available. While this may seem an odd consequence, it is one that I accept. I accept it because the rationale for the availability requirement is to help locate advocacy which is subject to principles, such as (5.2), which express the duty of responsible advocacy. It seems to me that there are circumstances in which advocacy must be engaged in responsibly even if it is addressed only to a small number of people.

Contributing to public political debate, like voting, is something citizens do as occupants of a certain social role: that of a citizen. It is therefore a role-specific activity. I have supposed so far that there is an obligation to participate in it responsibly, at least in some circumstances. If this is correct, that duty will be role-specific. How does that duty arise?

Public political debate is exchange among citizens as such about the political outcomes among which they must make a binding choice. When citizens engage in it, they speak as decision-makers addressing others as decision-makers. When someone speaks as a decision-maker, advocating a political outcome before others who will be affected by it, she engages in behavior that has the relevant features of commitment. It is because her advocacy has these features that taking part in public political debate, like voting, can subject citizens to the role-specific duty to participate responsibly. But the duty to participate responsibly gets its grip in more complicated ways than the duty to vote responsibly, at least when advocacy is addressed to one's fellow citizens. This suggests interesting and morally significant differences between the two. These differences ultimately explain why I differ from other philosophers in proposing different principles to govern voting and advocacy.

Unlike voting, participation in public political debate addressed to fellow citizens is not secret. When someone speaks as a decision-maker advocating an outcome, she engages in behavior that has the relevant features of a commitment. She not only expresses her preference for that outcome. She also evinces, or can reasonably be taken to evince, her willingness to help bring about the outcome. Others may reasonably conclude that she favors the outcome she advocates, favors it for the reasons she offers and intends to vote for it for those reasons. Revealing or seeming to reveal what outcome she favors and why can have important consequences when significant matters are at stake. This is so even if someone's vote for that outcome would be inconsequential. Irresponsible participation in public political debate – seeming to favor outrageous outcomes, for example, or seeming to favor outcomes for reasons they regarded as inadequate – can erode trust and civility between the advocate and her auditors or can keep trust and civility from developing. This is because others may reasonably infer that she thinks it would be acceptable for government to impose an outrageous outcome or that she thinks the reasons others regard as inadequate are adequate. Conveying this impression is especially bad if one's interlocutors believe they are being addressed as citizens, as those whose lives will be affected by political outcomes. Under those circumstances, they will expect someone advocating an outcome to take their interests properly into account and to offer what they reasonably take to be adequate reasons for impinging on them. The duty to participate in public political debate responsibly depends, in part, upon the costs to mutual trust and civility of failing to do so.

Because participation in public political debate is participation in a collective undertaking, the universalizability test can also be deployed to show that citizens are obliged to participate responsibly. If everyone participated in debate irresponsibly, offering reasons they regard as inadequate for the political outcomes they defended, then mutual distrust and incivility among citizens would be pervasive. This would be undesirable in itself. Moreover, because public political debate depends upon the mutual expectation of at least minimally responsible participation, universally irresponsible participation would destroy the possibility of such debate. In a world in which everyone offered and was known to offer only reasons they regard as inadequate, or offered and was known to offer reasons they regard as inadequate when it seemed convenient, every argument would be received as strategic, disingenuous or inappropriately self-interested. The conditions of exchange about the merits of possible political outcomes would no longer obtain. This would be especially bad when the political questions at issue are important ones the effects of which most need to be widely and honestly debated. A different application of the universalizability test brings to light another reason for responsible participation in public political debate. Instead of asking what would happen if everyone offered bad reasons for political outcomes, we can ask what would happen if everyone was persuaded by them. The collective decision reached because everyone was persuaded by such reasons would arguably be a flawed decision, even if it was arrived at unanimously.

Thus as with voting so with advocacy, the universalizability test shows the importance of acting responsibly. If we think of the universalizability test as a test of obligation, then it shows that citizens are obligated to advocate responsibly. Conceiving of participation in public political debate as participation in a collective undertaking by citizens to debate about the choice of political outcomes therefore shows why it is a role-specific activity and how the duty of responsible participation arises. It shows, that is, why their participation in public political debate when important interests are at stake is subject to principles like (5.2), just as conceiving of voting as a collective undertaking by citizens shows why it is subject to principles like (5.1). But, as I will argue in chapter 5, it is because advocacy has consequences for relations among citizens that (5.2) imposes a stronger requirement than (5.1).

I have said that citizens advocate outcomes in public political debate when they advocate or can reasonably be taken to advocate an outcome as citizens addressing either other citizens or public officials in their official capacity. Such advocacy satisfies the availability condition, and entails the right sort of commitment. It is subject to role-specific duties, though the reasons it is subject to those duties are far more complicated than the simple story suggested. Citizens who engage in advocacy of this kind advocate publicly, instantiating the public forum.

This account of publicity accommodates cases of advocacy that seem obviously to take place in the public forum. The reason town meetings, local hearings on affairs from legislation to zoning and Congressional testimony all take place in the public forum is because of the shared, reasonable expectations that participants bring to them. They reasonably expect that citizens will address one another as decision-makers about outcomes among which they must choose and which will affect them all. In these cases, the expectations are created by shared knowledge of what such occasions are typically for and of how participants typically behave. Letters addressed to public officials in their official capacity are part of public political debate because of their addressees. *Open* letters to public officials, such as Abraham Heschel's open letter to President Kennedy advocating "a Marshall Plan" for African-Americans,[9] or Martin Luther King's "Letter from a Birmingham Jail," also contribute to debate in the public forum, but for a different reason. To "open" a letter by divulging and publicizing its contents is precisely to change the addressee from the recipient of the letter to one's fellow citizens as such.

The account also accommodates judgments about advocacy that take place in civil society or in "private space" but which seem to be public nonetheless. A cleric, speaking in church, can speak as a decision-maker as well as a cleric to his congregants, addressing them as fellow decision-makers and as citizens whose interests will be affected by political outcomes. He can do so by, for example, changing the terms in which he addresses his congregants, altering the mode of argumentation he uses, inviting media to cover his homily and opening the text of the homily to a larger audience. As we saw, this is exactly what Cardinal O'Connor of New York did in the homily to which I referred earlier. By doing so, he transformed the pulpit temporarily into a public forum or, as I put it, he temporarily *instantiated* the public forum.

Taking the publicity of advocacy to depend upon its pragmatics not only avoids some of the puzzles that beset other ways of defining the scope of advocacy principles, it also sheds some light on why attempts to lay down necessary and sufficient conditions of publicity are so vulnerable to counterexample. Whether a given set of circumstances or instance

---

[9] Abraham Joshua Heschel, *Moral Grandeur and Spiritual Audacity* (New York: Farrar, Straus, Giroux, 1996), Susannah Heschel (ed.), p. vii.

of advocacy instantiates the public forum is highly context-sensitive. Expectations may not be clearly formulated; where they are, their reasonability may be disputable. Specifying conditions which will enable us to determine whether or not any imaginable case occurs in the public forum would require principles which resolve such disputes. It is highly unlikely that these can be formulated. I shall not try to formulate them here. I have concentrated on the pragmatic features of political advocacy that make responsible advocacy important and in some cases obligatory. I have not, however, tried to resolve thorny questions about when those features can reasonably be supposed to be present. This is a matter for citizens' educated judgment and one on which they may disagree.

The arguments that citizens should vote and advocate responsibly turned on the fact that political outcomes affect the interests of those who are subject to them. The argument that citizens should advocate responsibly also turned on the consequences of some citizens believing that others might affect their interests by voting for outcomes irresponsibly. But not all citizens' interests are equally important. Some outcomes are more important, and have more far-reaching impact, than others. Should voting and advocacy principles govern all votes and all advocacy in the public forum, or just votes and advocacy when certain sorts of political outcomes are under consideration?

WHAT INTERESTS MUST BE AT STAKE?

Some philosophers argue that principles governing the use of religious reasons apply to all and only political decisions about the use of coercion. These are decisions about laws and policies which mandate the use of state power to penalize specified forms of conduct. They include decisions about laws which touch on morally charged issues like abortion and physician-assisted suicide, as well as laws which settle important but less highly charged issues like speed limits and air quality. These decisions are singled out for special treatment because of the way some liberal theories specify the role of citizenship. According to that specification, citizens have a fundamental interest in their liberty or in the ability to act autonomously. They are, it is said, bound to respect one another's fundamental interests, hence to respect one another's fundamental interest in liberty or autonomy. This requires that when citizens advocate and vote for governmental infringements on one another's freedom of action, they must be prepared to show why they think those infringements would be justified if enacted. The demand for justification leads to the questions of what reasons can justify the infringement of liberty and what role, if any, religion can play in that justification. These questions are especially pressing for liberal theorists who attach a high value to public civility and to the avoidance of mutual resentment. For citizens naturally resent the prospect of being coerced for what they take to be inadequate reasons and are resentful when others offer only what they regard as inadequate reasons for coercing them. In societies committed to the separation of church and state, religious reasons may be regarded as especially bad reasons for coercion. Citizens' use of them in political argument and reliance on them when they vote may be especially resented.

But if what motivates restrictions on the use of religious reasons is citizens' fundamental interest in their liberty or autonomy, then it seems to be a mistake to focus only on decisions about coercion. Citizens do not simply have an interest in liberty or in autonomy action-by-action. They have an interest in exercising or using their liberty to form and execute plans of life. Laws can restrict or enhance the use we can make of our liberty by the way they distribute benefits and burdens, such as laws which determine how the tax burden shall be distributed, laws which govern the provision of economic and educational opportunity and laws which govern the distribution or withdrawal of welfare benefits. Some philosophers place great weight on the effects government action can have on this use of liberty. They therefore extend restriction on the use of religious reasons beyond decisions about coercion. Others argue that it is possible to single out political decisions which are especially important because the restrictions of liberty and its use that could result from them would have especially profound effects on citizens' ability to form and execute plans of life. These decisions, decisions which bear on what might be called the *essential use* of liberty, are in the greatest need of justification. It is therefore these cases that raise the most pressing questions about citizens' reliance on religious reasons and, it is said, in which restrictions on the use of such reasons are most urgently called for.

My differences with proponents of the standard approach concern political decisions bearing on the restriction of liberty and its use, since these are the cases in which they think reliance on religious reasons must be qualified or made good by other reasons. Despite the fact that these are where our differences lie, I want to draw attention to other cases which those who defend the standard approach pass over in silence. These other cases also raise questions about the place of religion in political decision-making. As I shall show, the significance of these decisions is not accounted for by the interest liberal theory says citizens have in their liberty and its use or essential use, but by quite different interests altogether: the interests citizens have in what government does in their name.

To see what these interests are, consider what might be called the *Agency Conception of Government.* According to this conception, the government is the agent of the people. Its only powers are those delegated to it by the people, who authorize the government to exercise those powers on their behalf subject to certain constraints. So stated, the Agency Conception is very general. It can be specified in different ways, depending upon how the conditions of delegation and authorization are spelled out. These different specifications may carry different specifications of citizenship with them. Still, some conclusions about citizens and their interests can be drawn even from the general statement of the Agency Conception.

If government is the agent of the people in this sense, then citizens should be thought of as having important interests in what government does, interests which do not depend upon their interests in their own liberty. One reason for this is that the actions of an agent authorized by someone to act on her behalf are, at least under some conditions, actions for which the authorizing party bears some moral responsibility. If a government which satisfies the Agency Conception puts criminals to death, deters aggression by threatening foreign civilian populations with nuclear annihilation or closes its borders to refugees, the citizens – those on whose authority it acts – bear some responsibility for these actions, at least under some conditions. Since citizens have an interest in the performance of actions for which they may be or may think they are responsible, an adequate specification of citizenship will include a *responsibility interest* in the outcome of political decisions about how government power is to be exercised. Furthermore, government action betrays moral qualities which can reasonably be attributed to the citizens in whose name it acts, at least when it acts on their authority and they are morally responsible for its actions. Harsh penal laws show a severity that can reasonably be attributed to a people which authorizes government to enact and enforce them. Immigration laws can reveal hospitality or callousness toward stateless persons and refugees. Stringent environmental regulations reveal concern for the natural world. And so a people can be judged to be harsh or hospitable, environmentally sensitive, generous or humane, on the basis of their government's authorized action. Since citizens have an interest in the moral qualities that can be ascribed to them, citizenship should be specified to include an *ascriptional interest* in the outcome of political decisions.

What I have said so far indicates that citizens have responsibility and ascriptional interests in *all* the political decisions of a government which satisfies the Agency Conception. They therefore have these interests in decisions in which they also have a liberty interest, decisions with implications for their liberty and its use. But because responsibility and ascriptional interests do not depend on their liberty interests, citizens should also be thought of as having these interests in decisions which do not have such implications.

Many of the actions performed by governments which satisfy the Agency Conception are actions in which citizens' responsibility and ascriptional interests are not urgently felt. Citizens may, with good reason, have no urgently felt interest in whether they are responsible for speed limits which government sets in their name or in arcane matters of administrative law which government enforces on their behalf. Other political decisions, however, may concern issues on which citizens feel, or have good reason to feel, these interests more urgently – such as decisions about major defense and immigration policies. Some citizens have religious convictions which bear on these matters. They may believe on religious grounds, for example, that certain policies of nuclear deterrence or certain ways of conducting armed combat are immoral. They might also believe that they would bear some responsibility if their government pursued those policies. Alternatively, they may believe they would bear some responsibility for government action if their government pursued those policies and they did not disavow responsibility by publicly opposing the policies. And so they might wish to rely on their religious convictions to oppose them. These possibilities raise questions about whether citizens who propose, advocate and vote for or against defense and deterrence policies, immigration policies, policies of humanitarian aid and other policies in which they do not have a liberty interest may rely on their religious convictions when they do so. I believe they may. I intend (5.1) and (5.2) to apply to these decisions, as well as to decisions which bear on citizens' liberty and their ability to use it.

The argument for including such decisions within the scope of (5.1) and (5.2) presupposes the correctness of the Agency Conception. These principles therefore seem to promise little guidance for the citizens of actually existing societies who face decisions about defense or immigration policies, since actual liberal democracies may fail to satisfy that conception. Their citizens find themselves subject to government without expressly consenting to their subjection. Still less do they do anything which can plausibly be construed as an authorization of government to act for them. If that is so, then some other account is needed of how they can be responsible for their government's action and how the moral qualities those actions reveal can be imputed to them. Without such an account, the argument for claiming that citizens have responsibility and ascriptional interests in political decisions fails.

Perhaps such an account can be provided. But even if it cannot, many of the governments which do not satisfy the Agency Conception conduct themselves as if they do. They claim to act on behalf of their citizens, prosecuting criminals, imposing punishment and conducting foreign policy in the name of the people. Government's public declarations that it acts in the name of the people encourages citizens to think of themselves as persons on whose behalf government acts. It thereby provides at least tacit encouragement to identify with a specification of citizenship which includes responsibility and ascriptional interests, and so provides tacit encouragement to develop those interests. Moreover, a government's claims to act in the people's name suggests that the people are complicit in the performance of its actions and bear responsibility for those actions, even if the conditions of responsibility are not in fact satisfied. This gives citizens a *reputational interest* in actions government performs in their name, even if they have not authorized and would not authorize their performance. Thus the fact that governments behave as if they are the authorized representatives of their citizens gives citizens an interest in all political decisions, including those which do not bear on their liberty. This interest raises questions about citizens' reliance on their religious views, even when their liberty is not at stake. These are questions to which, I have claimed, (5.1) and (5.2) provide the answers.

It might be granted that citizens have these interests as well as interests in liberty and its use. But it might be objected that not all these interests are equally important. Citizens' interest in their liberty and its use, or their interests in liberty and its essential use, might be thought more important interests than those I have seized on in this section. And so, it might be maintained, (5.1) and (5.2) are acceptable principles for cases in which these liberty interests are not at stake, but when they are, the urgency of these interests means tighter restrictions are called for. The most powerful versions of the standard approach get their plausibility from precisely this line of thought. They get their plausibility, that is, from the claim that liberty interests are especially urgent. That is why I said earlier that the arguments of this chapter are only partial defenses of (5.1) and (5.2). Completing the defense requires us to look at the arguments for thinking these interests are compelling enough to require tighter restrictions than (5.1) and (5.2). It therefore requires confronting the most powerful versions of the standard approach. This is what I shall do in chapters 6 and 7.

THE DECISIONS ORDINARY CITIZENS ACTUALLY MAKE

The promise of principles governing ordinary citizens' reliance on religion in political decision-making is that it will inform our critical moral judgment about liberal democratic politics. But, it might be objected, I have now specified the scope of those principles so that they apply only to decisions ordinary citizens rarely make. Ordinary citizens of most liberal democracies are not given the opportunity to cast votes on laws and policies. They vote on candidates. Much of their public political debate focuses on the merits and demerits, the promises and platforms, the deeds and escapades, of those seeking public office. It is not clear how, if at all, (5.1) and (5.2) apply to these common instances of voting and political argument.

Though ordinary citizens do typically choose among candidates rather than policies when they vote, and though much of their public political debate may be about candidates rather than about laws and policies, their support for candidates is often based upon candidates' positions on the issues. Citizens vote for and advocate candidates because of candidates' positions on taxes, school prayer, abortion, education policy, defense policy, the environment, or commercial development and because of citizens' belief that the candidates would, if elected, work to advance those positions. Abortion, taxes, education and other issues bear on the interests of citizens that I identified in the previous section. When citizens try to determine what the right position is on aid to the poor, how candidates' positions on welfare policy and capital punishment are to be balanced against one another and whether a candidate's position on abortion can be decisive regardless of his position on other issues, they often rely on their religious beliefs or religious authorities.

Suppose someone prefers candidates who support generous welfare policy and she thinks these policies represent the right position on welfare policy because of the pronouncement of religious authorities. Then her preference for the candidate is based on her religious views. If she votes such a preference, then her vote is based on her religious views. In that case, (5.1) requires that she believe her liberal democratic government would be justified in enacting the generous welfare policy. If she argues in favor of a candidate on the grounds that she favors a generous welfare policy and she publicly defends that position on religious grounds, then she offers a religious political argument. What (5.2) requires is that she believe her liberal democratic government would be justified in enacting the welfare policy and that she be prepared to indicate what she thinks would justify the enactment of that policy. So (5.1) and (5.2) apply to the votes and advocacy of ordinary citizens after all.

The crucial premise of this response is that the political preferences of ordinary citizens are based on candidates' stands on the issues. This may be true of some voters. There are many others, however, of whom it is not true or for whom candidates' stands on the issues are only part of the bases of their votes. It is these citizens at whom much of the religious discourse in American politics, at least, is aimed. It is they and not citizens who base their votes on the issues, it might be said, who raise the most interesting questions about religion and political decision-making. For in American politics, relatively little of candidates' religious discourse is religious argument. Much of it is evocative, emotive or biographical. It is intended to convince voters that they are trustworthy, likeable and of good character. And so, it might be concluded, it is religious discourse of this kind that principles should be framed to cover.

The citizens I have in mind in imagining this objection are a varied lot. Some have a Burkean or a quasi-Burkean view of elections. They are content to learn little about issues themselves. They believe their job as electors is to choose candidates who can be trusted to make the right decisions. Others believe office-holders should be persons of outstanding character. Still others want office-holders whom they find likeable and with whom they feel comfortable, since they know they will see and hear so much of the official once elected. Obviously many citizens who value comfort, wisdom and independent judgment, or good character as they conceive it, rely on their own religious beliefs and attitudes when they determine who satisfies their criteria. They may conclude that one candidate is more trustworthy than another or of better moral character because the candidate attends church or a church of a particular denomination, quotes scripture or talks about God. They may be unable to relate to a candidate who is obviously, even if nonaggressively, secular.[10]

Whether it is responsible for citizens to base their votes on judgments of trustworthiness and whether citizens may responsibly rely on their own religious views and attitudes to determine who satisfies their standards

---

[10] For an interesting case study that makes this point, see Garry Wills's discussion of Michael Dukakis in his *Under God* (New York: Simon and Schuster, 1990), pp. 60–61, 93.

are interesting questions. I want to stress, however, that they are very different questions from those with which I am concerned here. I have argued that votes and advocacy need to be responsible when they entail commitments to political outcomes that impinge on the interests of citizens. I have assumed that outcomes impinge on those interests via the exercise of government power to enact laws and policies. Thus a vote for or advocacy of a law restricting assisted suicide must be responsible because the law touches on citizens' liberty interests. A vote for or advocacy of a candidate because he favors that law entails the voter's or advocate's commitment to a law that touches on citizens' liberty interests. Votes that are based entirely on judgments of trustworthiness or comfort are different. If they are irresponsible, it is not because they entail a commitment that is irresponsibly made, though they may indeed entail such a commitment. They are irresponsible because they are cast without regard to the candidate's stand on the issues, and hence do not entail any commitment at all. Whether such votes, or advocacy based entirely on the same judgments, are as irresponsible as they seem are matters for a different inquiry.

There might, however, seem to be other cases that *are* or *should be* the subject of this inquiry and that I should therefore have principles to cover. Consider citizens who want a legislator whose character they think reflects their most deeply held moral values. They view the opportunity to choose a legislator as an opportunity to express those values by picking the candidate with the right image and character[11] and by allowing her to represent them for a set number of years. In making their choice, they may well rely on their religious views about what character traits are worth having or who is more likely to have them. These cases seem to fall squarely within the inquiry I have undertaken because I have introduced reputational and ascriptional interests as important. Once we recognize the possibility of cases like those I am now imagining, it is hard to see why we should assume that citizens' important interests are affected only by the exercise of power to enact legislation and policy. It is hard to see, that is, why they cannot be affected by citizens' choice of public officials as well. If I really am concerned about the conditions under which citizens may rely on religion to make political decisions when important interests are at stake, it seems clear that I should have principles to govern cases like the imagined one.

---

[11] The supposition that voting serves an expressive function for some citizens is hardly fanciful; see Geoffrey Brennan and Loren Lomasky, *Democracy and Decision* (Cambridge: Cambridge University Press, 1993), especially chapter 6.

It would be good to have principles saying what role religion can play when candidates are assessed for what we might call their "expressive value" – their fittingness to express the values of their constituencies. Unfortunately I do not have any such principles. What is most important to remember about these cases, however, is that elections should not be decided nor votes cast entirely or primarily on the basis of various candidates' expressive value. Votes should be based on candidates' positions on the issues or the most important of them. The conditions under which ordinary citizens can rely on their religious views to determine the right stand on issues and to balance positions against one another *are* covered by (5.1) and (5.2), the principles I defend in the next chapter.

CHAPTER 5

The principles

The principles I shall defend are:

(5.1) Citizens of a liberal democracy may base their votes on reasons drawn from their comprehensive moral views, including their religious views, without having other reasons which are sufficient for their vote – provided they sincerely believe that their government would be justified in adopting the measures they vote for.

(5.2) Citizens of a liberal democracy may offer arguments in public political debate which depend upon reasons drawn from their comprehensive moral views, including their religious views, without making them good by appeal to other arguments – provided they believe that their government would be justified in adopting the measures they favor and are prepared to indicate what they think would justify the adoption of the measures.

As I indicated when I introduced them, these principles put me at odds with what I call the "standard approach" to questions about religion and political decision-making. Unlike proponents of the standard approach, I distinguish voting from advocacy in public political debate and impose a higher standard on the latter than the former. According to (5.1) and (5.2), someone offering a religious political argument in public must be prepared to indicate what she thinks would justify enactment of the measure she favors. Someone voting for a measure must believe that enacting it would be justified, but she need not be prepared to indicate what the justification is. More important, these principles allow citizens to vote on the basis of their religious views and to offer religious political arguments in public, without having or being prepared to offer accessible reasons. The person who argues in public for a measure must be prepared to say what she thinks would justify the government in enacting it, but the justification she is prepared to offer may depend upon claims, including religious claims, which proponents of the standard approach would deem inaccessible.

The arguments of this chapter constitute only a partial defense of the principles. For reasons I shall mention in the conclusion of this chapter, completing the defense requires confronting the standard approach in its most nuanced and plausible forms. I shall take up those versions of the standard approach in the chapters that follow. Before I defend (5.1) and (5.2), I want to address a number of questions these principles raise.

SOME PRELIMINARY CLARIFICATIONS

(5.1) says that citizens may base their votes on their comprehensive moral views, including their religious views. I shall say more about comprehensive moral views in a moment. For now, note that in this context, "views" are systematically ordered sets of propositions. A moral view is a systematically ordered set of propositions that concern right or good conduct and, usually, that concern what makes conduct right or good. Religious moral views are moral views that use religious propositions to support their ethical or meta-ethical claims. As I said in chapter 2, I am operating with the concept of religion implicit in the educated common sense of most Americans. Thus religious propositions include propositions that presuppose the existence of God, propositions about the sacredness of texts, about the holiness of persons and ways of life, about the worship of God and about other devotional practices. They also include certain propositions about believing and acting, including the beliefs that some persons are authoritative interpreters of sacred texts, that some persons are authorities about dogma, worship or the way to holiness, and the proposition that the sacredness of some text provides grounds for accepting its authority.

(5.2) says that citizens may make arguments which depend upon reasons drawn from their religious views. But what is "dependence"? I am concerned with what people may do intentionally or what they may reasonably be taken to have done intentionally, not what they may do accidentally or unwittingly. The dependence I have in mind is therefore dependence as seen from the point of view of the person offering the argument or from what others reasonably suppose that point of view to be. Thus the principle allows citizens to offer arguments which seem sound to them only because they accept a religious conviction or which others reasonably believe seem sound to them only because they accept a religious conviction. It also allows them to offer arguments which seem valid to them only because they accept such a belief.

Consider an example. Suppose someone argues that the genetic uniqueness of the fetus implies its personality and that personality implies worthiness of legal protection. Suppose further that someone in his audience takes these inferences to be self-evidently valid in this sense: he thinks the inferences are valid and that any propositions adduced to support their validity would be no better warranted than the inferences themselves. For the sake of illustration, we may even suppose that the auditor is right. Still, if the person who offered the argument thinks it would be a mistake to accept the inferences unless one also accepts the supporting pronouncements of someone she regards as reliable because religiously authoritative, then she has offered an argument which depends upon her religious view. If she seems to think this, then she may reasonably be taken to have offered an argument which depends upon her religious view.

The term *comprehensive view* is, of course, adapted from John Rawls. Rawls speaks of "comprehensive doctrine" and refers to some moral conceptions as "comprehensive." He distinguishes moral conceptions which are "fully comprehensive" from those that are "partially" so. Thus Rawls says that a moral conception

is comprehensive when it includes conceptions of what is of value in human life, and ideals of personal character, as well as ideals of friendship and of familial and associational relationships, and much else that is to inform our conduct, and in the limit to our life as a whole. A conception is fully articulated if it covers all recognized values and virtues within one rather precisely articulated system; whereas a conception is only partially comprehensive when it comprises a number of, but by no means all, nonpolitical values and virtues and is rather loosely articulated.[1]

The phrase "comprehensive conception" as Rawls uses it is therefore very inclusive. Indeed it is so inclusive that it is most usefully thought of as a contrast term. The contrast is with what Rawls calls "political conceptions." These, as we shall see in chapter 7, are moral conceptions that are developed from ideas implicit in political culture, that apply primarily to what Rawls calls "the basic structure of society"[2] and only derivatively to other subjects and that can be presented independent of comprehensive conceptions. I use the term *moral view* to denote what Rawls denotes by the phrase "moral conception." When I speak of "comprehensive moral views," I am referring to comprehensive moral conceptions in the Rawlsian sense, including both fully and partially

---

[1] Rawls, *Political Liberalism*, p. 13.   [2] *ibid.*, pp. 257–88.

comprehensive conceptions. Like Rawls, I use the term *comprehensive moral view* as a contrast term. The relevant contrast is with political conceptions as he understands them.

(5.1) says that citizens who vote for a measure must believe government would be justified in adopting it; (5.2) says that citizens who advocate a measure in public political debate must be ready to indicate what they think would justify government's adoption of it. What is it to believe that government would be justified in adopting a measure? Are there any constraints on the sort of justification citizens must believe is available?

According to the standard approach, government must justify laws and policies to those affected by them by offering reasons for their enactment. Proponents of this approach then isolate the kinds of reasons capable of justifying government action. Reasons of this kind are "justifying reasons." They then argue that citizens must have and be prepared to offer one another justifying reasons for the measures they favor, at least when their most important interests are at stake. If my view were a version of the standard approach, then (5.1) would require that citizens who vote for a measure believe there are justifying reasons of sufficient strength for it. (5.2) would require that they be ready to indicate what those reasons are. But (5.1) and (5.2) do not constitute a version of the standard approach. My argument against that approach does not depend upon denying either that it is possible to isolate a set of justifying reasons, or that it is possible to specify properties justifying reasons must have, though as I shall show, I have doubts about the property of accessibility. What I do deny is that citizens are obligated to have or be ready to offer one another justifying reasons.

Government is justified in adopting some measure only if there are good reasons for government to adopt it given its legitimate ends and the moral constraints within which it must operate. When someone believes government would be justified in adopting a measure, what she believes is that there are good reasons for government to adopt it given what she takes its legitimate ends to be and the moral constraints within which she thinks it must operate. (5.1) and (5.2) refer to liberal democratic governments. If these principles are to express role-specific duties of democratic citizenship, the ends citizens impute to government and the constraints under which they believe government must operate must be aims of and constraints on liberal democratic government.

What are those ends and constraints? As I stressed in chapter 1, democratic states are committed to treating their citizens as equals. More specifically, democracies regard all their citizens as equally possessed of fundamental interests that government must respect when it pursues its legitimate aims. Furthermore, the aim of liberal democratic government is to serve the common interest rather than the interest of any one class or any one section of the economy. In order for (5.1) and (5.2) to express obligations of liberal democratic citizenship, citizens asking themselves whether their government would be justified in adopting the measure they favor must understand their government to satisfy these conditions. That is, they must impute to government what might be called a "common interest view of its aims." They must ask whether a government whose purpose is the promotion of the common good would have good reason to adopt the measure in question. Moreover, they must ask themselves whether adoption or enforcement of the measure would entail violating the requirement that government equally respect the essential interests of all its citizens. A plausible common interest view for liberal democratic government will require respect for the rights and liberties traditionally associated with liberal democracy. Perhaps a common interest view of governmental aims is best spelled out using the notions of participation and full participation I introduced earlier, but about this there will be reasonable disagreement. Thus while citizens may agree about some of the ends government must or may pursue to promote the common good, about some fundamental interests, constraints on government power and justifying reasons for government action, they may disagree about others. They may also disagree about how various considerations are to be weighted and balanced when a decision must be made. As I shall argue, these disagreements are reasonable in some circumstances. It is because they are reasonable in those circumstances that (5.1) and (5.2) allow citizens to rely on a wide range of reasons, including religious reasons.

Why do the principles require that citizens believe *their* government, rather than liberal democratic governments more generally, would be justified in adopting the measures they favor? I assume that different constitutional arrangements can be appropriate for different liberal democracies because of their history, traditions and culture, that citizens are generally at least somewhat aware of major differences between their own political systems and others, and that this awareness generally leads them to recognize that they may have to make different arguments for some political arrangements than citizens of a different democracy might have to make.

These legitimate differences in constitutional arrangements are not confined to differences in governmental structure, such as the differences between the presidential and Westminister systems. They extend to differences which may affect basic liberties. In Germany, for example, some liberties are entrenched and, while freedom of expression is permitted, it is a crime to deny the Holocaust. The United Kingdom has an established church. The United States, by contrast, has no entrenchment and no established church. Because of these differences, there are differences in what measures liberal democratic governments can justifiably enact. The British government, I am supposing, may justifiably impose taxes to support a church while the American government may not. Suppose the principles allowed citizens to advocate measures provided they sincerely believed liberal democratic government – rather than their liberal democratic government – would be justified in enacting them and were prepared to indicate why. Then someone could argue that the United States government should establish a church because he sincerely believes and is prepared to indicate why the British government is justified in establishing one. This seems unacceptable. An American who wants to argue for an established church in the United States must be prepared to make the case that his government would be justified in establishing one. That case would be a more difficult one to make in the United States because tradition has created a widely held and strong expectation that there shall be no establishment.

Finally, (5.2) is clearly more demanding than (5.1). While (5.1) requires citizens who vote for a measure to believe that government is justified in adopting it, it does not require that they be able to say what the justification is. (5.2), by contrast, requires that citizens who advocate a measure in public political debate be able to produce a justification. They must be able to indicate what would justify government's adoption of the measure they favor. Why impose a more stringent requirement on advocacy than on voting?

The answer is that there is a difference in the way reasons for voting and reasons adduced in advocacy are typically elicited and received. Advocacy is and is generally taken to be an exercise in persuasion in which someone volunteers considerations in support of her position. When she offers those considerations, the people she is addressing can reasonably take those considerations as reasons addressed to them. The person advocating the outcome, they can suppose, offers those considerations because she thinks others should regard those considerations as good reasons *for them* to support the outcome. By contrast, voting in large liberal democracies is usually secret. We do not usually know how others vote or why. When someone does give his reasons for voting, the reasons he gives are offered and received as reasons which were supposed to be good reasons *for him*.

To see the significance of these differences for present purposes, consider some examples.

Suppose that I read an editorial arguing for a legal ban on physician-assisted suicide. I find the editorial cogently argued. It persuades me both that legalizing PAS would have dire implications for women and minorities and that these concerns outweigh the liberty interests at stake. I decide to vote against a referendum legalizing PAS on the basis of the editorial's arguments. By election day, I know that I want to vote against the referendum even though I have forgotten why I once believed the liberty interests at stake are outweighed by other considerations. But I also know that my memory is reliable and that if I seem to remember having once been persuaded of things on grounds I then found compelling, I in fact was once persuaded of those things on grounds that I then found compelling. Moreover I believe that I have not since found grounds to believe that the reasoning I once found compelling was faulty. In this case, it seems to me, my vote against the referendum was responsible even though I do not suppose that my memory and my belief in its reliability provide others with good reasons to vote as I did.

Now suppose I am asked to vote on a ballot referendum imposing a new tax on industries which dump effluents into the water supply. The polluting industries insist that the taxes will drive them to a state with less strict environmental regulation and that the cost to the local economy of their departure will outweigh the value of the environmental gains realized when the polluters cease production. Proponents of the tax argue otherwise. They maintain that relocation costs are too high for the industries to bear and that their profits are such that they can easily afford the tax. The economic calculations may be too complex for me to perform and I may not have ready access to the requisite information. The proponents of the tax are, however, experts in environmental and industrial economics whom I trust because of their impartial position. I can, it seems to me, take their word over that of the industrial representatives and responsibly vote for the referendum.

The point of these examples is to illustrate how memory and testimony can function when someone decides how to vote. They can ground a voter's beliefs that there are good reasons for the measure the voter favors and that government would be justified in adopting that measure. But now consider someone who advocates a ban on PAS at hearings which are supposed to air views on the referendum and help citizens make an informed decision. She does so on the grounds that she once read an open letter on the subject that she found persuasive, but she cannot recall any of the reasoning. Her memory may furnish a good reason *for her* to think that the ban is a good idea and that government would be justified in enforcing it. She cannot assume that it provides *her audience* good reason to believe the same things, since she cannot assume they know the reliability of her memory. She must be ready to make good her appeal to her memory by indicating what she takes to be the reasons for the ban and for the claim that government would be justified in enforcing it. Why?

As I noted earlier, advocacy is an exercise in persuasion. The pragmatics of this exercise create certain expectations. Those who are addressed by someone trying to persuade them expect to be offered considerations that the speaker takes to be good reasons for them, reasons they should find rationally compelling. They may expect even more. They may, for example, also expect to be offered reasons that the advocate takes to be good ones for her – reasons she would find rationally compelling, reasons she recognizes as good ones or reasons that in fact move her. I leave these stronger expectations aside here, since it will be important to consider them later, in chapter 6. What matters for present purposes is the minimal requirement. If someone offers what she should know cannot be good reasons for others, those she addresses may feel insulted, condescended to or patronized. It may seem arrogant to suppose that others should regard one's own uncorroborated and impressionistic memories as a good reason to decide so important a political outcome. The resentment or mistrust engendered by the perceptions of arrogance and condescension may not always be justified. There are times when others overreact or are too ready to take offense in political debate. But I am assuming that resentment is justified when, as in this case, the advocate should have known better. If, as I also assume, citizens are obliged to avoid engendering justified resentment, then they should be prepared to offer what they evidently take to be adequate reasons for the outcomes they favor.

This conclusion gains further support when we turn our attention to what it is advocates try to persuade their audience to do. When someone advocates a measure banning PAS in public political debate, she tries to persuade her audience to support the ban – typically by voting for it. If they are to vote responsibly, then by (5.1) they must believe there are adequate reasons for the ban. It would surely be wrong for someone to urge others to vote for the ban while being unable to provide them with the grounds they would have to have to vote for it responsibly. It would, that is, be wrong to urge others to vote for a ban on PAS while not being prepared to show them what the reasons for it are. Therefore someone who advocates an outcome thereby incurs the stronger duty expressed by (5.2).

(5.1) does not require that citizens be ready to indicate what they think justifies government in adopting the measures they favor. It allows them to vote responsibly while relying on testimony about what political outcomes are good ones and what candidates endorse the best measures. Reliance of this kind is inevitable in elections in which a large number of important issues are at stake and in which issues are sufficiently complicated. But I do not deny that it is good for citizens to be informed about issues and candidates, to know why some measures are better solutions to political problems than others, and to know which candidates are better suited to hold office. I do not deny that it is good for citizens to know the reasons for their own political positions rather than to take those positions on trust from others. I merely deny that this is a duty of responsible citizenship. I therefore think that

(5.3) It is an excellence of citizenship to be able to offer reasons one thinks would justify government in enacting the measures one favors.

Of course this is not an excellence everyone has time to pursue. Other activities or other duties may keep them from learning enough about issues to realize the excellence singled out in (5.3). So, too, may other role-specific excellences, include other excellences of citizenship. Someone may, for example, be engaged in a kind of public service which allows her to satisfy her other duties but is too time-consuming to allow her to study political questions. By engaging in such demanding public service, she realizes a different excellence of citizenship which competes with the excellence of (5.3).

THE PRINCIPLES: THEIR DEPARTURE FROM THE STANDARD APPROACH

(5.1) and (5.2) are controversial principles. To bring out how controversial they are, let me give some examples of their implications.

- Mark's state has posed a referendum that would legalize physician-assisted suicide. While trying to decide how to vote on the referendum, Mark reads the open letter Cardinal Joseph Bernardin of Chicago wrote to the United States Supreme Court, urging the justices not to find a right to PAS in the Constitution. Were it not for the letter, Mark would be unsure whether the values Bernardin cites outweigh citizens' liberty interest in determining the time and manner of their deaths. After reading the letter, Mark concludes that they do because the author is a religious authority whom he believes to be reliable on difficult moral questions. Because he thinks that Cardinal Bernardin is correct about there being no right to PAS, he votes against the referendum. His vote is based on the deliverance of a religious authority. (5.1) implies that this is morally permissible.

- I mentioned that it is common for American presidential candidates to make campaign stops at African-American churches. Imagine that Sarah reads of such a visit in the paper or is present when a candidate visits her congregation. She believes that the candidate has the correct position on the issues, or at least the most important issues, of the campaign. She thinks this because she thinks that the candidate has the endorsement of her pastor and that the pastor, as a religious authority, has greater insight into the difficult moral questions at issue in the campaign. (5.1) implies that she may vote for the candidate on this basis.

- Mary must decide between two candidates for office, each of whom takes some positions she finds attractive. In order to make her decision, Mary must decide which issues – hence which positions – are most important. She believes on religious grounds that the poor have the most urgent claim on the nation's conscience and resources. She therefore decides that a candidate's stand on issues which bear most directly on the poor should be decisive. Mary may vote for the candidate whose stand on these issues she favors.

- Anne thinks targeting the innocent populations of other countries with nuclear weapons is offensive to God. To think that the nation-state is worth protecting in this way betrays, she thinks, an idolatrous nationalism and treats God's children as mere pawns in a geopolitical game. She therefore thinks it would be wrong for government to pursue policies of nuclear deterrence that depend upon aiming land-based missiles at civilian populations. (5.2) implies that she may present this argument at a public meeting about the federal government's construction of missile silos in her county, even if she has no other argument to offer.

- Jerry believes that the flourishing of his country and its vigor depend upon parts of its legislation conforming with the precepts of natural law which bear on the common good. He believes, for example, that legislation should strengthen traditional families. Not only does Jerry believe that legislation should conform to natural law, but his beliefs about the precepts of natural law depend upon his comprehensive view, a view elucidated by religious authorities. (5.1) implies that Jerry may vote for candidates because they would try to bring about the conformity Jerry favors, provided he thinks government would be justified in enacting the measures in question. (5.2) implies that Jerry may argue publicly for such candidates on the grounds that they would try to bring about the conformity he favors, even if he has no other argument to offer, provided he thinks government would be justified in adopting the measures in question and is prepared to say what would justify the adoption.

As I indicated, these examples are intended to show the controversial implications of (5.1) and (5.2). The riders to these principles may, however, make the view defended here seem like a version of what I have been calling "the standard approach." According to proponents of the standard approach, citizens should be prepared to offer one another justifying reasons for the measures they vote for and advocate. As the examples make explicit, (5.1) requires that someone who bases her vote on her comprehensive doctrine believe government would be justified in adopting the measures she favors. (5.2) requires that someone whose contributions to public political debate depend upon her comprehensive doctrine believe government would be justified in adopting the measures she favors and be prepared to indicate what she thinks would justify their enactment. Thus both (5.1) and (5.2) seem to make responsible voting and advocacy parasitic on the availability of justifying reasons. (5.1) seems to require that citizens believe there are justifying reasons for the measures they favor. (5.2) seems to require that citizens believe there are justifying reasons and that they be ready to offer them. I seem to have departed from the standard approach only by proposing a more demanding principle for advocacy than for voting. This seems a relatively insignificant difference.

(5.1) and (5.2) do bear some similarity to principles associated with the standard approach but that similarity masks deep differences. One important difference between (5.1) and (5.2) on the one hand, and principles associated with the standard approach on the other, is that the standard approach requires that citizens be ready to offer one another justifying reasons. (5.1) and (5.2) impose no such requirements. (5.1) says that citizens must believe government would be justified in enacting the measures for which they vote. It therefore implies that they must believe there is a justification. It does not, however, require that those reasons be of the kind that *actually would* justify government's enactment of the measures in question. Someone satisfies (5.1) if he sincerely but mistakenly believes that there is a justification for those measures. (5.2) imposes the additional requirement that citizens who advocate a policy be ready to say what they think would justify the government's enactment of it. Like (5.1), (5.2) can be satisfied by someone who is mistaken about what would justify governmental enactment of the measure she favors.

A more significant difference is that according to the standard approach, justifying reasons must be accessible reasons. The standard approach therefore implies that citizens must have and be ready to offer one another accessible reasons for the policies they favor. As will become apparent, I am deeply skeptical of the notion of "accessibility." There may be many considerations – from the promotion of public health, economic growth and environmental quality to the demands of basic human rights – that everyone agrees can be justifying reasons and that seem, intuitively, to be accessible. But if we are to decide whether religious reasons and other reasons drawn from comprehensive views are accessible, it will be necessary to go beyond these clear cases and develop conditions of accessibility. If accessible reasons are to play the role that they are assigned by the standard approach, insuring the right forms of mutual trust and civility, then the criteria of accessibility will have to be widely even if tacitly shared. This, in turn, will require that citizens identify with a certain specification of their citizenship. Citizens will have to think of themselves, perhaps implicitly, as persons who are owed reasons that satisfy those criteria.

The problem is that there is pervasive and reasonable disagreement about what kinds of reasons can be justifying reasons, about what reasons are accessible, about what reasons citizens owe to each other and hence about the specification of citizenship with which citizens should identify. It is because of these problems that (5.1) and (5.2) do not require that citizens must have or be ready to offer accessible reasons. The principles can be satisfied by someone who believes government action can be justified by reasons which proponents of the standard approach deem inaccessible. To return to some of the examples, Mark may believe that human law should promote the common good and that the violation of some precepts of natural law impedes that good. He may believe that clerics have insight into the requirements of the natural law and the common good that he does not. He may therefore believe that government would be justified in enforcing a ban on PAS because PAS goes against a precept of natural law the violation of which impedes realization of the common good. Anne may think that government actions ought not be repugnant to God. She might think that government would be justified in imposing a moratorium on the construction of missile silos because, of the available courses of action – moratorium or continued construction – the moratorium is the one that satisfies that condition. Neither Mark nor Anne would satisfy the requirements of the standard approach, yet they satisfy the principles defended here.

(5.1) and (5.2) allow religion to play a much more prominent role in political decision-making than the standard approach does. As a consequence, these principles allow votes and advocacy that proponents of the standard approach would regard as violations of the duties of citizenship. It may be that the principles permit votes and political arguments we do not like for measures that we hope will lose. This is not a possibility that I deny. I merely maintain that these votes and arguments do not violate citizens' role-specific duties. Acknowledging that they do not is consistent with working hard to insure the electoral defeat of those who cast or offer them.

The standard approach does point toward an important truth about responsible citizenship. To see this, consider the requirement that citizens be ready to offer one another reasons for law and policy that are of the same kind as government must offer citizens. This requirement lies at the heart of the standard approach. As we shall see, Robert Audi moves directly from a claim about the reasons government must offer to a claim about the kind of reasons citizens must be prepared to offer. Rawls is somewhat more expansive. He urges citizens to test the arguments they intend to offer by imagining that they are public officials who must justify government action to citizens generally.[3] This exercise of the imagination is supposed to help citizens identify the arguments they must be prepared to offer one another. Why do proponents of the standard approach move from the reasons government must offer to the reasons citizens must be prepared to offer?

Though they do not say so, I believe proponents of the standard approach think

(5.4) It would be irresponsible for a citizen to vote for or publicly advocate a measure if she does not reasonably think government would be justified in enacting it should her side win the political contest.

I believe they also think that if the issue at stake is important enough, citizens are obliged to behave responsibly. According to this line of thought,

[3] *ibid.*, p. 254.

they are therefore obliged to argue and vote only for measures that they reasonably think government would be justified in enacting. To insure mutual trust and civility, they should be ready to show others that they are voting and debating responsibly. They should therefore be prepared to adduce reasons they reasonably think are justifying reasons for the laws and policies they vote for and advocate. And, I believe proponents of the standard approach think, there are some kinds of reasons that all reasonable citizens can recognize as justifying reasons and that are sufficient to settle political questions or the most important political questions.

There may, as I have stressed, be significant overlap in the sets of reasons reasonable citizens take to be justifying. There are, however, considerations that fall outside the overlap. These are considerations that some citizens take to be justifying but that others do not. In light of reasonable disagreement about whether these reasons are justifying, the standard approach's claim about responsible citizenship is too strong. Rather than requiring that citizens advocate and vote only for measures that can be defended by reasons of the relevant kind if enacted, I am arguing that responsible citizenship requires that citizens advocate and vote only for measures that they *sincerely believe* would be justified. The subtlety of this important difference explains the superficial similarity between my view and the standard approach.

It may be that the citizen who satisfies the demands of the standard approach realizes some good of citizenship that is not realized by those who merely satisfy (5.1) and (5.2). It may be, that is, that

(5.5) It is an excellence of citizenship to be able to offer reasons of the sort that justify government in adopting the measures one favors.

It may also be an excellence of citizenship to strive to bring about a coincidence between the reasons that one thinks justify governmental adoption of some measure and the reasons that really do justify it. It may, that is, be an excellence of citizenship to try to bring it about that one realizes the excellence mentioned in (5.5) or to do one's part to bring about a society in which everyone realizes that excellence. Unfortunately I cannot pursue these suggestions here.

THE PRINCIPLES: A DEFENSE

(5.1) and (5.2) require that citizens who vote for a measure bearing on their own and others' fundamental interests believe that the government's adoption of the measure they vote for can be justified. (5.2) requires that citizens who advocate such a measure be prepared to indicate what a justification is. Yet the principles do not imply that citizens who satisfy them share a view of what justifies government action. Instead they are premised on the supposition that people disagree about what interests are fundamental and what justifies the government's adoption of a law or policy. They require only that citizens invoke the standards of justification that they sincerely believe to be correct. As a consequence, the principles depart significantly from the standard approach, allowing citizens to vote on grounds, and to offer arguments, that many philosophers would deem inaccessible and to do so in favor of political outcomes that many may not like. What tells in favor of the principles?

Principles governing voting and public political advocacy are supposed to be principles the general observation of which maintains civility among citizens or, to use a phrase I have employed elsewhere, keeps relations among citizens on their proper footing. To determine what the proper footing is, some philosophers begin by trying to determine what justifications or reasons citizens are obliged to offer one another. They then argue that the world in which the obligation to offer those reasons is generally honored sets the benchmark of civility. Others begin with intuitions about civility and argue that observing the obligations they defend seems to promote civility as they understand it. It is, however, a mistake to suppose either that civility can simply be defined in terms of principles which are defended on an independent basis or that our intuitions about civility can be taken at face value. I argued in the last chapter that voting and advocacy are collective undertakings. We cannot determine what responsible participation in those undertakings requires or what relations among citizens should be like without knowing what arguments they can reasonably expect others to offer them, on what basis they can reasonably expect others to vote, and how they can reasonably expect to be treated.

What expectations are reasonable depends, in turn, on how it is reasonable for citizens to think of their role and on what citizens can reasonably expect others to believe about the reasons they owe each other. If there are reasonable disagreements about what kinds of reasons are accessible and about what ends government must serve, then it would be unreasonable for some citizens to expect others to offer them reasons they regard as accessible. In that case they may resent being offered reasons they regard as inaccessible, but it would be a mistake to cite their resentment as evidence that those who offered them the inaccessible reasons have violated some moral obligation. Then the claim that the duty of civility requires offering or being prepared to offer others accessible reasons for one's political position would be too strong. Rather than defining civility as what results from compliance with voting and advocacy principles or beginning with a notion of civility and arguing that only the readiness to provide accessible reasons can bring it about, it is better to ask what sorts of reasons it is reasonable for citizens to expect and frame our account of civility accordingly.

The religious arguments citizens offer one another, the reasons on which they rely when they vote, the interests or some of the interests they regard as fundamental, their views about what justifies government action, and hence the specification of citizenship with which they identify, all may result from their exposure to the political arguments and activities of churches. Thus the political argument and activity of churches can lead to citizens holding different opinions on these matters. Of course it does not follow immediately that we should regard this disagreement as reasonable. Nor does it follow that the right accounts of civility and of citizens' reasonable expectations of one another should make allowances for those who rely exclusively on religious reasons and arguments. These conclusions depend upon what disagreements political philosophy should regard as reasonable and upon empirical data about the societies in question. The result is that different principles of responsible voting and advocacy may be appropriate for different societies. I want to argue that there *is* reasonable disagreement about what specification of liberal democratic citizenship is the right one, about what kinds of reasons justify government action and about what kinds of reasons citizens may rely on when they vote or publicly advocate political outcomes. Since I have said that the reasonability of such disagreement depends upon social circumstance, I shall be concerned with the United States and, by implication, with other societies in which religion makes similarly valuable contributions to liberal democracy.

There is reasonable disagreement about some subject when reasonable people reasonably endorse different conclusions about it. Whether people reasonably endorse different conclusions on some subject depends upon how they arrived at those conclusions. Thus whether a disagreement is reasonable depends upon whether some parties to the disagreement satisfy plausible standards of reasonability and whether they had adequate evidence available to them, whether they took adequate account of the evidence or whether their reasoning was in some way faulty or corrupted, and, most important, what explains their divergent opinions if their evidence and reasoning are adequate. Note that

Rawls's claim that disagreement about the good is reasonable depends upon just such considerations. Reasonable people, for these purposes, are people who are willing to cooperate with others on fair terms. Rawls thinks disagreement about the good is natural even among people who are reasonable in this sense and who live under free institutions, for human beings who reason adequately and have access to adequate information still labor under what he calls "the burdens of judgment."[4] Thus he says that reasonable pluralism about the good is "the natural outcome of the activities of human reason under enduring free institutions."[5]

Now let us turn to the disagreement with which I am concerned. The parties to this disagreement in whom I am most interested are, for obvious reasons, those who think they may rely exclusively on religious reasons and who effectively identify with a specification of citizenship that permits this. Consider those who fit this description and who, in addition, impute a common interest conception of legitimate aims to their liberal democratic government, think that government must respect the usual rights and liberties, think government should be responsive to the will of the people and who, when deliberating about what measures to advocate and vote for, are guided by what they think liberal democratic government may justifiably do. Such people seem to satisfy an intuitively plausible standard of reasonability. I am supposing that their views about their own citizenship and about the reasons on which citizens may rely when making political decisions result, at least in part, from the political activity of churches. This activity, I am supposing, explains or helps to explain the disagreements with which I am concerned. Does this, together with the claim that some parties to the disagreement are reasonable, establish that the disagreement is reasonable? To show that it does, it is necessary to advert to the empirical data.

One line of argument seizes on Rawls's claim that pluralism about the good is a *natural* outcome and maintains that the disagreement in which I am interested is no less natural. According to this line of thought, religiously inspired political movements in the United States, religiously motivated political behavior and the use of explicitly religious political argument are due in part to the political engagement of churches. While these institutions are not primarily political in their aims, the ways in which they pursue their institutional missions are influenced by their perception of the needs of their congregants and their society. They intervene in public political debate and civic argument because there are

---

[4] *ibid.*, pp. 54–58.   [5] *ibid.*, p. xxiv.

arguments they think need to be made and points of view that need to be represented. They attempt to promote realized citizenship because they think that otherwise their congregants would not be integrated into political life. They may succeed in these attempts because of a peculiarity of American political life: the absence or weakness of other institutions which might have been expected to mobilize those who now become politically involved through their religion. Thus, according to this line of thought, the political engagement of churches in the United States is the result, in part, of their having adapted to fulfill a function in American politics: the function of enabling certain segments of the population to participate in the political process. This is a function that other institutions of civil society might well have fulfilled if churches had not and that they do fulfill elsewhere. This is because, under conditions of freedom, it is natural for secondary associations to flourish. It is also natural for them to play the role of integrating citizens into political life in the ways I highlighted in chapter 2. Indeed, it might be said, a working liberal democracy depends on this. But it is also natural for free secondary associations which are politically involved – and not just churches – to develop and transmit differing views about citizenship and its duties, just as it is natural for some free secondary associations to develop and transmit differing views about the human good. Disagreement of the former kind among reasonable citizens is therefore just as natural as disagreement of the latter kind.

This line of thought can be supplemented by another which makes do without claims about what is natural. Secondary associations – according to the data I have adduced, churches – provide the only mechanism by which some citizens realize their citizenship. If the operation of these mechanisms results in disagreement about citizenship and its duties, this disagreement is reasonable in this sense: it would be unreasonable to expect the disagreement to vanish. This is because it would be asking too much of the citizens with whom I am concerned to expect them not to have the views about citizenship that they do, since the alternative entails disengagement from politics. In societies in which churches fulfill the political functions I have highlighted, the disagreement that interests me is reasonable disagreement.

What difference does it make if disagreement is reasonable? Some reasonable disagreement may be easily and unproblematically eliminated. Where elimination is not unproblematic, the features of disagreement that make it reasonable explain what is wrong with eliminating it. Thus Rawls says that disagreement about the good can be eliminated only by the oppressive use of state power. What would make the use of power to eliminate such disagreement oppressive is that it would be an objectionable infringement on the free exercise of practical reason by reasonable people. As we saw, it is because disagreement about the good is the natural result of the free exercise of reason by reasonable people that the disagreement is a reasonable one. Thus the reasons the disagreement is reasonable show why it would be objectionable to eliminate it. It may be that disagreement about citizenship and the reasons on which citizens may rely can also be eliminated only by the use of state power. Such use of state power would be oppressive for similar reasons.

But even if we are to imagine that it can be eliminated because churches ceased to engage in the activity that fosters religious political argument, religiously inspired political activity and the identification with the associated specifications of citizenship, the disagreement cannot be eliminated *ceteris paribus* without cost. To show the cost of eliminating it, it will be useful briefly to recall the contributions churches make to democracy. I said in chapter 2 that these contributions are of two sorts. Churches contribute to civic argument and to public political debate by circulating their teaching in civil society, by lobbying, by bringing about the satisfaction of conditions – especially the *minimally democratic agenda* and *adequate representation conditions* – on debate in governmental fora, and by oppositional advocacy. These contributions, I argued, enrich debate about economic justice, the environment, defense policy and international relations, immigration policy, assisted suicide and capital punishment. Part of what makes them valuable, I argued, is their employment of distinctive moral concepts to challenge accepted understandings of liberal democratic values.

The other contribution churches make is to widespread identification with citizenship, and thus to the realization of citizenship, especially by the poor and minorities. Churches serve as venues of political discussion. They also serve as places where people learn about issues and candidates, acquire organizational and parliamentary skills that can be transferred to politics, acquire a sense of self-worth that seems to be correlated with political participation and acquire a sense of themselves as persons who can join with others to hold public officials accountable. Effecting people's realization of their citizenship makes large-scale participation in collective debate and decision-making possible. Indeed, as I argued in the last chapter, the ability to participate in and to recognize debate as *public* debate depends upon identifying with one's citizenship. Furthermore, the realization of citizenship should be reckoned one of the components of subjective well-being. Thus effecting the realization of citizenship is an enormous social achievement. It is, or should be, one of the goals of liberal democracy. The contributions churches make to it, like the contributions they make to civic argument and public political debate, are too important to be lost. There may, of course, be costs involved in allowing exclusive reliance on religious arguments and religious reasons in politics. Doing so may result in the advocacy of policies which strike us as unjust and which cannot be defended on nonreligious grounds. But the greater cost to liberal democracy would be the political marginalization of those whom churches integrate into political life, most notably the poor and minorities.

It is because churches perform the valuable functions I have discussed that disagreements among reasonable citizens to which they give rise are reasonable. Showing that a disagreement is reasonable does more than show why its elimination or disappearance may be problematic. It also shows what citizens may reasonably expect of each other. Rawls would maintain that, given the burdens of judgment, it would be unreasonable for citizens to expect agreement on the good. Given the causes of the disagreement in which I am interested, it would be unreasonable for citizens to expect agreement on a specification of citizenship and on the kinds of reasons on which citizens may properly rely. Norms of voting and political argument the general observance of which requires such agreement, require too much.

I have said that the disagreements on which I have focused – and the seemingly problematic arguments and votes that result – will be eliminated only if churches stopped making these contributions. This is a social scientific conjecture. It cannot be proven definitively. The best I can do to defend it is to argue that what appears to be an alternative which allows churches to make these contributions without producing arguments and votes that seem problematic would not, in fact, allow churches to make the contributions I have highlighted. That alternative, which initially seems promising, is that churches draw some clear distinctions in their own theory and practice, distinctions which would be important in a fully developed version of the standard approach. The relevant distinctions are between contributions to public political debate and civic argument, and between grounds for voting and reasons for political action which does not contribute to a binding decision. Once they have drawn these distinctions, churches can make thoroughly theological contributions to civic argument. They can use those contributions to develop the social teachings of their tradition and challenge dominant social values. When they enter public political debate, however, churches must have and be ready to offer accessible reasons for their political positions and must encourage their members to do the same. They should encourage their members to participate in politics, provide them with political information and help them to develop civic skills. They should also encourage them to find accessible grounds for their votes and to be ready to offer those reasons to justify their votes, at least on fundamental issues. Thus according to this alternative, political discussion and political action will be governed by two sets of norms. Public political debate and voting will be governed by some version of the standard approach. Civic argument and other political action will be governed by (5.1) and (5.2) or by other, weaker principles. By teaching and example, churches should insure that these two sets of norms are honored.

This alternative, if feasible, would allow churches to make many of the contributions I have highlighted without producing the arguments and votes that proponents of the standard approach find problematic. Unfortunately the alternative is not feasible. The problem is that the norms which govern public political debate tend, as a sociological matter, to be taken as norms for other discourse as well. Those who think they should be ready to produce accessible reasons in public political debate tend to insist on them in civic argument as well. One result is that the distinctive moral argument which was to be among churches' contributions to democracy is eliminated even from discussions in which it is ostensibly permissible. Such self-censorship is not something for which I can produce rigorous empirical evidence but there is, I believe, ample anecdotal evidence to support it.[6]

The claim of self-censorship gains additional plausibility once we see why it is natural for people to apply norms from public political debate to civic argument as well. The disposition to comply with norms requiring accessible reasons in public political debate requires those who have other, nonaccessible reasons for their position to recognize that not all interlocutors regard their nonaccessible reasons as good ones for the political outcomes they favor. Only if they recognize this will those with nonaccessible reasons be prepared to supplement their arguments and explain their votes with accessible reasons. As a matter of psychological fact, it is easy to slide from the belief that not everyone regards nonaccessible reasons as good reasons for political outcomes to the belief that nonaccessible reasons are bad reasons for those outcomes. Once

[6] For just one example, see Stephen Carter, *The Culture of Disbelief* (New York: Basic Books, 1993), p. 53.

someone sees some kinds of reasons as bad reasons, he is more likely to refrain from using them, and to insist that others refrain from using them, whether engaged in public political debate or in civic argument. If this slide is widely made – if large numbers of people mistake the claim that nonaccessible reasons need to be supplemented for the claim that nonaccessible reasons are bad reasons which should not be offered – then the alternative will not be feasible.[7]

If, as I have argued, citizens' disagreements about what reasons can justify government action are reasonable disagreements – if the parties to this disagreement are reasonable and if the disagreement can be eliminated only at an unacceptably high cost – then the disagreement is one that voting and advocacy principles must accommodate. They must do so by allowing citizens to rely on their religious convictions when they cast their votes and to adduce religious arguments for their political positions even when they have no other reasons to which they can appeal. This is exactly what (5.1) and (5.2) allow.

Those who worry that religion is often used to support extreme political positions and that this causes resentment and incivility have, paradoxically, an additional reason to accept (5.1) and (5.2). It is often said that compliance with principles of the standard approach is necessary to keep relations among citizens on their proper footing. But it may be that compliance with these principles is less effective at producing civility in the long run than compliance with (5.1) and (5.2). Allegedly extreme political positions may be altered precisely because the religious groups that back them in the public forum on religious grounds cannot win adequate political support for their positions. Not all religious groups modify their position in response to political or cultural reversals; some thrive on the sense that they are embattled minorities and become more strongly oppositional.[8] Even churches and religious citizens who do modify their views may do so over the course of several election cycles rather than immediately. There is, however, evidence that conscious moderation takes place, at least in the United States.[9] Such moderation

---

[7] The best evidence that people will make such a slide is to be found in the scholarly literature on public reason itself. Despite Rawls's insistence that he defends an inclusive view, even well-informed readers commonly claim that his guidelines on public reason exclude religious reasons from political debate.

[8] Christian Smith, *American Evangelicalism: Embattled but Thriving* (Chicago: University of Chicago Press, 1999).

[9] A story entitled "GOP retreating from hard stand against abortion," *New York Times*, Monday, June 21, 1999, p. A13 reported: "Even Pat Robertson, founder of the Christian Coalition, asserted last month that pressing for a constitutional amendment [banning abortion] was unrealistic, saying 'A strategic, incremental approach is much more effective.' He added, 'We must win an election.'"

may, over time, reduce the polarization caused by the earlier adoption of positions that were regarded as extreme. The force of public opinion and the responsiveness of politically active organizations to it are among the moderating and equilibrating forces of liberal democracy. They are among the forces that, over the longer run, counteract forces of polarization and encourage social unity.[10] It would be very odd if those who fear religious extremism and incivility in liberal democracy argued that citizens violate a role-specific duty when they engage in conduct which is the first step to their adoption of more moderate views.

The empirical data laid out in chapter 2 have been crucial to the argument for (5.1) and (5.2). I have relied on the data to show that disagreements about citizenship and the reasons on which citizens may rely are reasonable and result from contributions to democracy which are too valuable to be lost. At this point it may be objected that I have drawn the wrong conclusions from the empirical data I have adduced about the contributions churches make to democracy. Those data do not help us uncover what the prima facie obligations of citizenship are. Those obligations are to be determined philosophically, from the value commitments of liberal democracy. Empirical data help us determine whether the prima facie obligations of citizenship are overridden because of the prevalence of special circumstances or nonstandard conditions.

The problem with this line of thought is that obligations, even prima facie obligations, are supposed to have normative force. They are supposed to guide our conduct and inform our critical judgment. If the normal conditions of human life were such that putative obligations were regularly overridden or evacuated of their force, it would be questionable whether the norms really were *obligations* at all. They might retain some normative force, but it would arguably be the force possessed by ideals rather than duties. Anyone proposing even prima facie obligations must therefore make some assumptions about standard conditions. This is especially so if the obligations are to be defended on consequentialist grounds, as voting and advocacy principles sometimes are. For then the claim that some norm expresses an obligation depends upon claims about the normal consequences of violating it. But what are standard conditions for present purposes? And what is special or nonstandard about actual conditions?

The objector may maintain that our target is a set of principles which express the prima facie obligations of the citizens of liberal democracies

---

[10] For the American case, see generally Alan Wolfe, *One Nation, After All* (New York: Viking Penguin, 1998), pp. 57–61.

as such. Principles as general as that must presuppose a description of standard conditions that abstracts away from the conditions of particular liberal democracies like the United States. The proper description must include only those conditions that are true of liberal democracies as such or, perhaps, conditions common to all and only liberal democracies. In these conditions, acts of ecclesiastical political involvement will not have the features or consequences to which I have pointed in this chapter; these are features, it might be said, that these acts have only in the United States. In light of their society's circumstances, citizens of and churches in this or that liberal democracy may be excused from the prima facie obligations the principles express. But the features acts may have in those special circumstances should not be taken into account in determining what prima facie obligations there are in the first place.

The problem with this argument is that it is far from clear if any description could be given of the conditions common to all and only liberal democratic societies. Or at any rate it is not clear that one could be given that is both detailed enough to show the characteristic features of ecclesiastical involvement in politics and general enough that it is not merely an abstract description of some one society. Even if such a description could be given, liberal democracies surely change over time so that what was true of all of them at one time may not be true of all of them at another. Therefore some argument must be given for designating the conditions common to liberal democracies at one time rather than another as the standard ones for purposes of determining prima facie obligations. It is, however, hard to see why prima facie obligations should be based upon the features certain acts have at a given time in the history of liberal democracy rather than on the features they have in one or another liberal democracy. An attempt to describe the conditions characteristic of liberal democracies "as such" will fare no better.

Alternatively it might be said that the conditions of an ideally just liberal democracy are the ones relevant to determining the prima facie obligations of citizens. This thought will be especially appealing to someone interested in determining what prima facie obligations citizens have in virtue of their commitment to just liberal democracy. For in a liberal democracy which is ideally just, it might be thought, citizens act from their commitment to liberal democracy. They would willingly satisfying the obligations this commitment entails. Ideal conditions might therefore seem to afford a clear and uncluttered view of the actions citizens would perform when they are moved by their liberal democratic commitments. An ideally just liberal democracy would also be one without unjustifiable economic and political inequality for churches to combat, nor would it be one in which the poor need churches to help them realize their citizenship. Once ideal conditions are taken as standard, the data to which I have referred are seen to be irrelevant to citizens' prima facie obligations.

This line of thought assumes that in an ideal liberal democracy churches would not need to endorse some economic policies as more just than others because such a society would be economically just, or very nearly so. It therefore overlooks that possibility that church involvement in politics could be among the ways an ideal liberal democracy might maintain economic justice. A more serious problem with the reply is that an ideally just liberal democracy does *not* afford a clear view of citizens' actions when they are moved by the relevant commitments. If anything, it affords a view of the morally significant features such actions have when citizens are moved by those commitments, when each person's willingness to act on her commitments is mutually recognized and when institutions are designed so that action on these commitments results in economic and political justice. It is hard to see how the morally significant features acts have in such ideal conditions bear on the prima facie obligations citizens are under in actual ones, where there is deep disagreement about what justice demands and when social institutions quite conspicuously fail to produce just outcomes. It is therefore hard to see that our prima facie political obligations could depend only upon the morally significant features our political acts would have under ideal conditions, remote as they are from our own experience.[11]

It still might be maintained that I have focused on the actual circumstances of one society – the United States. While some set of actual conditions may be standard for purposes of determining the duties of liberal democratic citizenship, those so clearly peculiar to a particular society cannot be. The answer to this objection is that it is not at all obvious that the conditions I have discussed are peculiar to one society. As I said when I introduced empirical data in chapter 2, it could well be that in other countries, churches make the same contributions to democracy that they do in the United States. Even if they do not, it may be that other organizations in civil society – such as ideologically oriented labor unions – do and that they convey comprehensive views. It is precisely

---

[11] On idealization and abstraction, see Onora O'Neill, "Constructivisms in Ethics," in *Constructions of Reason* (Cambridge: Cambridge University Press, 1989), pp. 206–18, especially p. 210, where she remarks: "Idealization masquerading as abstraction produces theories that may appear to apply widely, but in fact covertly exclude from their scope those who do not match a certain ideal. They privilege certain sorts of human agents and life by presenting their specific characteristics as universal ideals."

because this possibility cannot be foreclosed that (5.1) and (5.2) apply to comprehensive views generally, and not just to religion.

Finally, to return to the main line of argument, note that religious contributions to public political debate can be appreciated by citizens who are not of the same denomination as the advocate and by those who are not religious at all. Whether or not they are religious, they can see that a religious argument draws on claims which are, from the advocate's point of view, moral claims. This will be evident from the fact that the advocate regards them as categorical claims which preempt the claims of self-interest. They may also be able to feel the force of religious discourse by sympathetically recasting it so that it refers to experiences with which they are familiar, claims which they can accept or aspirations which they share. That is what many Americans presumably did and continue to do with the religious arguments of Martin Luther King. King's biographer, Taylor Branch, wrote that King thought "religion and democratic politics are united in their purest essences and yearnings."[12] The possibility that citizens will sympathetically interpret one another casts some doubt on the claims that religious reasons are inherently inaccessible or that their use in politics inevitably leads to resentment and the erosion of mutual trust.

Whether citizens are willing or able sympathetically to interpret one another no doubt depends upon the prevalence of certain conditions. It depends, for example, on citizens' sharing background knowledge about the religious views appealed to in public political debate, so that they can understand and sympathetically interpret the premises that are relied upon, the stories and imagery that are used and the rhetorical devices that are employed. It may be that increasing pluralism makes the requisite background knowledge harder to maintain, though perhaps this problem could be addressed with an aggressive program of multicultural education. Citizens' readiness to interpret others sympathetically may also depend upon the moral authority of or respect for those who advocate on religious grounds. Alan Wolfe once wrote of Martin Luther King that he

managed to build upon America's religious and moral foundations to uphold the dignity of the individual . . . [h]e said of civil rights demonstrators "The patter

---

[12] Taylor Branch, "Uneasy Holiday," *New Republic*, February 3, 1986. The essay is reprinted in Dorothy Wickenden (ed.), *The New Republic Reader* (New York: Basic Books, 1994), pp. 419–48; the quoted passage is from p. 426. For a sophisticated attempt to find a basis of agreement in King's views, see Joshua Cohen, "The Arc of the Moral Universe," *Philosophy and Public Affairs* 26 (1997): 91–134, especially 133–34.

of their feet as they walked through the Jim Crow barriers in the great stride toward freedom is the thunder of the marching men of Joshua. And the world rocks beneath their tread. My people, my people, listen, listen, the battle is in our hands." In the aftermath of the Birmingham bombing, King spoke not of retribution but of redemption . . . Words like this are rarely heard in American politics these days, because so few have the moral stature to utter them.[13]

Such respect can easily be lost. It would be prudent for churches and religious citizens to conduct themselves in ways that do not squander the respect and moral authority on which a sympathetic reception of their religious advocacy depends. This may require limiting their explicitly religious interventions in politics or making good those interventions with nonreligious arguments. What matters for present purposes is that the imperative to do so is one of prudence rather than of moral obligation.

CONCLUSION

As I mentioned at the beginning of the last chapter, the defense of the role I allow religion in political decision-making falls into two parts. The first part of the defense consists of the arguments found in this chapter. Those arguments leave some important questions unanswered and some important claims to be vindicated. In the last chapter, I noted that the standard approach gains considerable plausibility from the claims that citizens have a fundamental interest in their liberty or its essential use and that it is most important for citizens to qualify their reliance on religious considerations when deciding on political outcomes which bear on those interests. I noted that proponents of the standard approach claim citizens' general willingness to offer one another accessible reasons keeps their relations on the proper footing. But, I said, it is not possible to isolate kinds of reasons which do for relations among citizens what accessible reasons are supposed to do when citizens' liberty interests are at stake. This, I shall argue, is because the notion of accessibility – so central to the standard approach – cannot be adequately spelled out. In order to complete my defense, I therefore need to confront the standard approach in its most developed forms. That is the task of the next two chapters.

---

[13] See Wolfe's review of Taylor Branch's *Pillar of Fire: America in the King Years, 1963–65* (New York: Simon and Schuster, 1997), *New York Times Book Review*, January 18, 1998, p. 13.

CHAPTER 6

Robert Audi on secular reasons

In this chapter I look at Robert Audi's arguments that citizens must qualify their use of religious claims in politics. Audi's view is one version of what I called "the standard approach" to questions about religion's place in democratic decision-making. In the fourth chapter I said that this family of approaches derives much of its plausibility from specifications of citizenship according to which citizens have especially urgent interests in some form of liberty. Their urgency is said to be such that infringements on liberty or its essential use require special justification. As we shall see, Audi's arguments for his principles depends upon the claim that citizens have an urgent interest in one particular form of freedom, autonomy of action. According to his version of the standard approach, it is because citizens have this interest that laws and policies which restrict liberty must be justified by "accessible" – or what Audi calls "intelligible" – reasons.

Unlike some proponents of the standard approach who assume that accessibility is self-explanatory, Audi lays down a condition of accessibility or intelligibility. Unlike other proponents of this approach, he lays down only a necessary condition: secularity. The standard approach requires citizens to offer or be ready to offer one another accessible reasons for the laws and policies they support. Since Audi thinks secularity is a condition of intelligibility, one of his principles – the Principle of Secular Rationale – demands, roughly, that citizens have and be ready to offer secular reasons for their political positions. Audi differs from almost every other proponent of the standard approach in explicitly concerning himself with citizens' motives as well as their arguments. He claims that the accessible reasons citizens must be prepared to offer should also be reasons which move them. And so another of his principles, the Principle of Secular Motivation, demands that citizens be motivated by secular reasons when they support laws and policies which are coercive.

Audi's version of the standard approach is an especially interesting one given the arguments I have made so far in defense of my own views. Audi implies that his principles are part of a specification of citizenship with which he thinks religious citizens can and should identify. He thinks that general observance of his principles is compatible with churches' making many of the valuable contributions to liberal democracy I identified in earlier chapters. Finally, he defends his principles by arguing that their general observance conduces to the realization of various liberal democratic ideals. His is also one of the most thoroughly developed and widely cited versions of the standard approach. Seeing the problems with it shows how hard it is for the standard approach to accommodate the contributions churches make to democracy. It also shows how difficult it is to make precise the notion of accessibility which lies at the heart of that approach.

Audi defends a number of principles governing the political conduct of churches, clergy and ordinary citizens. The two I am going to concentrate on are the two I have mentioned already: the Principle of Secular Rationale and the Principle of Secular Motivation. I will furnish more precise statements of them below. First I want to say something about how the principles are defended.

AUDI'S TWO LINES OF ARGUMENT

I said that Audi claims compliance with his principles promotes various liberal democratic ideals. This way of putting it obscures the fact that Audi offers two very different kinds of argument for his principles. One line of argument that is especially prominent in Audi's earlier work depends upon the consequences of compliance, or generalized compliance, with his principles. Audi argued that observing his principles preserves liberty,[1] "facilitate[s] good relations *between* different religious traditions and between religious and non-religious people,"[2] encourages reciprocity[3] and autonomy,[4] establishes conditions under which citizens can respect one another "as free and dignified individuals,"[5] reduces suspicion,[6] resentment[7] and the risk of religious polarization,[8]

---

[1] Robert Audi, "Liberal Democracy and Religion in Politics," in Robert Audi and Nicholas Wolterstorff (eds.), *Religion in the Public Square: the Place of Religious Convictions in the Political Debate* (New York: Rowman and Littlefield, 1997), pp. 25–46, at p. 28.

[2] *ibid.* (emphasis original).   [3] *ibid.*, p. 30.   [4] *ibid.*, pp. 32, 42–43.

[5] Robert Audi, "The Place of Religious Argument in a Free and Democratic Society," *San Diego Law Review* 30 (1993): 677–702, at 701.

[6] Audi, "Liberal Democracy," p. 32.   [7] *ibid.*, pp. 32, 34.   [8] *ibid.*, p. 43.

and encourages mutual trust.[9] He also implies that violating them could lead to civil strife.[10]

While this line is not absent from his more recent work,[11] Audi now seems equally anxious to defend his principles by appealing to an ideal of civic virtue "that has independent moral force."[12] According to the second line of argument, someone realizes an ideal of citizenship when she is moved by and is prepared to offer others intelligible reasons for the coercive policies she favors. Since Audi thinks reasons must be secular to be intelligible, he thinks complying with this principle is necessary for realizing that ideal. The excellence of the disposition to offer intelligible, hence secular, reasons does not depend upon the consequences of someone's having or acting from the disposition or on the consequences of citizens' generally acting from it. It depends, Audi thinks, on the fact that intelligible reasons enjoy a special status in liberal democratic theory.

It is important to distinguish the two lines of argument because they have complementary strengths and weaknesses. The first type of argument looks more promising as a defense of obligations since it seems plausible that liberal democratic citizens have an obligation to promote the ideals Audi singles out, or at least a duty not to interfere with them. It is hard to tell, however, exactly how the consequences of complying with or violating the principles figure in the argument that the principles are obligatory. Audi may think that in typical cases, someone's violation of the principles interferes with one or more of the liberal democratic ideals. Then the principles would be hypothetical imperatives addressed to each person, specifying what he is obligated to do to bring about ends he is obligated to promote. A problem with this reading is that it is not clear under what conditions adherence to the principles is supposed to promote the desirable consequences and what to do if those conditions do not hold. A more serious difficulty is that the ideals Audi lists can be promoted, if at all, only by general adherence to the principles. No one citizen's compliance with them will do. This raises questions about what any one person is obligated to do when others are patently unwilling to comply with them. What makes this problem pressing is that Audi clearly wants his principles to guide citizens under current conditions.

---

9 Robert Audi, "The Separation of Church and State and the Obligations of Citizenship," *Philosophy and Public Affairs* 18 (1989): 259–96, at 281–82.

10 See the remarks about intramural strife in "Liberal Democracy," p. 28; also the closing remarks of "Separation."

11 See, for example, Robert Audi, *Religious Commitment and Secular Reason* (Cambridge: Cambridge University Press, 2000), p. 145.

12 *ibid.*

Under current conditions, each person knows that the principles will be pervasively violated regardless of what he does.

A different reading, albeit one that strains the texts somewhat, is quasi-Kantian. According to this interpretation Audi takes very seriously the fact that realizing liberal democratic ideals depends upon general conformity with his principles. Indeed, on this reading, those principles express obligations precisely because the maxims of violating them cannot be universalized without sacrificing liberal democratic ideals. The problem with this reading is that Audi's principles are motivated in part by the possibility that the nonreligious will be dominated by the religious. Part of what makes his principles obligatory, he thinks, is that they preclude such domination. The universalizability test is not only supposed to show that actions are wrong, it is also supposed to show why they are wrong. Applied to Audi's principles, however, the universalizability test would be unable to do this. For a world in which everyone violated Audi's principles would be one in which everyone, including those who are *ex hypothesi* nonreligious, relied on and was moved exclusively by religious reasons for coercive laws. It would not be a world in which this domination could occur.

The problems with the first line of argument can most easily be disposed of by supplying an argument that does not depend upon the consequences of citizens' violating Audi's principles at all. This is just what the virtue theoretic defense does, since the moral ideal citizens realize when they comply with the principles is said to have "moral force" independent of consequences. The difficulty is that it is not obvious the defense yields an obligation. It seems at most to establish that citizens realize some excellence when they comply with the principles, but not that they are blameworthy for failing to do so. Audi says that his ideal of citizenship "represents a high standard" of citizenship, which might indicate that in meeting the standard someone realizes a nonobligatory excellence. He immediately adds, however, that the use of "ought" in claims like "she ought to realize that standard" is "not an unusual one" and he clearly means this "ought" to be the "ought" of obligation.[13] But this only shows that the virtue theoretic defense is consistent with the claim that Audi's principles express obligations. It does not imply that they do.

In what follows I shall contend that neither line of argument shows compliance with Audi's principles to be either obligatory or virtuous. Let me begin with the Principle of Secular Motivation.

[13] *ibid.*, p. 86.

THE PRINCIPLE OF SECULAR MOTIVATION

Audi thinks that the consideration he gives to citizens' motives constitutes an important advance over theories like Rawls's, which leave motivation aside.[14] There are, however, serious difficulties with the Principle of Secular Motivation. I want to devote most of my attention to problems with the Principle of Secular Rationale and with the view of justified coercion that is alleged to support it. But because Audi attaches such significance to the Principle of Secular Motivation, I want to give it some critical attention. The difficulties with that principle may explain why there are no comparable principles in other views.

The principle says:

(6.1) One has a (prima facie) obligation to abstain from advocacy or support of a law or public policy that restricts human conduct unless one has and is sufficiently *motivated* by (normatively) adequate secular reason.[15]

One of the problems with the principle grows out of Audi's view about how religious and secular motives can work together in the person who satisfies it. Many religious citizens claim they want to lead or think they should lead a "religiously integrated existence."[16] One way to take this is as a claim about what they think should give unity to their characters and plans of life.[17] Some religious citizens want to be people whose lives are unified by the role religion plays in motivating their actions. Indeed they may want to be persons whose every act, including their political action, proceeds from religious motives.

This is not an unusual aspiration. The thought that all actions should proceed from a love of God and of God's law has long been prominent in the Judaeo-Christian tradition. It is found in the Psalms[18] and the Pauline epistles.[19] It receives its most extensive development and defense in Thomas Aquinas's discussion of charity.[20] If the tradition sets an ethical

---

[14] *ibid.*, p. 160.   [15] *ibid.*, p. 96.

[16] The phrase is Nicholas Wolterstorff's.

[17] What follows is, I believe, the most natural way to take Wolterstorff's remark in light of other things he says; see Audi and Wolterstorff, *Religion in the Public Square*, p. 105. It is not, however, the only way to take it; see Nancy Rosenblum (ed.), *Obligations of Citizenship and Demands of Faith* (Princeton: Princeton University Press, 2000), pp. 15ff.

[18] Psalms 1.1; 16.8; 18.23ff.

[19] I Corinthians, 14.1 cited by Timothy Jackson, "Love in a Liberal Society," *Journal of Religious Ethics* 22 (1994): 29–38.

[20] See Thomas Aquinas, *Summa Theologiae*, IIaIIae, qq. 23ff. An especially clear and instructive discussion is found in IIaIIae, q. 25, a. 1, where Aquinas discusses the reason for loving one's neighbor. I am grateful to Fred Freddoso for helpful conversation about these passages.

standard that believers cannot or frequently do not reach, that standard still functions as an ideal to which many aspire. When some religious citizens assess their characters and motives, they may resolve to make themselves persons for whom religious motives are more central and pervasive. Can Audi's principles accommodate them?

Audi argues that his principles "do not ask more of religious citizens than a free and democratic society should."[21] His standards of citizenship, he thinks, are standards to which religious citizens can and should try to conform. They are at the heart of a specification of citizenship that he thinks should be theirs. And he seems to think that this is true of citizens who want a "religiously integrated existence" and that their aspiration is consistent with the Principle of Secular Motivation. Thus he notes that religious reasons may come first for someone complying with the principle, so that she favors a policy for which she subsequently seeks and finds motivationally adequate secular reasons. He also suggests that for such a person, religious reasons can remain in play even after she finds motivationally adequate secular reasons. He says, for example, that for religious citizens, "the ideal . . . is a special kind of cooperation between the religious and the secular, not the automatic supremacy of the former over the latter"[22] and later that religious reasons can "contribute" to the religious citizen's "motivation to be moral."[23]

To see whether Audi can accommodate those who want a religiously integrated existence, it is necessary to see *how* religious and secular reasons "cooperat[e]" when someone complies with the principle and what religious reasons "contribute" to secular ones. One way in which religious motives might cooperate with and "contribute" to secular ones would clearly be too weak. For someone who wants a religiously integrated existence, it is not enough that her religious reasons do not oppose her secular reasons or that they make her readier to do what she is moved to do by secular reasons. In that case religious reasons would *facilitate* her action, but they would not *motivate* it. That Audi does not intend this weak reading of "cooperation" is clear in any case from other remarks. He says that the principle "allows that one may have and be motivated by religious reasons *as well as* secular ones," that it "allow[s] being more strongly motivated" by one's religious reasons, and that in someone complying with the principle "religious reasons may be motivationally *sufficient* for a political stance."[24] Perhaps Audi thinks that if

---

[21] Audi, *Religious Commitment*, p. 116.   [22] *ibid.*, p. 112.   [23] *ibid.*, p. 132.
[24] All quotes in this paragraph are from *ibid.*, pp. 112–13 (emphases original).

someone's secular and religious reasons cooperate in these ways, she can satisfy the Principle of Secular Motivation while living up to, or trying to live up to, the integrationist ideal.

To see whether she can, suppose Joan aspires to a religiously integrated existence. Suppose further that she publicly advocates policy P, satisfies the Principle of Secular Motivation but also has and is sufficiently motivated by religious reasons for publicly advocating P. The Principle of Secular Motivation requires that citizens who advocate restrictive laws "ha[ve] and be sufficiently *motivated* by (normatively) adequate secular reasons." "Sufficiency of motivation," Audi continues

(6.2) here implies that some set of secular reasons is motivationally sufficient, roughly in the sense that (a) this set of reasons explains one's actions and (b) one would act on it even if, other things remaining equal, one's other reasons were eliminated.[25]

To see one of the problems with the Principle of Secular Motivation, it will help to draw out one of the implications of (b). (b) implies that someone who has a set of motivationally sufficient secular reasons in the actual world W would act on the set in a different world W' in which the other reasons she has in W for performing the same act were eliminated. The phrase "other things remaining equal" in (b) implies that W' is just like W in all other respects. Since Joan satisfies the Principle of Secular Motivation, she has a set of secular reasons which explain her advocacy of P in W and which she would act on in world W', a world which is just like W except that the religious reasons she has for advocating P are eliminated.

Nothing in conditions (a) and (b) depends upon the *secularity* of motivationally sufficient reasons, so I assume that a set of religious reasons is motivationally sufficient "roughly in the sense that" it satisfies (a) and (b). Since Joan also has and is sufficiently motivated by religious reasons for publicly advocating P, she has religious reasons which explain her action in W and on which she would act in world W", a world which is just like W except that the secular reasons Joan has for advocating P in W are eliminated. Note that by advocating P in W" without motivationally sufficient secular reasons, Joan violates the Principle of Secular Motivation in W". Since W" is just like W except for the difference in Joan's reasons, that principle expresses an obligation in W" if it expresses one in W. So if the Principle of Secular Motivation expresses an obligation in W, someone who publicly advocates P in W, satisfies that principle in

[25] *ibid.*, p. 96.

W and has motivationally sufficient religious reasons for publicly advocating P in W has reasons which are sufficient to move her to violate her obligation in W".

This does not, of course, imply any inconsistency in W. Compliance with the Principle of Secular Motivation in W is consistent with the possession in W of reasons which would move someone to violate the principle in W". Therefore someone can both satisfy the Principle of Secular Motivation and have a religiously integrated existence in W. The problem is that Audi also says the Principle of Secular Motivation is a principle of civic virtue. It is part of a standard or an ideal of virtuous citizenship to which citizens should try to conform. Treating the Principle of Secular Motivation as a principle *of virtue* is, I shall argue, incompatible with aspiring to the integrationist ideal.

Virtues are ordered families of intellective and affective dispositions. One of the civic virtues Audi thinks citizens should try to cultivate includes the disposition to comply with the Principle of Secular Motivation. But the virtue must include other dispositions as well. Though Audi thinks that the excellence of that virtue does not depend only upon the consequences of violating or complying with it, the virtue must include a disposition to be appropriately sensitive to the consequences of violating the principle. It must also include an effective desire to act so as not to produce those consequences. So someone in W who treats the Principle of Secular Motivation as a principle of virtue must want to have the effective desire to act so as not to produce the consequences that would result in W from publicly advocating policies without motivationally sufficient secular reasons.

Note that this cannot merely be a desire not to produce those consequences in W. If those consequences are bad in W, they are bad in worlds sufficiently similar to W. The virtuous person would want to act so as not to produce them in those worlds either. While it is difficult to lay down criteria of similarity and to list all the worlds in which the virtuous person would want so to act, she certainly will want to act so as not to produce them in a world which is just like W except for the absence of the secular reasons she has in W publicly to advocate P. Indeed this, we might think, is just the world in which the virtuous person would want to have that disposition. Someone who regards the Principle of Secular Motivation as a principle of civic virtue regards the presence of this effective desire as an excellence of character and its absence as a defect. The person who aspires to civic virtue as Audi understands it therefore values and tries to cultivate this desire. Not only *does* she not act in W without motivationally sufficient secular reasons. She tries to be a person who *would* not act without motivationally sufficient secular reasons if her doing so would have those consequences.

But now note that Joan, who aspires to a religiously integrated existence, cannot try to cultivate this desire or regard it as an excellence. For she wants to have motivationally sufficient religious reasons for everything she does, including publicly advocating P. These are reasons on which she would act to advocate P in W", the world in which she lacks motivationally sufficient secular reasons for publicly advocating P. Since W" is just like W except for the elimination of her secular reasons, Joan's public advocacy of P in W" for religious reasons has the consequences that it would in W if she publicly advocated P without sufficient secular reasons. So what Joan wants is to have religious reasons on which she would act despite these consequences. She cannot also want an effective desire to act so as not to bring about those consequences, on pain of inconsistency. So while compliance with the Principle of Secular Motivation is compatible with actually leading a religiously integrated existence, regarding that principle as a principle of virtue is inconsistent with aspiring to lead such an existence.

The ideal of a religiously integrated existence is one that may be encouraged by churches. The ideal of a citizen whose political actions proceed from religious motives is one that they may be encouraged to identify with or aspire to by churches and religious organizations that encourage political involvement and that contribute to public political discussion. It seems even more likely that the ideal will be promoted by churches and religious organizations that engage in explicit reflection on the relationship between discipleship and citizenship. In chapter 2 I mentioned one example of this: the volunteer from Habitat for Humanity who said "I tend to think of myself living my life as a disciple and that being also how I am a citizen [*sic*]."[26] This is, I believe, an ideal or specification of citizenship that it is reasonable to aspire to. It is one citizens are led to, in part, when churches make the valuable contribution to liberal democracy that I discussed in earlier chapters. An ethics of citizenship that cannot accommodate it, such as an ethic that includes the Principle of Secular Motivation, is seriously deficient.

To see another difficulty with the Principle of Secular Motivation, imagine someone who attends a public meeting about a referendum which would ban physician-assisted suicide (PAS). At the meeting she

---

[26] See chapter 2, note 51.

speaks in favor of the referendum by offering a secular argument which she believes will be rationally persuasive to the others in attendance. She argues, we may suppose, that legalization of PAS would be very bad for the poor, minorities and women. Suppose further that whenever she considers PAS and her own reasons for opposing it, she finds herself powerfully moved by her religious reasons. She thinks that human life is a gift from God and that taking innocent life is a blatant infringement on God's prerogatives. The prospect of permitting so blatant an infringement fills her with a revulsion which leads her to support the referendum. Indeed she finds herself so powerfully and consistently moved by her religious reasons that she is unable to discern any "pull" from any secular reasons. On the other hand, insofar as she is able to think about what she would do if she no longer believed life were a gift from God, she sincerely thinks she would be moved by the argument she offered at the meeting and so would support the referendum anyway. That is part and parcel, she might say, of thinking that the argument is not just persuasive but rationally persuasive.

The agent in this case has secular reasons which would move her were her religious reasons eliminated, and so her secular reasons satisfy (b). On the other hand, those reasons seem not to explain her advocacy of the referendum, so they fail (a). She is not sufficiently motivated by secular reasons and so does not comply with the Principle of Secular Motivation. Yet it is hard to see that she has done anything even prima facie wrong. She defends her political position by what she regards as good, secular arguments. It is true that those arguments seem motivationally inert in her present condition. But she thinks they should be rationally compelling to those in a different condition than she is and she thinks they would be rationally compelling to her were she in that condition. Whatever she thinks of that condition, she does not think it a condition of deficient rationality. Her advocacy of the referendum is therefore not like the action of someone who offers a child arguments she thinks would rationally compel her if she were a child as well.

Audi *could* reply that what moves her to advocate coercive legislation is a reason that is not a good one for the purpose. Advocating coercive law on the basis of bad reasons is wrong regardless of the fact that other reasons would move her if her actual reasons did not. That it is wrong, he might say, can be brought out by considering other cases in which people favor coercive legislation for what they regard as bad reasons. If someone supports a coercive measure because he wants to bend others to his will, he does something wrong even if he would be moved by reasons he knows to be good were his will to power eliminated. If someone supports a measure because it will yield economic benefits for those in his sector of the economy, he does something at least questionable even if he would be moved by good reasons were his economic self-interest eliminated. In each case, Audi might say, the fact that the conduct is defective is reflected in the fact that others can be expected to object to it. And in each case, what is defective about the conduct in question can be brought out by focusing on the motive from which the support proceeds. That is exactly where the Principle of Secular Motivation suggests the problem lies.

There is, however, an important difference between the opponent of PAS on the one hand and the citizens moved by their will to power or economic self-interest on the other. The opponent of PAS is moved by what she takes to be moral, though not secular, reasons. Those to whom she addresses her arguments may not take the reasons to be moral ones; that is why she offers them secular reasons instead. But they are still in a position to recognize that *she* takes her reasons to be moral ones. They can, for example, recognize that she takes them to be universalizable and to have priority over considerations of selfishness, group interest, ambition and convenience. This is something they are equipped to recognize by their background knowledge of their fellow citizens and of the religious traditions represented in their society. Recognizing that someone is motivated by reasons she regards as moral, they should not resent her action in the way that they might if it proceeded from reasons of self-interest. At least they should not if, as I have supposed, she recognizes that others may not take her religious reasons to be good ones and therefore offers secular reasons instead.

It is crucial to the example that, while the agent would oppose the legalization of PAS for secular reasons if her religious reasons were eliminated, she is unmoved by secular reasons in the presence of her religious ones. Someone might try to defend Audi by maintaining that a properly demanding interpretation of (b) precludes this. If someone recognizes a secular reason as a reason for which she would act in the absence of religious reasons which are consistent with it, she must recognize the secular reason as a sufficient reason for action. That recognition, the defender might say, normally carries with it enough motivational force to elicit the action.

Note first, though, that the strong interpretation of (b) makes (a) redundant. For if (b) entails that the secular reasons in question provide enough motivational pull to elicit the action, then it entails that they explain the agent's action. That is just what (a) says. Furthermore, the strong reading of (b) is clearly mistaken. Many religious people would have a very difficult time determining what they would do if their religious reasons for action were eliminated. They may find it very difficult to determine what they would be moved by if their characters and beliefs were so fundamentally altered that they no longer loved God or thought life was a gift from God. Insofar as they can think cogently about this possibility at all, there seems to be no inconsistency in their thinking – as the person in my example does – that certain secular reasons would move them then which do not move them now. To see this, consider a parallel case. A doctor may find it very hard to know how he would behave if he did not think it wrong to have a sexual relationship with a consenting patient. He could believe that under those circumstances, he would be deterred from having such a relationship by having sworn not to do so when he took the Hippocratic Oath. He could believe this even though the relevant clause of the Oath has no discernible motivational force for him now because his other moral reasons preempt it. And we would certainly see no difficulty in his reminding a colleague who did not share those reasons that he too was obligated not to have such relationships because he too swore the oath.

The counterexample to the Principle of Secular Motivation – which turns on the possibility of recognizing a good reason but not being moved by it because of other moral considerations – is not an aberrant case. To insist that it is, is to insist on a mistaken view about how our motives respond to reasons. As cases of akrasia make clear, recognizing some set of considerations as a good reason to do something does not always move us to do it. Another important class of cases in which it may not are cases in which we have what we think are other moral motives to do the same thing. It is clear that there are limitations on what we can will. The complexity of higher-order objects of volition limits the objects to which we can be responsive. Perhaps the stringency of what we take to be moral reasons gives them a preemptive character that normally limits the number of such reasons to which we are simultaneously responsive. It may be an excellence of character to respond to some moral reasons rather than others; indeed this is precisely what those who aspire to a religiously integrated existence assert. Even if it is, the examples show that failure to realize that excellence does not entail the violation of a duty, even a prima facie one.

It would be possible to cope with the counterexample to the Principle of Secular Motivation by falling back on a Principle of Counterfactual

Secular Motivation. Such a principle might weaken the Principle of Secular Motivation by requiring that people who support a coercive policy either be sufficiently motivated by normatively adequate secular reasons or have normatively adequate reasons that would move them in the absence of the moral reasons that in fact move them to support the policy. But the Principle of Counterfactual Secular Motivation is hopelessly weak as a basis for mutual trust, since others' claims to have reasons which satisfy the weaker disjunct would be so difficult to credit. In light of these difficulties, it would be better to avoid thorny philosophical questions about how citizens are obligated to respond to the good reasons they have and simply insist that they should have and be prepared to offer good reasons. This is the route taken by other philosophers. It is just what Audi thinks is required by the Principle of Secular Rationale.

THE PRINCIPLE OF SECULAR RATIONALE

The *Principle of Secular Rationale* says that

(6.3) One has a prima facie obligation not to advocate or support any law or public policy that restricts human conduct unless one has, and is willing to offer, adequate secular reason for this advocacy or support (say for one's vote).

As I mentioned at the beginning of the chapter, one defense of Audi's principles depends upon causal claims about the use of religious arguments in politics. More specifically, it depends upon the claims (i) that citizens' exclusive reliance on religious arguments to explain why they support coercive laws, or on secular arguments that are clearly insufficient, will threaten civil strife, and engender justified resentment and mistrust, and (ii) that these consequences can be avoided, and ideals of mutual trust and civility promoted, by general compliance with the principle.

Clearly the causal connections these claims assert might hold in some circumstances but not others. It is worth asking about the conditions in which Audi thinks the causal claims supporting his principles are true. Audi remarks at one point that his principles "lay out what we ought to do in something like an ideal case."[27] This might suggest that he thinks the connections hold in ideal conditions. But he also seems to think his principles should be observed in current debates, so he must think that the causal connections he alleges also hold under prevailing conditions

[27] Audi, *Religious Commitment*, p. 114.

in liberal democracies like the United States. Whether they do is at least open to question. Whatever may be true elsewhere, religiously inspired civil strife seems extremely unlikely in the United States and in most other north Atlantic democracies. While some mistrust and resentment might result from the violation of the principle under current conditions, Audi must assert that violation of the principle will result in *justified* resentment and mistrust. It is not obvious that that assertion is true.

Under current conditions many citizens receive political information from their churches, become politically involved through their churches and are encouraged effectively to identify with their citizenship through their churches. The involvement of churches in civic argument and public political debate exposes citizens to diverse political points of view. I have argued that adherents of very different democratic theories should regard these as valuable contributions to liberal democracy. Thus the conditions that Audi's principles presuppose are conditions in which churches help to promote certain democratic ideals, like informed and vigorous political participation, particularly among minorities and the poor. I conjectured that the ways in which they do so result in their congregants having religious arguments on which they believe they can rely. Thus liberal democracies may have to balance two competing sets of liberal democratic ideals: those advanced by the political activities of churches and the trust and civility that Audi says would come from general adherence to his principles. Before we can conclude that violating the principle leads to justified resentment and distrust, we need to know how much resentment and distrust should be tolerated in order to realize the competing ideals. We need, that is, to know how the two sets of ideals are to be balanced. The need to defend a balance cannot be evaded by pointing out the obligation expressed by the Principle of Secular Rationale is merely prima facie. Even the prima facie obligation depends upon the existence of resentment and mistrust that are justified, at least prima facie. This is just what I mean to question.

The argument for the Principle of Secular Rationale now under consideration seems to require looking at the immediate consequences of an action for relations among citizens and the implications of uncivil relations for their well-being. But perhaps citizens can be as well-off, or well enough off, even if relationships among them are frayed by religious political arguments. That citizens can be well-off despite a certain amount of incivility and mutual wariness seems more probable if incivility and mutual wariness vary over time. If all citizens pull together in times of national crisis, this could do much to restore trust and civility that have previously been dissipated. Even the ordinary dynamics of politics can restore trust and civility. Religious groups, including churches, which at one time advocate political positions regarded as extreme or intolerant may moderate their political positions to increase their chances of political success. This moderation may reduce the polarization caused by the earlier adoption of positions that were regarded as extreme. The force of public opinion and the responsiveness of politically active organizations to it are among the equilibrating forces of democratic society. They are among the forces that, over the longer run, counteract forces of polarization and encourage social unity.[28]

If the quality of citizens' relationship can return to equilibrium over time, it is hard to see why the immediate consequences of religious argument, or immediate consequences alone, are relevant. What matters may be the quality of that relationship over the course of an election cycle, a decade or a generation. Perhaps in specifying the obligations of citizenship, we should take the long view. Without knowing a good deal more about exactly what forms of civility, civic friendship and mutual trust ought to characterize the relationship among citizens and over what period of time, it is hard to see why the fact that reliance on religious argument threatens them in the short run should ground a prima facie obligation to comply with the Principle of Secular Rationale.

To see another difficulty, note that the principle applies to voting. It applies most obviously to votes on referenda and initiatives that would restrict liberty, like the referendum on PAS I imagined earlier. It also applies, albeit less obviously, to the votes citizens are usually asked to cast, votes for candidates. Consider two citizens who vote against a candidate because he supports a welfare reform bill that will forestall the imposition of new taxes but that the two voters believe will force a large number of people deeper into poverty. In addition to their reasons for believing that the reform bill will make large numbers of the poor even worse off, they must have reasons for thinking this important. Indeed they must have reasons for thinking it important enough to be decisive when they cast their votes.[29]

Suppose one of the voters is prepared to argue that justice normally requires society to give first priority to the needs of its least advantaged. Since no other issues bearing so directly on the poor are at stake in the election, she thinks welfare reform which adversely affects the poor is the most important matter dividing the candidates. While she does not

---

[28] See generally Wolfe, *One Nation*, pp. 57–61.
[29] This seems to be the kind of case Audi has in mind at *Religious Commitment*, p. 177.

make this the sole basis of her vote, she thinks it important enough to be decisive and feels morally bound to vote against a candidate who supports it. Suppose the other voter says she allows the candidate's stand on welfare reform to be decisive because her church has said the poor have the most urgent claim on the nation's conscience and resources,[30] she believes her church is a reliable indicator of what the most important moral issues are and she accepts its moral authority because she accepts its religious authority. She has no other argument to offer for allowing the issue to be decisive. Clearly the only rationale the second voter is prepared to offer for her vote depends upon a religious claim: the claim that her church is morally authoritative because it is religiously authoritative.[31] She has violated the Principle of Secular Rationale while the first has not. Are the two voters in different moral positions and, if so, does the Principle of Secular Rationale account for the difference?

The case is not a fanciful one. Many citizens believe their churches are moral authorities capable of reliably identifying the moral implications of social and political issues. Though Audi thinks that churches should not take political positions, he is in no position to argue that citizens should not accord their churches this sort of authority since he says that churches and religion can play a heuristic role in politics, "leading citizens to the discovery of new truths,"[32] and that they can inspire public policy.[33] They are most likely to do this when their adherents recognize them as moral authorities with insight into social questions. Thus the most sympathetic way to read Audi is as thinking, not that the second voter should change her beliefs about the authority of her church, but that she should find and be ready to offer sufficient secular reasons for making a candidate's stand on welfare reform decisive.

But it is questionable whether the two voters are in significantly different moral positions in the first place. To see this, it is useful to ask about the contexts in which they would typically put forward the arguments they are prepared to offer. The citizen in my example who violates the principle, like the citizen who does not, has an argument she will offer if pressed about what reasons she took to be good ones for voting as she did. In the context, we need not suppose that she thinks others should vote the same way for the same reason. What is likely to be at issue if she is pressed for a rationale is what reasons she took to be good ones for her. The context in which this argument is elicited from her is therefore

---

[30] See the source cited at chapter 2, note 50.
[31] cf. the criteria of secular reasons at Audi, *Religious Commitment*, p. 89.
[32] *ibid.*, p. 77.   [33] Audi, "Separation," p. 293.

quite different from that of a public meeting in which someone volunteers only a religious argument for her candidate. There her typical use
of the argument will be attempts to persuade, implying that she thinks it
provides reasons that others should take to be good ones as well.

The implication that others should take religious reasons to be good
ones is likely to elicit far more mistrust and resentment than someone's
claim that she regarded them as good reasons for herself, given her background beliefs. On one reading of Audi's argument, his principles depend
upon the consequences their violation can normally be expected to have.
If this is so, then perhaps the significant moral distinction is not between
voters who can and cannot offer secular rationales for their votes.
Perhaps it is between two quite different uses of religious argument: uses
which typically imply that others should regard religious reasons as good
ones, and uses which typically carry no such implication. This is not a line
which divides the two voters of my example. It is one which divides them
both from those who use exclusively religious arguments to persuade.

The claim that the two voters are in different moral positions looks
even less plausible when we realize that both base their votes on moral
grounds. Audi insists that secularity is merely a necessary condition on
rationales for voting and not a sufficient one. There are some secular
rationales he would regard as inappropriate bases for voting and other
forms of support for coercive law, though he says little about what they
are. In the absence of any indication to the contrary, I assume he allows
some secular moral reasons as the bases for voting, including moral
reasons like those the first voter relies on. The question raised by the
example is why secular but not religious moral reasons are allowed to
be decisive. Why has the second voter done something wrong while
the first has not? The force of the question becomes especially clear if
the case is varied so that the first voter supports reform which forces
large numbers into poverty and does so on classical utilitarian grounds.
Why is it permissible for someone to base her vote on the utilitarian
claim that total satisfaction is more important than individual well-being,
but impermissible for someone else to base hers on the deliverance of
religious authority who denies that?

It may be that the use of religion as a basis for voting will lead to resentment, incivility and the erosion of mutual trust. What is needed is some
argument that these reactions are justified. Audi offers some reasons for
thinking that religious reasons differ from secular moral reasons in ways
that would justify these reactions to citizens' reliance upon them. He suggests, for example, that religious reasoning is more subject "to cultural

influences that may distort" and that religious arguments are "more liable to bias stemming from political or other non-religious aims."[34] These suggestions seem hard to sustain in light of powerful cultural pressures to conform with the dictates of political correctness. But Audi does not intend these suggestions to bear much weight. The most significant difference Audi alleges between religious reasons and reasons that may be used as the basis of political decisions is that the latter are "intelligible" while the former are not. "Intelligible" reasons have a special place in liberal democratic decision-making, Audi thinks, and because they do the good citizen must be ready to appeal to them. As this talk of the good citizen suggests, the distinction between intelligible and unintelligible reasons is one Audi draws in the virtue theoretic argument for the Principle of Secular Rationale.

SECULARITY, INTELLIGIBILITY AND COMPREHENSIBILITY

Audi writes:

As advocates for laws and public policies, then, and especially those that are coercive, virtuous citizens will seek grounds of a kind that any rational adult can endorse as sufficient for the purpose. Virtuous citizens tend to be motivated in this direction in proportion to the burdensomeness of the coercion, for instance to be more concerned with the rationale for military conscription than with the basis for requiring drivers to be licensed. This adequacy condition for justifying coercion implies intelligibility of a certain kind (allowances being made for technical considerations in some cases); more to the point, it implies secularity.[35]

The conclusion we are supposed to take away from this passage is that virtuous citizens will seek secular reasons for the laws and policies they support. But the passage compresses a very complicated argument for this conclusion, an argument that needs considerable unpacking. To see how that argument is supposed to go, it is helpful to ask why virtuous citizens should "seek grounds of a kind that any rational adult can endorse as sufficient for the purpose." The "then" in the first sentence of this passage provides a clue, indicating that the passage builds on a previous line of argument. The conclusion of *that* argument is that liberal states must defend coercion "in terms of considerations – such as public safety – that any rational adult citizen will find persuasive and can identify with."[36]

---

[34] Audi, *Religious Commitment*, p. 130.
[35] Robert Audi, "The State, the Church and the Citizen," in Weithman (ed.), *Religion and Contemporary Liberalism*, pp. 38–75, at p. 48.
[36] *ibid.*

Thus Audi moves from talk about the grounds to which a *liberal state* must appeal to justify coercion to talk of the grounds to which a *citizen of a liberal state* must appeal, or must be prepared to appeal, when advocating coercion.

In the article I have quoted, Audi does not say what licenses this crucial move, but his discussion of the virtues of good citizenship suggests some possibilities. Perhaps he thinks that a good citizen would not support coercive measures that would not be justified if enacted. He may think she can avoid this only if she has and is prepared to offer reasons for the measures she favors that would justify it if enacted. Or perhaps he thinks that the good citizen would *do her best* to avoid supporting coercive measures that would not be justified if enacted. And he may think that she can do her best only if she has and is prepared to offer reasons she has good grounds for thinking would justify the measures she favors if they were enacted. On either of these readings, refraining from supporting coercive measures unless one has and is willing to offer such reasons would then be a virtue of citizenship. Its status as a virtue would not be due to the consequences of citizens' singly or collectively offering or being disposed to offer such reasons. It would be a virtue because the good citizen advocates or does her best to advocate only measures which can be justified.

More puzzling is the relationship between justifying reasons – the reasons to which states must appeal – and those to which citizens must be prepared to appeal. Audi says states must defend coercion by appealing to considerations "any rational adult citizen will find persuasive and can identify with." How are these considerations related to those Audi explicitly says citizens must be prepared to appeal to – "grounds of a kind that any rational adult can endorse as sufficient for the purpose"?

One way to solve the puzzle is to read Audi as claiming that the two descriptions pick out the same set of reasons. This interpretation, how-ever, creates problems of its own. The first description – considerations "any rational adult citizen will find persuasive and can identify with" – contains an indicative and a modal. The indicative "will" suggests that the considerations in question are those rational adult citizens *do* find persuasive or will in fact find persuasive at some unspecified time in the future. Surely Audi does not mean that states and citizens must defend coercion by appealing to considerations that will in fact persuade *any* rational adult citizen. On the assumption that most actual adults are ra-tional, that would be an implausibly high demand. He can more plausibly be taken to require the state to appeal to considerations adult citizens *would* find persuasive if they satisfied certain standards of rationality. This modal reading brings "will" into line with "can." As I shall show, it also comports with the conditions Audi imposes on justified coercion.

Unfortunately even the modal reading of the first description is not enough to make it coextensive with the second since the descriptions include two different counterfactuals. One speaks of considerations that would persuade while the other speaks of *kinds* of reasons that would be endorsed. This suggests a different reading. Perhaps Audi thinks that reasons that would persuade all rational adults exhibit some important and relevant property or fall into some salient and relevant kind. If the property or kind in question is or implies secularity, then this would allow Audi to claim that the state must appeal to secular reasons. And if we grant that the good citizen would appeal to the same *kinds* of reasons when she advocates a measure that the state would appeal to in justifying it, this would complete the argument for the Principle of Secular Rationale. Since the principle characterizes the behavior of the good citizen, that principle will then be vindicated by reference to an ideal of citizenship that, as Audi promised, has "independent moral force."

Why think that justifying reasons, the reasons the state must appeal to to justify coercive legislation, must be secular? In the passage I quoted at the beginning of this section, Audi says that secularity follows from "intelligibility" or – as he calls it elsewhere – "comprehensibility."[37] Thus the claim that justifying reasons must be secular depends crucially on the claim that they must be comprehensible. Audi says that for reasons to be comprehensible, it must be possible for "an adequately informed, rational adult citizen" to see their reason-giving force.[38] But why think that adequately informed, rational adults cannot see the reason-giving force of religious reasons or would not take them as sufficient reasons for action? And what is wrong with citizens or the government relying exclusively on reasons for coercive legislation that are not comprehensible? Audi's answers to these questions depend upon what he calls "the Surrogacy Conception of Justified Coercion."

THE SURROGACY CONCEPTION EXAMINED

True to the liberal tradition, Audi thinks that citizens have a strong interest in their liberty and that that interest must be respected. The need to respect that interest requires, he thinks, that restrictions on their

---

[37] Audi, *Religious Commitment*, p. 157.   [38] *ibid.*, p. 158.

freedom must be justified to them. It is because he accepts these tenets of liberalism that Audi is interested in what role, if any, religion can play in public justification. The question is whether Audi can show that the nature and urgency of citizens' liberty interests can ground his principles.

The Surrogacy Conception lays down conditions that must be met if coercion for a given set of reasons is justified. The coercion Audi has in mind is coercion by law or more precisely, the restriction of liberty by laws that carry sanctions for violation. The conception imposes three conditions on coercive laws. "Coercing a person, for a particular reason, to perform an action in a given set of circumstances, is fully justified," Audi says, only if

(a) Someone else (most often, fellow citizens in the cases that concern us) has a (moral) right, in the circumstances, to have this action performed by this person . . . or at least the person morally ought to perform the action in the circumstances, for example to abstain from stealing from others.

(b) If fully rational (hence willing to imagine a reversal of positions or roles between oneself and others) and adequately informed about the situation, the person would see that (a) holds and would, for the reason in question, say from a sense of how theft creates mistrust and chaos, or for some essentially related reason, perform the action or at least tend to do so.

(c) The action in question is both an "important" kind of conduct . . . and one that may be reasonably believed to affect someone else.[39]

Why is this a *Surrogacy* Conception? I believe Audi begins, understandably enough, with the view that we ought to govern ourselves by choosing on the basis of good reasons. Lapses of rationality and inadequacies of information are, however, inevitable. Even if they were not inevitable in our own case, we would need some assurance that others will behave well when they suffer lapses. The basic idea of the Surrogacy Conception is that government enacts coercive laws to govern us when lapses occur and to solve the associated assurance problems. Such laws, to be justified, must require actions that we would perform if we were adequately informed and fully rational. To put this condition another way, coercive laws must require actions that would be performed by the persons we would be if we were adequately informed and fully rational – by our adequately informed and fully rational counterparts or surrogates. I shall abbreviate this condition by saying they must require actions that would be performed by our "full and adequate surrogates." Because laws must satisfy this condition to be justified, the condition expresses what can appropriately be called a "surrogacy conception" of justified coercion.

---

[39] *ibid.*, pp. 66–67.

The Surrogacy Conception is one version of what I called in chapter 4 the "Agency Conception of Government." According to the Agency Conception, government is the agent of the people. Its exercises of power must be justifiable to those on whose authority it acts. But the Surrogacy Conception is a particularly strong form of the Agency Conception. According to (b), restrictions on liberty are justified only if we can be expected to see that we would have so acted of our own volition, or as Audi says "on our own" – given adequate rationality and enough information. The imposition of a coercive law is therefore justified only when government requires conduct of us that we would have performed of our own volition, and requiring it for reasons that would lead us to that conduct anyway.

The Surrogacy Conception has a certain prima facie appeal. When we take a legal prescription as our reason for action, we substitute the legislature's judgment of what we should do for our own.[40] When there are penalties for violating the law, the substitution can seem forced. The forced substitution of another's practical judgment for our own threatens to alienate us from our actions and to engender resentment toward the agent who coerces us. By contrast, laws which require conduct that would be performed by our full and adequate surrogates might be thought to be laws we would give ourselves. When we recognize this, Audi thinks, we see that the substitution is justified. We can then identify with our action and, Audi thinks, the ground for resentment vanishes.[41] Furthermore if, as Kant thought, we are autonomous when we obey laws we would give ourselves, then coercive laws which are justified according to the Surrogacy Conception are laws which preserve an important form of freedom. The conception thus promises to address what Rousseau identified as the fundamental problem of political theory: that of showing how someone can be subject to the force of all while he "obeys no one but himself and remains as free as before."[42]

The Surrogacy Conception also promises to show what is wrong with coercing someone to perform an action for what Audi calls "incomprehensible reasons." Considerations which are incomprehensible in the relevant sense, Audi says, are those that "cannot be seen to have any force given the powers of an adequately informed rational citizen."[43]

---

[40] See Joseph Raz, "Authority and Justification," *Philosophy and Public Affairs* 14 (1985): 3–29. Raz offers a number of subtle qualifications to the substitution view of political authority. Those qualifications do not affect the points made here.

[41] See Audi, *Religious Commitment*, p. 67.

[42] Jean-Jacques Rousseau, *The Social Contract*, Book 1, chapter 6, §4.

[43] Audi, *Religious Commitment*, p. 158.

Considerations which cannot be seen to have reason-giving force are not reasons for which a fully rational and adequately informed person would perform that action. Coercing someone on the basis of such considerations therefore violates (b). Such coercion is wrong if the Surrogacy Conception is right. Furthermore, suppose that religious reasons are not such that they would move fully rational and adequately informed persons to do what is required by some law enacted for religious reasons. Then coercing someone for religious reasons violates condition (b). This would not itself show that religious reasons are not publicly comprehensible, since the person or persons in question could still see them to have *some* force. It would, however, show that coercing someone for religious reasons is wrong if the Surrogacy Conception is right.

Finally, the Surrogacy Conception promises to show what is wrong with coercing someone for incomprehensible reasons without appealing to the consequences of doing so. Explaining the rationale for the conception, Audi says:

> If I am coerced on grounds that cannot motivate me, as a rational informed person, to do the thing in question, I cannot come to identify with the deed and will tend to resent having to do it. Even if the deed in fact *is* my obligation, where only esoteric knowledge . . . can show that it is, I will tend to resent the coercion. This kind of coercion breeds alienation.
>
> It is part of the underlying rationale of liberal democracy that we not have to feel this kind of resentment – that we give up autonomy only where, no matter what our specific preferences or our particular world view, we can be expected, given adequate rationality and sufficient information, to see that we would have (or would at least tend to have) so acted on our own.[44]

Though Audi mentions the resentment that results from coercing people for reasons which cannot move them, we can take him to mean that the wrongness of coercing people for incomprehensible reasons depends – or also depends – on the disrespect it shows for their interest in acting autonomously.

But how plausible is the Surrogacy Conception on closer examination? Problems with it begin to appear when we look more closely at the second condition. According to that condition, coercing a person P to do A for reason r is justified only if, if P were fully rational and adequately informed, P would see that others have a right to his performance of A or that he ought to do A, and P would perform or tend to perform A for r or some essentially related reason.

44　*ibid.*, p. 67.

One difficulty with this requirement is that Audi does not lay down conditions of adequate information and full rationality beyond saying that those who are fully rational are "willing to imagine a reversal of positions or roles between [themselves] and others." Are most people fully rational and adequately informed most of the time, so that I am identical with my full and adequate surrogate most of the time? If not, which of my current beliefs, desires and dispositions to act does my surrogate have and which does he lack? What is adequate information? The deliverance of science or perhaps science plus common sense? What of the deliverances of theology, moral philosophy or social theory? Are they part of adequate information? If not, does my surrogate believe them, or may he? Does he have all of my beliefs and desires *plus* those beliefs that result from adequate information, or does the provision of adequate information lead him to disbelieve some things I believe? And if the provision of adequate information persuades him to favor one course of action, can he also be persuaded to favor another which excludes the former, or does practical rationality preclude this? Is my full and adequate surrogate an impartial spectator, an ideal observer or perhaps a party in Rawls's original position? And most important, what is my relationship to my surrogate? Do I believe that if he would do A for reason r, I should do A for r? Does he believe that I should believe that if he would do A for r, I should do A for r? What if I do not have that belief – is the resentment that I feel for being coerced to perform an action he would perform justified resentment or not?

Unless Audi can provide convincing answers to these questions, the Surrogacy Conception cannot do the job it is introduced to do. Consider first the question of what constitutes adequate information. Audi's example of an incomprehensible reason is a consideration that "cannot be seen to have any force given the powers of an adequately informed rational citizen, [one that,] for example, cannot be so understood without initiation into a subculture." The implication seems to be that initiation into a subculture of the relevant kind involves the acceptance of beliefs or norms of rationality that the adequately informed rational citizen does not or need not accept. The Surrogacy Conception is supposed to show that it is wrong to coerce people for such reasons. What counts as a subculture and what does not – hence what counts as an incomprehensible reason and what does not – depends upon what adequate information and rationality are. Audi wants to argue that religious beliefs are incomprehensible in the relevant sense and that the problem with advocating coercion for religious reasons is that such coercion would violate the conditions of the Surrogacy Conception. If he is to make the argument credibly, he cannot simply assume standards of adequate information and full rationality according to which our adequately informed and fully rational surrogates do not or need not believe religious claims or are not moved by religious reasons.

Consider next the question of which of my beliefs, desires and dispositions my full and adequate surrogate has. When I discussed the Principle of Secular Motivation, I argued that people can recognize reasons for laws which do not move them because they have other, preemptive reasons for doing what the law requires. Suppose I am a person who is subject to a law requiring A, that the law is justified for one set of reasons r but that I have other, preemptive reasons for doing A. If my surrogate has my preemptive reasons to do A and my disposition to act on them, then he does not do or tend to do A for r even though the law requiring A is justified by r.

Audi concedes that he merely sketches the Surrogacy Conception. Perhaps the worries I have raised so far can be addressed by the provision of a more detailed account of it. There is, however, a deeper problem that will not be fixed by the provision of more detail. It lies with the basic idea of the Surrogacy Conception.

To see how this problem arises for Audi's version of the Surrogacy Conception, recall that according to his condition (b), if coercing P to perform A for reason r is justified, then if P were fully rational and adequately informed, P would see that others have a right to his performing A or that he ought to perform A, and P would perform A or would tend to perform it for r. So if coercing P to do A is justified for reason r, then in a world W* populated by our full and adequate surrogates, P's surrogate sees that others have a right to his doing A or that he ought to do A and P's surrogate performs A for reason r. In the case of justified coercive laws which apply to everyone, every full and adequate surrogate in W* sees that other surrogates have a right to his doing A or that he ought to do A, and every full and adequate surrogate does A for r. Therefore if some law requiring everyone in the actual world to do A is justified and if the Surrogacy Conception is correct, there are reasons r for which every full and rational surrogate in W* does A and every surrogate sees that others have a right to his doing A or that he ought to do A. Do laws which intuitively seem justified satisfy this requirement? And what conditions of rationality and informational adequacy must our surrogates meet if such laws do satisfy it?

I do not believe the requirement is satisfied by laws which solve pure coordination problems, like whether everyone should drive on the right or the left, or by laws establishing certain uniform standards, like the number of witnesses needed to validate a will. Laws of these kinds are, however, the sort of peripheral cases of law which pose problems for many legal theories. Rather than focus on them, I want to argue that the condition is not satisfied by more central cases of law that intuitively seem to be justified.

Suppose that I live in a town in which air pollution has reached disturbingly high levels. I and other citizens are asked to decide among two measures to combat it. One would require local industries to comply with strict antipollution standards; the other would severely restrict auto usage on local streets when climatic conditions are unfavorable. I study the matter carefully and decide to support the first. The stockholders of local industries, including myself, can afford air filters. The costs of relocation are so expensive that I think we stockholders are more likely to decide to install the filters than to move. The majority, who have also investigated the matter thoroughly, fear the adverse economic impact of enforcing antipollution measures and believe that more pollution is due to automobiles than to industry in any case. A referendum restricting auto usage wins overwhelmingly on these grounds and I am forced to rely more heavily on public transportation.

It seems to me that this restriction on my liberty and the liberty of other residents of my town is justified. If the Surrogacy Conception is correct, then there are reasons r for which all of our full and rational surrogates restrict or tend to restrict their auto usage. What could those reasons be? The reasons over which r ranges are not reasons which presuppose that a law is in place, reasons such as "The law requires restrictions on auto usage" or "The majority voted to restrict auto usage." They are reasons for enacting a coercive law, reasons citizens might offer one another to vote for it such as "the cost of enforcing antipollution standards on industry would outweigh the inconvenience of restricting auto usage." It is precisely because the reasons over which r ranges do not include reasons like "the law requires restrictions of auto usage" that – when he introduced the Surrogacy Conception – Audi said we should have to "give up autonomy only where . . . we can be expected, given adequate rationality and sufficient information, to see that we would have (or at least tend to have) so acted *on our own*." Are there reasons r which do not presuppose the existence of a law restricting auto usage for which all full and adequate surrogates of the residents of my town do "on their own" in W* what the law requires of us in W?

The claim that there are such reasons has odd implications. For one thing, had the majority of my fellow citizens voted to impose antipollution restrictions on industry, then I assume that the restrictions of liberty that that measure entailed would have been justified. In that case, there would be reasons for which my full and rational surrogate would have complied with *those* restrictions on his own. It seems odd to claim that the existence of reasons for which full and adequate surrogates act on their own in W* – the existence of reasons on which I would act if I were fully rational and adequately informed – depends upon what the majority in W decides to do.

Furthermore, if there are reasons for which all our surrogates in W* do on their own what laws require in W, then the existence of disagreement in W about what laws there should be must be due to the fact that we in W are not fully rational and adequately informed. This seems highly implausible. What restrictions of behavior solve the problem legislation is supposed to address depend upon complicated economic and scientific questions. To insist that everyone would arrive at the same conclusion to these questions if adequately informed and fully rational and that everyone would voluntarily restrict his behavior in the same way in response to the pollution problem seem to require that persons who are adequately informed in Audi's sense are informed about the future and that they have information about psychology, economics and social theory that far exceeds what experts in those fields currently have. This seems an implausibly high standard of informational adequacy. We shall see in a moment why such a standard undermines the Surrogacy Conception. First I want to look at what standard of adequacy the Surrogacy Conception presupposes when the disagreement about legislation is moral.

Imagine that the costs of pharmaceuticals have become so high that it is clear most people need a prescription insurance plan. At issue is whether they will be allowed to purchase coverage from private insurers or whether everyone will have to subscribe to a government plan financed through a special payroll tax. It is granted all around that private plans provide the cheapest coverage for those who can afford any plan at all, but that reliance on private insurers would leave the poorest without access to drugs. A government program would cover everyone, but only by imposing more costs on those who could have afforded private insurance than they would bear if they were allowed to subscribe to private plans. Moreover, the inefficiencies of administering a plan that covers every last person entails that the marginal cost of covering the poorest would be extremely high, so that cost-benefit analysis favors privatization. Those who support the government plan do so because they think a decent society should provide universal drug coverage and because they think cost-benefit analysis should not be determinative on so important a policy question. Those who oppose are moved by cost-benefit considerations. They also think that the plan provides morally objectionable disincentives to work, that enough is already done for society's poorest through expensive transfer programs, that the government plan would unfairly burden the working poor and the middle class, and that foreclosing the possibility of self-help remedies like private insurance makes government too intrusive.

Are there reasons for either solution to the problem which would be acted on by everyone if fully rational and adequately informed? Moral disagreement that infects politics in the actual world seems to depend upon different interpretations of past and current events, different hopes and fears for the future, differences in political philosophy and deep differences of sensibility. The Surrogacy Conception seems to imply that these differences are due to someone's deficiency of knowledge or rationality, since it implies that our full and adequate surrogates would agree on what legislation to enact. This, however, seems highly implausible. What is more plausible is that the Surrogacy Conception is too strong and that persons may justifiably be coerced to perform some actions on the basis of some reasons that would not move them to perform the action even if they were fully rational and adequately informed. The problem is to identify those reasons. As we shall see in the next chapter, this is in effect the problem John Rawls takes up.

Audi's aim in laying down the Surrogacy Conception is to state conditions under which I can identify with actions I am coerced to perform. The basic idea of the conception is that I can identify with those actions only if I am coerced for reasons for which my surrogate would perform or tend to perform that action on his own. These are reasons I would act from if I satisfied certain norms of rationality and information. Such counterfactual analyses of identification with our actions are difficult to evaluate because it is hard to get a grip on the notion of identifying with our actions except through such analyses. Still it seems clear enough that if such analyses are to succeed, the norms of rationality and information they employ must be norms we should satisfy or aspire to satisfy or that it would be good for us to satisfy, given the kind of creatures we are. Call this the *desirability condition* on norms used in such analyses. The desirability condition implies that it cannot be a necessary condition on identifying with an action that I would perform it if I were grossly defective in some way. Nor is it a necessary condition of identifying with an action that

I would perform it if I were a well-functioning bat or a well-functioning member of some other species very different from human beings as we know them. Nor, I assume, is it a necessary condition that the action be one I would perform if I were God and satisfied the norms of rationality and information that God satisfies. The norms satisfied by bats and by God are not norms that apply to us.

What of norms of rationality and information that are satisfied by our full and adequate surrogates? Do they satisfy the desirability condition? Those norms are such that when persons who satisfy them confront a problem we address by enacting law, they all do or tend to do the actions the law requires of us for the reasons which justify the law we would enact. Perhaps they all do or tend to do those actions because each arrives independently at the same decision about what to do. Or perhaps they all do or tend to do those actions because they reach unanimous agreement after collective deliberation. For my purposes it does not matter which of these two is correct. What matters for my purposes is that they do not need to reach a binding decision in the face of enduring disagreement about what it is best to do. Not only do they agree about fundamental political questions or about the grounds for settling fundamental questions. They agree about all the political questions which we address with coercive laws. Therefore those who satisfy Audi's norms of full rationality and adequate information either do not enact laws at all or they enact them under circumstances and to meet needs that are very different from ours. I want to suggest that norms the general satisfaction of which have this consequence – norms the general satisfaction of which have the consequence that persons who satisfy them do not need to make laws in the face of enduring disagreement about the best solution to common problems – are norms which do not satisfy the desirability condition.

I cannot develop the argument in detail. Briefly, the reason they do not is that the world inhabited by our full and adequate surrogates would be a world without either politics or political philosophy as we know them. But politics – understood as including the processes by which legislation is enacted in the face of enduring disagreement – is or can be an activity in which human beings realize important goods. These include the goods realized when we confront other agents as equals, the goods of satisfaction and mutual respect that come from reaching a mutually agreeable compromise, the self-respect that comes from having successfully defended one's interests and the education that comes from negotiating differences of opinion and finding common ground. The fact that the solution to the problem at hand will be binding and will be backed by coercion, I suggest, raises the stakes of decision-making so that these goods are available in a special way. Politics also provides the occasion for the goods we realize by reflecting on the need for laws to regulate behavior, including the goods we realize when we practice and study political philosophy. The capacity to enjoy the realization of these goods is an important element of human nature. The political disagreements that characterize our world are the result of features of our imagination and our cognitive limitations that are important ingredients of who we are. To imagine them away is to imagine away an important part of the human condition. Creatures who could reach unanimous agreement behavior because of their rationality and the information at their disposal would not be creatures sufficiently like us that the norms of rationality and informational adequacy they satisfy are norms that apply to us or that it would be desirable for us to satisfy.

The Surrogacy Conception implies that if laws of general application are justified, then there are reasons for which all full and adequate surrogates do what the law requires on their own. But as I have just shown, in order to agree in this way our surrogates must satisfy norms of information and rationality that it would not be desirable for us to satisfy. The desirability condition on norms is a condition on norms used in counterfactual analyses of identification with our action. If some set of norms does not satisfy it, the analysis in which they are used fails. Since the norms used in the Surrogacy Conception fail to satisfy it, the Surrogacy Conception does not impose a condition on our identification with actions we are coerced to perform. It therefore cannot be exploited to show what is wrong with the state's coercing people for reasons that are not intelligible or publicly comprehensible. It is therefore hard to see how it can be exploited to show what is wrong with a citizen's advocating coercion for religious reasons or for reasons that are not intelligible or publicly comprehensible. Hence it cannot be exploited to show why the Principle of Secular Rationale expresses an obligation of citizenship.

CONCLUSION

As I have shown, Audi thinks that citizens must be prepared to offer one another secular reasons because he thinks they must be prepared to offer one another "intelligible" reasons and only secular reasons are intelligible. The intelligibility condition is similar to the conditions other proponents of the standard approach have imposed on the reasons citizens must offer or be prepared to offer for coercive public policy.

Kent Greenawalt says these reasons must be, not intelligible, but "accessible."[45] Amy Gutmann and Dennis Thompson also impose an accessibility requirement, saying that citizens should "press their public claims in terms accessible to their fellow citizens."[46] Their accessibility requirement, like Audi's and Greenawalt's, has implications for citizens' use of religious arguments. As we also saw, Audi's intelligibility requirement follows from his endorsability requirement, the requirement that justifying reasons be "of a kind that any rational adult can endorse as sufficient for the purpose."[47] In a language reminiscent of Audi's endorsability requirement, Gutmann and Thompson impose a reciprocity requirement, saying citizens should "justify public policy by giving reasons that *can be accepted* by those who are bound by it."[48]

These requirements suggest that those who offer them all propound some version or other of the standard approach. These versions – and many others besides – imply that the reasons citizens must be ready to offer one another are those that satisfy some counterfactual condition. The reasons citizens must be ready to offer must be such that they can or could or would be accessed, accepted or endorsed, or such that they do not fail some counterfactual test of inaccessibility, unacceptability or unendorsability. Unfortunately few proponents of the standard approach state the conditions under which this can or could or would happen. The reason I believe the notion of accessibility cannot be adequately spelled out is because I do not believe the counterfactuals needed to make the notion clear express plausible conditions on the reasons citizens should be ready to offer. Audi's view is more developed than many other versions of the standard approach in that condition (b) of the Surrogacy Conception states a relevant counterfactual. But Audi would have to say far more than he does about rationality and adequacy of information to show that coercing people for religious reasons fails condition (b). Even that will not salvage this argument for the Principle of Secular Rationale since condition (b) presupposes undesirable norms of informational adequacy and rationality.

If my reading of Audi's argument for the Principle of Secular Rationale is correct, then he attempts to specify the kind of reasons citizens must be ready to offer one another by first asking what reasons justify coercion.

---

[45] Kent Greenawalt, *Private Consciences and Public Reasons* (Oxford: Oxford University Press, 1995), pp. 23ff.
[46] Gutmann and Thompson, *Democracy and Disagreement*, p. 57.
[47] Audi, "Liberal Democracy," p. 17.
[48] Gutmann and Thompson, *Democracy and Disagreement*, p. 52.

He locates these reasons by asking what reasons would move them to action if they were fully rational and adequately informed and looks at what properties such reasons have. He then concludes that citizens must be ready to offer one another reasons of that kind. I have argued that there are serious problems with this approach. It would, of course, be possible to try identifying the relevant kinds of reasons by using different counterfactuals. One counterfactual condition that might be imposed on reasons used in political justification is that they must be of a kind that our properly informed and rational surrogates would endorse if asked to choose among kinds of reasons they will use to defend restrictions on liberty. This, as we saw, is suggested by Audi in passing when he says that legal coercion must be justified by appeal to "grounds of a kind that any rational adult can endorse as sufficient for the purpose." It is roughly this counterfactual that John Rawls employs in his treatment of public reason. Rawls thinks that this condition leads to a very different requirement than that expressed by the Principle of Secular Rationale, a requirement he calls "the duty of civility." I examine Rawls's treatment of public reason in the next chapter.

CHAPTER 7

John Rawls on public reason

In his first published treatment of public reason, "The Idea of Public Reason," John Rawls defended an obligation of citizenship he called "the duty of civility." This duty requires citizens to "be able to explain to one another on those fundamental questions how the principles and policies they advocate and vote for can be supported by the political values of public reason."[1] More recently, in the essay "The Idea of Public Reason Revisited," Rawls has qualified the duty with an addendum he refers to as "the proviso." This "allows us to introduce into political discussion at any time our comprehensive doctrine, religious or nonreligious, provided that, in due course, we give properly public reasons to support the policies and principles our comprehensive doctrine is said to support."[2]

While the duty of civility and the proviso obviously raise a number of questions, Rawls's basic idea seems clear enough. Participants in public debate may publicly offer arguments for their political positions which are drawn from their comprehensive views. But in a pluralistic society, they should also be aware that not everyone will accept all their premises or regard their arguments as providing good reasons for the policies and principles they favor. They must therefore be ready to make good their religious arguments by supplementing them with what Rawls calls "properly public reasons."

Rawls's view is a version of what I have been calling "the standard approach." Properly public reasons – the reasons citizens must be prepared to offer one another – are therefore justifying reasons – reasons of the kind government must offer citizens to justify its actions. They are also accessible reasons, in a very sophisticated sense of "accessible." They are reasons of a kind that reasonable and rational citizens would endorse as an appropriate basis for settling fundamental political questions. As

---

[1] Rawls, *Political Liberalism*, p. 217.   [2] Rawls, *Law of Peoples*, p. 144.

will become apparent when we look more closely at what these reasons are, it is Rawls's insistence on the readiness to provide properly public reasons that rules out exclusive reliance on arguments that (5.1) and (5.2) say citizens do not need to supplement.

Rawls's work on public reason has generated a great deal of discussion. Most of this discussion concerns the reasonability or fairness of requiring citizens to supplement arguments drawn from comprehensive doctrine. Surprisingly little of it has been devoted to teasing out just what public reasons are and exactly how Rawls defends the claim that citizens must be prepared to appeal to them. The dispatch with which commentators have moved to the *implications* of Rawls's view for the use of arguments drawn from comprehensive doctrine suggests that they share one of two unspoken assumptions. They may assume that Rawls's view of public reason is clear enough as it stands – that his central concepts are well defined, his distinctions perspicuous, his premises innocuous or self-evident, and his inferences not just sound but obviously so. Or they may assume that Rawls should simply be granted his definitions and distinctions, his premises and inferences, because the real interest of his view lies in the implications rather than the arguments.

Though I have said that the basic idea of the proviso is clear enough, I do not think either of these assumptions is correct. Much of Rawls's exposition and argument is extremely puzzling. The anomalies multiply when some of his more recent remarks in "Public Reason Revisited" are juxtaposed with some of his earlier ones in *Political Liberalism*. Some of these puzzles are especially important because they raise the possibility that Rawls's view of public reason is not really an alternative to the view I have put forward. For example, various of Rawls's remarks suggest that his guidelines do not apply to actual societies or that they do not apply to the public political debate of ordinary citizens. Even once it is clear that they *do* apply to the ordinary citizens of actual societies, other remarks raise questions about *why* they apply. Ultimately I want to challenge Rawls's view by pressing two questions:

(7.1) How must citizens think of their authority if they accept and comply with the duty of civility and the proviso?

and

(7.2) Is it reasonable for some citizens to reject this view of their own collective authority?

First, however, I want to sort through some of the puzzles about Rawls's view, beginning with those that suggest that his guidelines are not genuine competitors to (5.1) and (5.2).

ACTUAL SOCIETIES, ORDINARY CITIZENS AND ROLE-SPECIFIC DUTIES

So much of Rawls's work is premised upon idealizing assumptions that it would be natural to think his account of public reason is part of ideal theory as well. As if to confirm this, Rawls opens "The Idea of Public Reason Revisited" by saying that "[t]he idea of public reason, as I understand it, belongs to a conception of a well ordered constitutional democratic society."[3] That the idea belongs to the conception of a *well-ordered* society raises obvious questions about its bearing on societies that are not well ordered, as many actual liberal democracies are not. For it could be that Rawls intends his discussion of public reason to do no more than furnish details about the conduct of political debate in a well-ordered society, details that previous descriptions left unstated. While the details would then round out Rawls's theory of justice, it would have no more (or less) bearing on actual societies than, say, his discussion of justice between generations.

If this were the right way to understand Rawls's treatment of public reason, then his discussion would be irrelevant to the obligations of citizenship in actual democracies. There are, however, reasons for thinking that this is not the correct interpretation of Rawls's discussion and that his guidelines of public reason are intended to apply to actual societies and their citizens as well. One is his treatment of issues like abortion.[4] Both the tone in which he discusses these issues and the examples he gives of arguments bearing on them suggest that he thinks citizens in actual societies are required to abide by the guidelines of public reason when they debate these matters. Even more telling is the fact that Rawls's original discussion of public reason made provision for societies that are not well ordered.[5] When Rawls later decided to drop these provisions, he commented that his revised account "secures what is needed."[6] The implication clearly is that this revised account is intended to cover the cases covered by the original one, including cases in which society is not

---

[3] *ibid.*, p. 131.
[4] See Rawls, *Political Liberalism*, p. 243, note 32, the explanation of this at pp. lv–lvii, notes 31–33; also *Law of Peoples*, pp. 169–70, notes 80–83.
[5] Rawls, *Political Liberalism*, pp. 248ff.   [6] *ibid.*, p. lii.

well ordered. Perhaps the opening remark of "Public Reason Revisited" should therefore be understood to say that "the idea of public reason belongs to a conception of a well-ordered constitutional democratic society" in this sense: no society is well ordered unless its citizens and public officials perfectly comply with the requirements of public reason. This does not imply that the duty of civility and the proviso are binding *only* in well-ordered societies or that they *do not* bind in actual ones. Since other remarks clearly suggest that they do, it is safe to conclude that Rawls intends them to apply to actual societies.

Do they, like (5.1) and (5.2), apply to *ordinary citizens* in actual societies? In "Public Reason Revisited" Rawls says that the idea of public reason applies to "government officials and candidates for public office";[7] he immediately expands this to include their campaign managers. Ordinary citizens, citizens who are not candidates or office-holders, "fulfill their duty of civility and support the idea of public reason by doing what they can to hold public officials to it."[8] This they presumably do by complying with what Rawls earlier said that "public reason asks" of them: namely, that they be "able to explain their vote to one another in terms of a reasonable balance of political values."[9] For when candidates know that citizens will only cast votes that can be explained in this way, they know those citizens will repudiate candidates who base crucial parts of their campaigns on nonpublic reasons alone. Candidates are thus held to the idea of public reason by the need to secure their constituents' votes.

Rawls's claim in "Public Reason Revisited" that citizens who do not hold public office fulfill the duty of civility by voting in the right way is hard to square with suggestions in *Political Liberalism* that the idea of public reason applies to citizens' *discourse*. There he says that "in *discussing* constitutional essentials and matters of basic justice we are not to appeal to comprehensive religious and philosophical doctrine"[10] and that "[t]he point of the ideal of public reason is that citizens are to conduct their fundamental *discussions* within the framework of public reason."[11] Furthermore, where *Political Liberalism* does mention how the requirements of public reason apply to voting, those requirements are said to fall out of its implications for discussion.[12] Rawls's more recent emphasis on voting is even harder to square with his remarks about Martin Luther King and about Joseph Bernardin, the late Catholic archbishop of Chicago. Rawls says that King's arguments for civil rights and Bernardin's arguments against

---

[7] Rawls, *Law of Peoples*, p. 133.   [8] *ibid.*, p. 136.   [9] Rawls, *Political Liberalism*, p. 243.
[10] *ibid.*, pp. 224–25.   [11] *ibid.*, p. 226.   [12] See the text cited at chapter 4, note 1.

abortion rights were cast in terms of public reason.[13] His clear implication is that they should have been. What is not obvious is why. Neither King nor Bernardin held or campaigned for public office, so we would think that what mattered is how they voted rather than what they said.

A natural response – suggested by the central place Rawls now gives to ordinary citizens' votes – would be that, as moral and religious leaders, King and Bernardin provided their followers grounds for voting by what they said about how pressing questions were to be settled. They were obligated to comply with the guidelines of public reason because, if they had not, they would have encouraged their followers to support politicians who offered only religious arguments for civil rights or the prohibition of abortion. According to this line of thought, then, King's and Bernardin's obligation to offer arguments in public reason depended upon their followers' obligation to hold politicians to the guidelines by voting only for those who comply with them.

Rawls has consistently said the guidelines of public reason apply to speech in the public forum or, as he now says, "the public political forum." The difficulty with the reply I have just imagined on his behalf is that neither King nor Bernardin spoke there. That forum, Rawls now says,

> may be divided into three parts: the discourse of judges in their decisions, and especially of the judges of the supreme court; the discourse of government officials, especially chief executives and legislators; and finally, the discourse of candidates for public office and their campaign managers, especially in their public oratory, party platforms, and political statements.[14]

This restrictive definition of the public political forum no doubt reflects Rawls's increasing realism about actual societies. Though Rawls's early work was not explicit about the boundaries of the public forum, it was clear he wanted to claim that a great deal of political speech takes place outside it. This enabled him to exempt that speech from the guidelines of public reason. At the same time, his talk of "fundamental discussions" suggested that he thought ordinary citizens do regularly discuss fundamental political issues in public fora. As Rawls thought more deeply about where to draw the boundaries of the public forum and about how his views of public reason apply to actual societies, he may have realized that actual societies have relatively few public fora in which citizens can engage in the "fundamental discussions" to which *Political Liberalism* referred.[15] And so by the time he wrote "Public Reason Revisited"

---

[13] For King, see Rawls, *Political Liberalism*, p. 250, note 39; for Bernardin, see *ibid.*, p. lvi, note 32.
[14] Rawls, *Law of Peoples*, pp. 133–34.   [15] cf. *ibid.*, p. 24, note 19.

he defined the public political forum so that it excludes discussions by ordinary citizens.

While Rawls's increasing explicitness about the public political forum may explain the inconsistencies between his earlier and later treatment of ordinary citizens, it does not resolve them. King and Bernardin did not speak in the public political forum as Rawls now understands it, yet he still seems to think their arguments should have complied with the guidelines of public reason. If the only discourse to which the idea of public reason applies is discourse in the public political forum, then the fact that their arguments affected the votes of their followers should be immaterial. But the real problem with Rawls's definition of the public political forum is not, of course, that it leads to an inconsistent treatment of examples to which he gave relatively little attention in the first place. It is that Rawls now seems unable to accommodate the plausible intuitions that underlay his original treatments of King and Bernardin. Those intuitions are that when citizens who do not hold office discuss fundamental questions they give evidence of how they will vote and they affect the votes of others, that the consequences of their doing so may sometimes be such that they have an obligation to discuss those questions responsibly and that expressing that obligation is part of what guidelines of public reason are supposed to do.

Rawls could preserve these intuitions by maintaining that discourse in "the public political forum" is just one part of the discourse to which the idea of public reason applies. Rawls distinguishes speech which takes place in what he calls "the background culture" from that which takes place in the public political forum.[16] He could maintain that political speech in the background culture can sometimes have the features of speech in the public political forum in virtue of which the idea of public reason applies to the latter. Or he could maintain that the guidelines of public reason apply to argument in the public forum but could claim that a great deal more takes place in "the public political forum" than the speech he singles out in "Public Reason Revisited." Either would lead him toward the more capacious understanding of the public forum found in chapter 4. That understanding is, I think, the correct one and one that allows the guidelines of public reason to apply to ordinary citizens.

Is the duty to comply with those guidelines, like the duty to comply with (5.1) and (5.2), a *role-specific* duty? Rawls seems to think so but the

---

[16] Rawls, *Political Liberalism*, p. 215.

remark which implies that it is is initially very puzzling. He writes: "the ideal of citizenship imposes a moral, not a legal, duty – the duty of civility – to be able to explain to one another on those fundamental questions how the principles and policies they advocate and vote for can be supported by the political values of public reason."[17]

If the duty of civility is imposed by the ideal of citizenship, the duty would seem to be role-specific. It would apply to agents because a role-specific ideal applies to them. The problem is that it is not immediately clear how moral *ideals* can impose moral *requirements*. The problem cannot simply be dismissed, since Rawls repeats the association of the duty of civility with moral ideals in a second passage.[18] To see what is so puzzling about this association, suppose we think of the ideal of citizenship as an abstract conception of a citizen who realizes to a perfect or an exemplary degree all of the excellences associated with that role. It may well be that we instantiate very great goods when we realize that ideal. It may also be that we can realize that ideal only if we comply with the guidelines of public reason. This implies that it is in some way good to comply with those guidelines, but not that we are required to do so.

One way to get from the ideal of citizenship to the duties of civility would be to deflate the notion of an ideal so as to narrow the difference between the two. Then the ideal of citizenship might be understood not as a conception of someone who exemplifies the virtues of citizens perfectly, but as a conception of someone who has the virtues desirable in a good citizen to a lesser but still satisfactory degree,[19] including the settled disposition to honor her duties. With a description of the ideal in hand, we could work backwards to the duties of citizenship. If those duties could be shown to include the duty of civility and if that, in turn, can be shown to include the duty to abide by the guidelines of public reason, then the ideal of citizenship might be said to impose the requirement to honor those guidelines, as Rawls suggests it does.

Unfortunately, this attempt to derive requirements from ideals seems to go wrong in at least two ways. First, the attempt depends upon a deflation of ideals that makes them too flat. Though I cannot pursue this matter here, I believe it is a mistake to think of personal ideals as entailing no moral excellences more demanding than a propensity perfectly to perform one's duty. Deflating ideals allows the part they play in the moral life to escape. Second and more worrisome, this line of

---

[17] *ibid.*, p. 217.   [18] *ibid.*, p. 218.   [19] See Rawls, *Theory of Justice*, p. 436.

thought seems to include an unnecessary shuffle. It must begin with a specification of citizenship and the associated duties in order to elaborate a conception of the citizen who performs those duties ideally. It must then read the duties back off the ideal in order to salvage the claim that it is the ideal which imposes them.

My suggestion is that instead of taking the ideal of citizenship as a conception of a citizen who has the virtues of a good citizen or who realizes the excellences of citizenship to an exemplary degree, we take it as a *partial specification* of citizenship. That partial specification gives the powers and interests of citizens as such. When Rawls says that the ideal "imposes" the duty of civility, we could take him to mean that the duty of civility follows from or can be derived from that specification. Later I shall try to give this reading some textual and philosophical support. What matters for the moment is that if we take the ideal of citizenship as a partial specification of that social role, we can see why Rawls thinks that the duty of civility and the proviso are role-specific duties while avoiding the puzzles that beset alternative readings.

In this section I have argued that the duty of civility, as qualified by the proviso, expresses a role-specific duty that applies to ordinary citizens in actual societies when they vote or when they present political arguments in the public forum. I suggested that Rawls's view would be more intuitively plausible if he adopted the account of the public forum given in chapter 4. His principles therefore seem to be competitors to (5.1) and (5.2). One important difference between them, however, is their scope. As I indicated in chapter 4, principles (5.1) and (5.2) apply when citizens vote on and debate issues touching on a large number of interests. The duty of civility applies to a much narrower range of issues. Since I implied in chapter 4 that Rawls's view derives some of its plausibility from the urgency of the interests at stake when it applies, it is necessary to say something about the scope of the duty of civility.

THE SCOPE OF THE DUTY OF CIVILITY

Rawls's guidelines of public reason apply only[20] to questions about what he calls "constitutional essentials and questions of basic justice."[21] While the boundaries of this set are somewhat hazy,[22] I am prepared to grant Rawls the category for the sake of argument. Whatever else the category includes, it includes questions about the scope of the basic liberties and

[20] Or apply in the first instance; see Rawls, *Political Liberalism*, p. 215.   [21] *ibid.*
[22] Greenawalt, *Private Consciences and Public Reasons*, pp. 113ff.

about the minimally just distribution of income and opportunity.[23] The inclusion of distributive questions signals a departure from other views about the proper scope of public reason, most notably Audi's. Audi's principles apply to deliberations about all and only policies which restrict conduct.[24] Why does Rawls take a different view, singling out constitutional essentials and questions of basic justice for special treatment?

Rawls famously thinks of citizens as having two moral powers: the capacity to form, pursue and revise a conception of the good and the capacity for a sense of justice. My hunch is that he thinks questions about constitutional essentials and matters of basic justice are special because of the way they bear on the exercise of those powers. The distribution of rights and liberties, opportunity and income all affect what citizens can do in pursuit of their conceptions of the good. More important, they affect citizens' reflective or higher-order exercise of their powers to form and revise their conceptions of the good. They affect what aims citizens can consider and adopt, what possibilities they think are open to them and what they can hope to be. Political debates about constitutional essentials and matters of basic justice therefore concern the fundamental social conditions under which citizens form their life-plans and identities. Because they have such profound effects, the outcomes to those debates must, Rawls thinks, be supportable by public reasons. Audi, by contrast, thinks it is the public advocacy and legal imposition of coercion that must be supportable by the kinds of reasons *he* thinks are justifying. This difference of focus is explained by a deeper and more interesting difference between their specifications of citizenship.

As we saw in the last chapter, Audi thinks citizens should be conceived of as having a fundamental interest in a certain kind of autonomy: an interest in performing only those actions they can identify with or can recognize as their own.[25] This is an interest which government and other citizens must respect. According to the Surrogacy Conception, this interest is frustrated when someone is forced to perform an action by a law enacted for reasons she would not act from if fully informed and rational. Legal infringements on citizens' freedom of action must be justifiable by reasons they would accept under those conditions; citizens who advocate legal infringements should have and be ready to offer such reasons. Thus Audi defends his guidelines of public reason – via the Surrogacy Conception – as necessary to safeguard citizens' fundamental interest in performing autonomous actions.

[23] Rawls, *Political Liberalism*, pp. 228–29.
[24] See Audi, *Religious Commitment*, pp. 86ff.   [25] *ibid.*, pp. 65ff.

Rawls thinks citizens should be conceived of as having a fundamental interest a different sort of autonomy: an interest in the autonomous endorsement and pursuit of the aims and aspirations that shape their plans of life.[26] This is an interest in what I called the "essential use" of liberty in chapter 4. It is an interest Rawls thinks government must respect. Citizens endorse and pursue their plans of life by the reflective exercise of their moral powers. Their interest in being able to endorse and pursue their own central aims and aspirations autonomously is frustrated if the essential social conditions for the reflective exercise of those powers – the distribution of rights, liberties, income and opportunity – are determined by laws and policies which they cannot see as justifying the distribution. Laws and policies bearing on those essential social conditions must be supportable by reasons they can be expected to accept. These are properly public reasons.

Furthermore, Rawls would insist, citizens must respect one another's fundamental autonomy interest. To show mutual respect for that interest, citizens voting on laws and policies which bear on that interest or discussing them in the public forum should have and be ready to offer reasons they reasonably think "may reasonably be accepted by other citizens."[27] This, he thinks, requires them to have and be ready to offer properly public reasons – hence the duty of civility and the proviso. Crudely put, whereas Audi's guidelines of public reason are intended to safeguard citizens' interest in performing autonomous actions, Rawls's are intended to safeguard their interest in leading autonomous lives.

The forms of autonomy to which I have said Audi and Rawls attach such importance are both political values in Rawls's sense. The interests citizens have in these forms of autonomy are interests they have as citizens. Those interests are ascribed to them for political theoretic purposes, to frame theories about how political power must be exercised so that those subject to it can still enjoy important forms of political freedom.

What might seem objectionable about the reading of Rawls I am urging is not that it blurs the distinction between the political and the metaphysical, but that it misdescribes the threat liberals typically think political authority poses to citizens' autonomy. Liberals, it is often said, think the defining – or at least the most salient – feature of political authority is its reliance on coercive power, a power in the face of which citizens need to

---

[26] For the notion of a plan of life, see Rawls, *Theory of Justice*, pp. 407ff. The fundamental interest in being able to affirm central features of our plans of life as our own is suggested, in a different connection, at Rawls, *Political Liberalism*, p. 313.

[27] Rawls, *Political Liberalism*, p. xlvi.

carve out space for autonomous action. Audi's recognition that coercive laws need to be justified locates him squarely within the liberal tradition so understood. The premium he places on the autonomy of every action is clearly reminiscent of Kant. For Rawls as I have been reading him, the most salient feature of political authority – and the feature which motivates a key element of his account of public reason – seems to be the pervasiveness of its distributive functions. Autonomy is threatened, on this reading, when government power is used to effect unjustifiable distributions. This initially seems to be a very different view of government than that held by the authors of seminal texts in the liberal tradition.[28]

But Rawls does not ignore the coercive power by which political authority exercises its distributive functions and maintains its monopoly on them.[29] A more detailed exposition of his argument would show that he relies on a premise about the coerciveness of political power at a crucial juncture. It would also show that he subscribes to a strong version of what I called the "Agency Conception of Government," according to which political power is delegated to government by the people. Rawls thinks that that power *just is* the power of the people. The fact that the power which has such profound effects on citizens' lives is ultimately their own power makes justification of its exercise especially important.[30] Moreover, a concern to show how citizens can form and execute their plans of life autonomously while they are subject to these distributive functions would not place Rawls outside the tradition. A similar concern surely underlies Rousseau's insistence that laws should insure citizens' economic independence.[31] Finally, I do not mean to deny that Rawls values autonomous actions. I could hardly do so in light of some of his remarks in *Theory of Justice*.[32] And of course the reflective planning of a life is itself an action or a set of actions which Rawls thinks must be performed

---

[28] Indeed, as Cass Sunstein once emphasized in conversation, it may be a view of government's most salient features that only became plausible in America with the advent of the New Deal.

[29] Rawls's list of the "distinctive aspect[s] of the political" includes both its reliance on coercion and the profound effects it has on "citizens' character and aims, the kinds of persons they are and aspire to be." Rawls, *Political Liberalism*, p. 68.

[30] I provide such an exposition in "Citizenship and Public Reason."

[31] Jean-Jacques Rousseau, *The Social Contract*, Book II, chapter 11, §2. I say "similar" not only because Rousseau must always be interpreted with caution but also because I said Rawls is interested in showing how citizens can lead autonomous lives. Autonomy may be a different ethical value from the authenticity of life Rousseau is said to have valued so highly and which he may have had in mind in the passage I have cited. Far from undermining the claim in the text, this difference tells in favor of my point that the liberal tradition houses thinkers with quite different concerns and priorities. For the difference between autonomy and authenticity, see Charles Taylor, *The Ethics of Authenticity* (Cambridge, MA: Harvard University Press, 1991), pp. 27–29.

[32] Rawls, *Theory of Justice*, p. 515.

autonomously. What matters for my purposes is this. Rawls thinks guidelines of public reason apply where they do because he recognizes that the higher-order activities involved in adopting and pursuing one's central aims comprise a distinct kind of action that is especially important for political theory. Thus he is best read, not as departing from the liberal tradition, but as attempting simultaneously to address concerns that have motivated different thinkers within it – including both Kant and Rousseau.

What seems most questionable about the line of argument I attributed to Rawls earlier in this section is the move *from* the requirement that citizens discussing and voting on fundamental matters should have and be ready to offer reasons they reasonably think "may reasonably be accepted by other citizens" *to* the duty of civility and the proviso. Perhaps each citizen's interest in leading an autonomous life is urgent enough to ground a requirement that other citizens respect it. Perhaps respect requires that when we vote on or publicly discuss measures bearing on that interest, we must offer others reasons we reasonably think they might reasonably accept.[33] But why does Rawls think these claims license a conclusion about the content of those reasons? Why does he think they license the conclusion that those reasons must be, as the duty of civility puts it, "the political values of public reason"? The answer is to be found in the notion of the reasonable. Properly public reasons, the political values of public reason, are the only political values or reasons Rawls thinks we can *reasonably* expect that others may *reasonably* accept. Seeing why he thinks this requires us to look more closely at what the political values of public reason are and how they are determined, beginning with how they are determined in justice as fairness. This will bring us, at last, to the two questions I want to ask about Rawls's view.

THE POLITICAL VALUES OF PUBLIC REASON: JUSTICE AS FAIRNESS

A variety of interests and desires, ideologies and beliefs can incline us to political positions. We can favor laws and policies because they enrich our class or our sector of the economy, because they will make our communities safer or the poor better-off, because they advance our nationalist impulses or the triumph of the proletariat. These are putative goods or values that we may hope to realize in politics. They may, with some propriety, be called "political values." They are not, however, the

33 cf. Rawls, *Political Liberalism*, p. xliv.

political values *of public reason*. The political values of public reason are the values which provide, not just *motives* for political action, but *reasons* for it. To see the difference, it is helpful to recall a point Rawls would make about reasons.

Reasons are considerations that can play a role in justification. Considerations can play a justificatory role, Rawls thinks, only if they are picked out or "specified" by a moral conception, an ordered network of principles and values that help spell out a justification should one be required. Thus Rawls says: "liberal political principles and values . . . are specified by liberal political conceptions of justice and fall under the category of the political." Liberal political conceptions, Rawls continues, have the following three features:

First, their principles apply to basic political and social institutions (the basic structure of society); second, they can be presented independently from comprehensive doctrines of any kind (although they may, of course, be supported by a reasonable overlapping consensus of such doctrines); and finally, they can be worked out from fundamental ideas seen as implicit in the public political culture of a constitutional regime, such as the conceptions of citizens as free and equal persons, and of society as a fair system of cooperation.[34]

He concludes "the content of public reason is given by the principles and values of the family of liberal political conceptions of justice meeting these three conditions."[35]

What does it mean to say that a conception of justice "specifie[s]" principles and values? Rawls says that the content of public reason is given by "the *family* of liberal political conceptions," so we will eventually have to see what he means by this. But since justice as fairness is a liberal political conception that explicitly includes an account of public reason, it is useful to begin there.

Rawls says that in justice as fairness "the parties in the original position, in adopting principles of justice for the basic structure, must also adopt guidelines and criteria of public reason for applying those norms."[36] He reiterates the thought in "Public Reason Revisited," saying that "one way to identify [the] political principles and guidelines [of public reason] is to show that they would be agreed to in what in *Political Liberalism* is called the original position."[37]

At the end of the last chapter I noted that various theories of accessible reasons depend upon conditionals which are rarely spelled out in any

---

[34] Rawls, *Law of Peoples*, p. 143.   [35] *ibid.*   [36] Rawls, *Political Liberalism*, p. 225.
[37] Rawls, *Law of Peoples*, p. 140.

detail. The requirement that guidelines of public reason be adopted in the original position promises to make precise the counterfactual condition public reasons must satisfy. Unfortunately Rawls never says how parties in the original position choose the guidelines of public reason. Parties are presumably supposed to choose from a menu of options, as they did in opting for Rawls's principles of justice.[38] It is easy enough to imagine what options would be on the menu. What is less easy to see is how parties are to decide among them. The alternatives are not ways of distributing primary goods. They are sets of reasons and principles which will, if chosen, be used to justify applying distributive principles. It will therefore be far more difficult for parties to predict how shares of primary goods would be affected by their choice from this menu than from the menu of principles of justice. They may still be able to identify the social position that would be least advantaged by each of the options. But the least advantaged may be, not the person with the lowest index of primary goods, but the person whose possession of her primary goods is in fact least secure or the person whose possession of primary goods feels least secure to her because of the (public) reasons for which they can legitimately be taken away. This way of identifying the least advantaged position would avoid the problem of predicting distributions under various alternatives. Unfortunately it would raise a problem about what principle of choice parties should use when adopting political values of public reason. Maximin is appropriate for choosing principles of justice precisely because of the parties' desire to maximize the primary goods of the least advantaged. When security of possession or perceived security of possession is what's at issue, perhaps things are different. These may not be things that can be maximized. Even if they can be, perhaps they need not be. Satisficing rather than maximizing may be the rational thing to do.

In light of all these difficulties, some will be tempted to explain away Rawls's remark about choosing guidelines in the original position as either a vaguely written promissory note that he never intended to redeem or lip-service to his claim in *Theory of Justice* that all duties are given by principles that would be chosen in the original position.[39] I do not think we should accede to either of these temptations. We can learn a great deal about Rawls's view by taking seriously his claim that guidelines of public reason would be chosen in the original position even if the details of the choice are not spelled out.

---

[38] Rawls, *Theory of Justice*, pp. 122–26.   [39] *ibid.*, p. 115.

The original position is, Rawls insists, a "device of representation."[40] Its defining features represent the powers and interests of liberal democratic citizens as Rawls conceives them. They therefore represent what I have been calling a partial specification of citizenship. The original position is also a fair choice situation. It is constructed so that the powers and interests of citizens as such determine the outcome of the choice made by their representatives in the original position – including, presumably, their choice of guidelines of public reason. More specifically, the adoption of guidelines of public reason is determined by the freedom, equality, reasonability and rationality of those represented – the freedom, equality, reasonability and rationality of liberal democratic citizens. Rawls thinks that those guidelines, were they fully spelled out, would allow citizens to appeal to "presently accepted general beliefs and forms of reasoning found in common sense, and the methods and conclusions of science when these are not controversial."[41] They would also say what political principles and political values citizens should be prepared to appeal to when discussing and voting on constitutional essentials and matters of basic justice. And they would express the duty of civility and the proviso by saying that citizens *must* be ready to appeal to them.

The original position therefore enables Rawls to derive the duty of civility from his partial specification of citizenship. Since I said earlier that Rawls uses the phrase "ideal of citizenship" to refer to his partial specification of citizenship, the possibility of this derivation explains why Rawls says that the duty of civility is imposed by that ideal. Furthermore, because the guidelines of public reason can be represented as the objects of choice in the original position, the political values and principles they specify are connected to a larger moral view: justice as fairness. It is because of these connections, and because the moral view satisfies the three conditions of liberal political conceptions, that those values and principles count as public *reasons*.

As I said a moment ago, the original position is a fair choice situation constructed so that the freedom, equality, reasonability and rationality of liberal democratic citizens determine which guidelines of public reason parties in the original position adopt. The political values and principles they single out can therefore be seen as the values and principles citizens – considered as free, equal, reasonable and rational – *would* choose as the basis for settling fundamental political questions. I mentioned at the end of the last chapter that proponents of the standard approach require

---

[40] Rawls, *Political Liberalism*, p. xxxi.   [41] *ibid.*, p. 224.

that justifying reasons be endorsable or acceptable. Because the political values and principles singled out by guidelines adopted in the original position are those citizens would choose, they are acceptable to citizens considered as reasonable and rational.

These acceptable reasons are included in the set of considerations government must draw on to justify legislation bearing on the constitutional essentials and matters of basic justice. It is important that Rawls does not think governmental justification must appeal to reasons that do persuade everyone subject to the law or that would move those subject to do what the law requires "on their own" if they were adequately informed and rational. Rawls insists only that the justification appeal to a certain kind of reason: the political values of public reason, as specified by justice as fairness and other liberal political conceptions. These, he says, are reasons citizens reasonably think others reasonably *could* – not reasonably *would* – accept. This is a very different requirement than that imposed by Audi's Surrogacy Conception, according to which coercion for reasons is justified only if citizens would be moved by those reasons on their own were they fully informed and rational. It is also a more plausible requirement. It allows for the possibility that laws are justified if they require actions citizens would not perform on their own, even if fully rational and adequately informed, because if fully rational and adequately informed they would still be moved to perform actions required by other, incompatible legislation. It is therefore compatible with the claim that not all political disagreement is due to deficiencies of rationality or information.

Acceptable reasons are also reasons that citizens are, as it were, to have at their command should the occasion arise. The duty of civility and the proviso require that when ordinary citizens of actual societies vote and publicly debate these questions in particular instances, they must be ready to show how their position can be supported by reasons which are members of the set. This is weaker than the requirement that citizens be ready to offer others reasons for their positions that they would accept in a given case. If I have decided to vote against a referendum that would permit assisted suicide, I must have an argument against the referendum that turns on reasons I think others would recognize as good ones for settling the question, such as considerations about the impact of PAS on the poor, women and minorities. I need not have an argument that would – or that I think would – persuade all others to vote against it. I can comply with the duty of civility while knowing full well that others might not think PAS would have disastrous implications for the groups I am worried about, hence while knowing full well that others, even if fully rational and adequately informed, might arrive at a different balance of concern for those groups and the liberty interests of the terminally ill.

This point is sometimes overlooked because readers mistake what is supposed to be accomplished by the readiness to offer public reasons. My appeal to reasons others would recognize as good is not supposed to persuade them that I am right. It is supposed to show them that I am reasonable. That is why Rawls says public reason

asks of us that the balance of those values we hold to be reasonable in a particular case is a balance we sincerely think can be seen to be reasonable by others. Or failing this, we think the balance can be seen as at least not unreasonable in this sense: that those who oppose it can nevertheless understand how reasonable persons can affirm it.[42]

It is because others recognize the political values of public reason as good reasons that I have grounds for thinking they *may* or *might* – not *would* – accept my argument in a given case. This, as we have seen, is all Rawls requires.

THE POLITICAL VALUES OF PUBLIC REASON: OTHER MEMBERS OF THE FAMILY

Justice as fairness is one example of a liberal political conception of justice. Consider another. Rawls says that what he calls "the Catholic doctrine of the common good" can be worked up into the kind of moral conception from which values and principles of public reason are drawn.[43] To indicate how this might be done, let us start with John Finnis's characterization of the common good of a political community. The common good is, he says, "the securing of a whole ensemble of material and other conditions that tend to favor the realization, by each individual in the community, of his or her personal development."[44] Finnis further insists that everyone is "equally entitled to respectful consideration" and to legal protections in the distribution of common goods.[45]

Is the common good conception a political conception from which public reasons can be drawn? Finnis's claims about equal entitlement to respectful consideration and about legal protections, as well as his view of the common good, are arguably fundamental ideas implicit in democratic political culture. The common good conception therefore satisfies

---

[42] *ibid.*, p. 253.   [43] Rawls, *Law of Peoples*, p. 142, note 29 and accompanying text.
[44] John Finnis, *Natural Law and Natural Right* (Oxford: Oxford University Press, 1980), p. 154.
[45] *ibid.*, p. 223.

the third of Rawls's three conditions. Because it applies to the basic structure, the conception also satisfies the first. It seems plausible that a theoretical structure could be developed which derived principles of justice from these ideas without ineliminable reliance on comprehensive doctrines of natural law or magisterial authority. If so, then the common good conception satisfies the second condition. Finally, it seems plausible that this conception could specify considerations that, from its point of view, count as good reasons for settling fundamental political questions. As if to confirm this, Finnis says that the phrase "the common good"

refer[s] to the factor or set of factors (whether a value, a concrete operational objective, or the conditions for realizing a value or attaining an objective) which, as considerations in someone's practical reasoning, would make sense of or give reason for his collaboration with others and would likewise, from their point of view, give reason for their collaboration with each other and with him.[46]

These considerations are among the common good conception's "principles and values of public reason." Because the common good conception satisfies the three conditions, it is a liberal political conception. *Its* principles and values of public reason can therefore be included in "the content of public reason."

To determine the "content of public reason" as Rawls understands it, then, we must first identify the family of liberal political conceptions of justice. Members of the family will include justice as fairness, the common good conception of justice and any other liberal conceptions which satisfy the three conditions Rawls lays down. Each of these family members singles out considerations that, from its point of view, count as good reasons for debating and settling fundamental political questions – considerations that, from its point of view, are justifying reasons or have reason-giving force when such questions are at issue. All of these considerations taken together are "the principles and values of the *family* of liberal political conceptions of justice meeting [the] three conditions." Together they make up the content of public reason – the considerations citizens can appeal to in public argument to show that their positions are justifiable, the considerations they can appeal to to make good on their religious political arguments and satisfy the obligation expressed by the proviso.

It might seem surprising that Rawls identifies the content of public reason with all of these considerations taken together. He is not, after all, impartial among various conceptions of justice. He is the framer and defender of a conception which specifies its own values and principles of

[46] *ibid.*, p. 154.

public reasoning. Rawls's refusal to identify the contents of public reason exclusively with the values and principles of justice as fairness might
seem puzzling. But this is just what we should expect given the aims of
public reason and the features of liberal political conceptions. The aim
of an account of public reason is to isolate reasons citizens can appeal
to to assure one another that they are reasonable. Since liberal political
conceptions are reasonable conceptions, the values and principles specified by any one of them will suit the purpose. Unfortunately Rawls is
not as forthcoming about this as he might be. This, I think, is because
he is not as clear as he might be about the somewhat diminished role a
well-ordered society now needs to play in his theory.

A well-ordered society is defined early in *A Theory of Justice* as a society which is "effectively regulated by *a* conception of justice."[47] In a
society well ordered by justice as fairness, everyone would endorse that
conception of justice. Everyone would presumably debate fundamental
questions on the basis of values and principles specified by that conception alone. There would be unanimous, if tacit, consensus that it alone
is the source of the principles and values of public reason. The important role accorded such a society in *Theory of Justice* can suggest that
debate which presupposes such a consensus is the *telos* of public debate
in a liberal democracy.[48] This, in turn, can suggest that Rawls identifies
the content of public reason with the values and principles specified by
justice as fairness.

The well-ordered society – understood as a society in which there is
consensus on a single conception of justice – is, while not a merely logical
possibility, clearly an unrealistic case. It plays so prominent a role in *Theory
of Justice* because of assumptions Rawls made to answer the questions
about stability that remained his abiding concern. By the time he wrote
Political Liberalism, however, Rawls had rethought his earlier assumptions
and arrived at different answers. He came to see that showing how a just
liberal democracy can be stable requires showing how an overlapping
consensus – not a well-ordered society – is possible.[49] The existence
of such a consensus is, Rawls guardedly admits, compatible with some
disagreement about justice. Thus he says that even in a society with an
overlapping consensus, the consensus is more likely to be on a "class of
liberal conceptions that vary within a more or less narrow range"[50] than

---

[47] Rawls, *Theory of Justice*, pp. 4–5 (emphasis added).   [48] See note 56 below.

[49] Alternatively, he came to see that a well-ordered society is a society in which there is an overlapping
consensus on a family of liberal political conceptions of justice rather than agreement on a single
conception.

[50] Rawls, *Political Liberalism*, p. 164.

on a single conception. The society in which everyone accepts justice as fairness, once front and center in discussions of stability,[51] is now treated as an example[52] or a limit case.[53] Rawls does talk about the well-ordered society as a limit it would be desirable to reach. But this, I suspect, is because, even while acknowledging that reasonable people can differ about which liberal political conception they endorse, Rawls cannot help showing that he thinks justice as fairness is the most reasonable.[54]

My point is not that an overlapping consensus is compatible with robust disagreement about justice. The phrase "narrow range" suggests that it is not; the qualifier "more or less" drives the suggestion home. My point, rather, is that its compatibility with any disagreement at all shows why the content of public reason should not be identified simply with the values and principles picked out by justice as fairness. Political contests among conceptions of justice may be a permanent feature of public life in a society with an overlapping consensus.[55] In these contests, the adherents of each may offer or be prepared to offer others the sorts of considerations their favored conception of justice singles out as good reasons.[56] Provided that the competing conceptions are drawn from the family of liberal conceptions which satisfy the three conditions, Rawls will grant that their adherents have satisfied the standards of acceptable political argument.[57] Since Rawls thinks, as we saw, that the guidelines of public reason apply to actual societies, he will grant that those who offer or are prepared to offer one another reasons drawn from any one of such conceptions satisfy the standards of acceptable argument – even in societies in which there is no overlapping consensus. They have offered

---

[51] Rawls, *Theory of Justice*, pp. 453ff.   [52] Rawls, *Political Liberalism*, p. 164.

[53] See *ibid.*, p. 167.   [54] *ibid.*, pp. xlviii–xlix.

[55] Supposing, with Rawls (*ibid.*, p. 165), that "a full overlapping consensus is never achieved but at best only approximated."

[56] See *ibid.*, p. xlix: "Public political discussion, when constitutional essentials and matters of basic justice are at stake, are [*sic*] always, or nearly always, decidable on the basis of reasons specified by one of a family of reasonable liberal conceptions of justice, one of which is for each citizens the most (more) reasonable."

[57] Jeremy Waldron, in *Justice and Disagreement* (Oxford: Oxford University Press, 1999), p. 154, writes: "Part of what we are trying to sort out in that argument is which one of the competing approaches to justice would be acceptable as a consensual basis for public reason. If we come up with an answer, then we can say *ex post* that the other views are unreasonable, because they have failed as candidates for criterion of public reason." I interpret Rawls as saying that (i) in societies which do not come up with *an* answer, citizens can argue on the basis of any liberal political conception which satisfies Rawls's conditions without being unreasonable or violating the duty of civility, and (ii) even in societies which do come up with an answer on which everyone agrees at time t, someone could subsequently argue at time t* on the basis of a different liberal political conception without being unreasonable or violating the duty of civility. For once we recognize the possibility of permanent reasonable disagreement about justice, it is hard to see why episodic or recurrent reasonable disagreement should be ruled out.

others reasons that they reasonably think "may reasonably be accepted by other citizens." But why are they the *only* reasons citizens reasonably think "may reasonably be accepted by other citizens"?

WHY PUBLIC REASONS MUST BE DRAWN FROM LIBERAL POLITICAL CONCEPTIONS

Rawls's guidelines of public reason have been criticized for precluding the introduction of novel ideas about justice.[58] It would be interesting to ask how much variety of political argument Rawls's guidelines allow if my interpretation is correct. I shall not pursue the question here. Instead I want to look into Rawls's insistence that, if I am to offer others reasons I reasonably think they may reasonably accept, I must be prepared to draw on conceptions of justice that satisfy the three conditions. The condition on which I want to focus is the second. It says that the political values of public reason are drawn from conceptions of justice, like justice as fairness, which "can be presented independently from comprehensive doctrines of any kind." This condition, together with the duty of civility, implies that citizens must be ready to offer one another reasons drawn from conceptions of justice that can be presented independently of comprehensive doctrine.

It is tempting to press hard on the phrase "*can* be presented" since Rawls does not say much about exactly when conceptions satisfy this condition. What is most important about it, however, are the clear implications of Rawls's view. There are clearly some conceptions of justice that he thinks support political outcomes only by appealing to metaphysical or religious claims, or to a comprehensive ethical theory. Rawls does not mean that citizens cannot appeal to such conceptions; appeal to them is permitted by the proviso. What he means is that someone making that appeal cannot reasonably assume that others will see the argument he offers as based on good reasons, on considerations with reason-giving force. The argument is therefore deficient and needs to be supplemented or qualified. This is true even of arguments appealing to comprehensive doctrines such as natural law, which has been developed precisely because it was thought to be accessible in ways that religious doctrines are not.[59] It is also true of natural rights views, of perfectionism and of comprehensive liberalisms. Given these implications and the

---

58 Jeremy Waldron, "Religious Contributions in Public Deliberation," *San Diego Law Review* 30 (1993): 817–48.
59 See Murray, *We Hold These Truths*; also chapter 4, note 3.

frequency with which citizens and politicians appeal only to conceptions of justice that violate the second condition, it is hard to overstate the condition's importance. When conjoined with the duty of civility, it rules out arguments and votes of the sort I said (5.1) and (5.2) permit. It is this condition that I believe many critics really mean to object to when they reject Rawls's view of public reason. Why does Rawls impose it?

Suppose, as I believe Rawls thinks, citizens can recognize that they have been treated reasonably only if their fundamental interests as citizens have been respected and they are in a position to see that they have been. I claimed earlier that Rawls thinks citizens should be thought of as having a fundamental interest in living autonomous lives or, more precisely, a fundamental interest in the autonomous higher-order exercise of their moral powers. This, I have suggested, is the fundamental interest that citizens respect in others when they comply with the duty of civility and the proviso. Why does Rawls think that when fundamental questions are at issue, citizens must be ready to appeal to reasons drawn from political conceptions in order to respect this interest?

One explanation begins with the thoughts that government must respect its citizens' interest in leading autonomous lives and they can lead autonomous lives only if a negative autonomy condition is satisfied. Citizens can lead autonomous lives only if fundamental social conditions are not supportable or seen to be supportable exclusively by values drawn from a comprehensive conception they reject. For, rejecting that conception, they are not positioned to see these values as good reasons. From their point of view these are values that lack reason-giving force. They still need to be made good. Values that have reason-giving force because they are specified by a conception that can be seen as standing free of comprehensive doctrine do not encounter the same problem. So fundamental social conditions should be supportable and seen to be supportable by such values. To show respect for others' autonomy interests, citizens should offer such values in due course when they publicly advocate outcomes bearing on those conditions.

How is someone's autonomy threatened when outcomes are only supportable by reasons linked to a comprehensive doctrine she rejects? The idea would be something like this. The fundamental conditions for the exercise of the moral powers are *fundamental* precisely because they are causally connected to the way those powers are reflectively exercised, and thus to the lives citizens fashion for themselves. If those conditions can only be supported by a conception someone rejects, she is subject to conditions which she finds rationally impenetrable, conditions for which she cannot see good reasons. Her situation can plausibly be described as one of subjection to a cause which is rationally or intellectually alien. Those whose plans of life are subject to such a cause can plausibly be described as living heteronomously rather than autonomously.

According to this line of thought, what makes the political values of public reasons *reasons* is that no one – regardless of her religion or ideology – sees them as considerations which need to be made good. Public reasons have this feature because they are drawn from political conceptions of justice, which by definition can be presented independently of comprehensive doctrine. Thus what explains Rawls's insistence that public reasons be drawn from political conceptions of justice is, ultimately, the negative autonomy condition.

Unfortunately this explanation is too weak to do the work required of it.

One thing it leaves unexplained is why our autonomy is compromised when fundamental questions are settled on the basis of someone else's conception of the good, but not when they are settled on the basis of someone else's conception of justice. Even if someone else's conception of justice can be presented as free-standing, it is still *someone else's* conception. Why doesn't the settlement of fundamental questions on *its* basis compromise the autonomous fashioning of our plan of life? Furthermore, initial appearances to the contrary notwithstanding, it remains unclear why public reasons must be drawn from political conceptions of justice. Perhaps citizens' interest in living autonomous lives can be respected only if the conditions for exercising the moral powers are not supportable exclusively by an alien comprehensive doctrine. But this leaves open the possibility that fundamental political questions could be settled on the basis of reasons drawn from their own comprehensive view or on the basis of what their view shares with others. More generally, it leaves open the possibility that grounds for settling fundamental questions can be located by surveying the comprehensive doctrines which happen to have adherents in a society, seeing what political values they share and settling questions on the basis of those shared values. This, clearly, is not what Rawls has in mind. As we have seen, he thinks the way to locate values and principles on the basis of which fundamental questions should be settled is by identifying the family of liberal political conceptions of justice and seeing what values and principles *they* specify. Proceeding otherwise would, to adapt a phrase he uses elsewhere, make public reason "political in the wrong way." Finally, even if the explanation succeeds in showing why no one regards reasons drawn from free-standing views as reasons that still need to be made good, it does not show why anyone should regard them as good reasons capable of publicly justifying political outcomes. That they are not seen as bad reasons is not enough to show why they are good ones.

To arrive at the explanation that has now been found wanting, I supposed that citizens' interest in leading autonomous lives can be respected only if a negative autonomy condition is satisfied. But now suppose that that interest can be respected only if an additional, positive condition is satisfied. Fundamental conditions must be supportable and seen to be supportable by considerations which are appropriately connected to citizens' rational capacities. The connection I have in mind – and that I believe Rawls has in mind – is that there are political values that count as reasons because of their relationship to those capacities. More specifically, they count as reasons *because* they can be seen as values of a kind that reasonable citizens would accept as the appropriate basis for settling fundamental political questions. Fundamental social conditions must be supportable by such values. To show that they respect one another's autonomy interests, citizens who advocate outcomes bearing on those conditions must offer values of this kind in due course.

These are just the kinds of reasons political conceptions of justice single out. To see this, consider one thing that would have to be done to spell out the required connection with citizens' rational capacities. We would have to be provided with some way of identifying the kind of considerations reasonable citizens would accept for settling fundamental questions. One way to do that would be to place citizens in a choice situation in which the rational interests and powers they have as citizens determine the outcome, and ask them to choose kinds of reasons. This, as we have seen, is exactly how Rawls says justice as fairness specifies the values and principles on the basis of which fundamental questions are to be settled. They are, as I have shown, specified by guidelines chosen in the original position.

As we have seen, Rawls says that the original position is the way *justice as fairness* specifies values and principles. He is at pains to stress that "others will think other ways to identify these principles are more reasonable."[60] I believe he means other members of the family of liberal political conceptions will have functionally equivalent means of specifying *their* principles and values. The means might be an idealized speech

---

[60] Rawls, *Political Liberalism*, p. li.

situation or a different choice situation. Or a conception could, like the common good conception, eschew idealized situations altogether. But if those values and principles are to be part of the content of public reason, the means used to specify them must, in this sense, be functionally equivalent to the original position: like the original position, they must pick out values which are acceptable to citizens considered as free, equal, reasonable and rational.

Thus each of the liberal political conceptions that has currency in a society will specify kinds of values and principles that are appropriately connected to citizens' rational capacities. And it will specify them *as* reasons *because* they are the kinds of considerations reasonable citizens would accept as the basis for settling fundamental questions. When adherents of these different conceptions of justice are prepared to appeal to the considerations of a kind citizens would accept for this purpose, they are prepared to offer arguments they can expect others may reasonably accept in a given case. Others may *reasonably* accept them because they are premised on reasons that they would accept, as reasonable and rational, for settling fundamental questions.

What explains Rawls's insistence that public reasons be drawn from political conceptions of justice is that political conceptions specify reasons which satisfy the positive autonomy condition. This explanation seizes on a plausible condition of citizens' autonomy. For suppose outcomes on fundamental questions are supportable by considerations of a kind citizens themselves would adopt as the basis for deciding on important outcomes. Then not only are the outcomes justifiable, but they are justifiable by values which count as reasons because of citizens' choices. The outcomes can then plausibly be described as ones free, equal, reasonable and rational citizens *could* give themselves. These outcomes set the conditions for the reflective exercise of the moral powers. Plans of life formed under such conditions are plans in which, as it were, citizens' own reasoned authorship goes all the way down. For not only do they rationally form their plans, they could rationally endorse the conditions under which they form those plans. At any rate, their authorship seems to go further down than when plans are formed under conditions determined by a conception of the good, even if that conception is their own. If this is correct, then the second explanation appeals to a more plausible condition of autonomy than the first one. Crudely put, what underlies the first explanation is the equation of autonomy with nonheteronomy, with freedom from alien conceptions of the good. Underlying the second is the more plausible view that an autonomous life is not *just* one which is lived nonheteronomously. It requires living under social conditions citizens could give themselves.

The second explanation also suggests why Rawls thinks living under conditions determined by someone else's conception of justice does not necessarily compromise citizens' autonomy. When conditions are determined by someone else's conception of the good, what compromises autonomy is not the fact that that conception is someone else's. What compromises it, Rawls would say, is that outcomes determined by comprehensive doctrines we reject are not outcomes that we can see as reached on the basis of good reasons. When outcomes are determined on the basis of someone else's political conception of justice, on the other hand, we know or can know that there are reasons available to support the outcome which are of the right kind. Even if we do not accept the supporting arguments, Rawls thinks we can still see the outcome as one reasonable people as such *could* give themselves. If we think of ourselves as reasonable, we can see them as outcomes *we* could give ourselves.

This last line of thought rests a great deal of weight on what Rawls would claim is a crucial difference between conceptions of the good and the right: conceptions of the good which we reject are alien or impenetrable in a way that rejected conceptions of the right need not be. Among the conceptions of the right we reject may be political conceptions of justice. We may, for example, reject justice as fairness in favor of the common good conception. But because justice as fairness is a political conception of justice, it satisfies Rawls's three conditions. It is, by the third condition, "worked out" from ideas implicit in a shared political culture. Those who share in that culture can accept its key elements or, at least, see how reasonable people could accept them. This allows us to see its principles and values, the principles and values to which its adherents appeal in argument, as considerations to which reasonable people could appeal. Thus we can see justice as fairness as a reasonable conception of justice adhered to by reasonable people, even if we reject it in favor of the common good conception. And, Rawls thinks, the reverse is true. Those who adhere to justice as fairness can see other political conceptions and their adherents as reasonable. Comprehensive doctrines, by contrast, include claims that cannot command the same widespread assent. This is why, Rawls thinks, we cannot reasonably assume others might reasonably accept values and principles which cannot be seen as reasons except by those who accept comprehensive doctrine.

This line of argument seems questionable on two counts. First, it is questionable that our recognition of considerations as reasons is all-or-nothing, correlated with our acceptance or rejection of moral conceptions as wholes. I may reject utilitarianism, but I can still see utilitarian considerations as reasons of a sort.[61] I can still see the people who offer them as not unreasonable, even when they offer them as the basis of settling fundamental political questions. Second, it is not so clear to me that rejecting all liberal political conceptions in favor of nonpolitical liberalisms is unreasonable. Or so I shall suggest in a moment. I now want to pick up the thread of the main argument, for the explanation I have offered may seem to have explained too much. If the political values of public reason count as reasons because of their connection with citizens' rational capacities, why must they be drawn from conceptions that can be presented independently of comprehensive doctrine? How, exactly, does this feature of political conceptions come into play?

I have said that the considerations on the basis of which fundamental questions are to be settled count as reasons because they can be seen to be connected with citizens' rational capacities and, in particular, with their reasonability. The phrase "can be seen" might seem to add a needless epicycle to what is already a complex account. In fact it is a necessary qualification. Those by whom public reasons are offered and those to whom they are offered may feel the force of those reasons because the reasons have a place in their comprehensive doctrines. Thus someone may be moved by values specified by the common good conception because of her religious views. Her opponents may be moved by them, at least prima facie, because those values are also found in their own comprehensive utilitarianism. What matters is that everyone knows the outcome they reach can be supported by reasons which can be seen as good without appeal to either comprehensive doctrine. This is insured if the reasons given for the outcome can be seen as considerations of a kind free, equal, reasonable and rational citizens would accept as appropriate for settling fundamental questions and if the crucial notions of freedom, equality, reasonability and rationality are spelled out independently of utilitarianism, Kantianism or any other comprehensive doctrine.

CONCLUSION

The settled readiness to comply with the proviso requires the ability to tell which reasons are public and which are not. It requires the ability to make complex judgments about context in order to determine when

---

[61] See the very helpful remarks in Waldron, "Religious Contributions," pp. 841–42.

public reasons are called for. It requires the intellectual and emotional capacities to respond appropriately when offered the right or the wrong kinds of reasons. To answer the two questions I shall pose of Rawls's view, I want to ask briefly about the capacity that interests me most: the capacity to recognize another's argument as respectful or disrespectful of one's fundamental interests as a citizen.

Talk of respect and disrespect suggests that citizenship carries with it a certain status. If I am to recognize that someone has or has not respected my fundamental interests as a citizen, I must have a sense of myself as a person with that status. Somewhat more technically, I must identify with a specification of citizenship according to which citizenship confers that status. The identification may be one I make simply for political purposes, but it is an identification I must make. A parallel may help to make the point. Suppose that someone offers me an argument for severely curtailing religious liberty. Suppose, for example, he proposes legal measures for closing the churches of my denomination except for very brief periods early Sunday morning while leaving other churches to open as their members wish. The person offering the argument insults and disrespects me by blithely ignoring my status as a citizen. He ignores the fact that I am a person with rights, that I have rights to worship freely and to gather with others to worship in places we have lawfully built for the purpose. He also ignores the fact that, regardless of my religion, I am a full participant in my society's political life, entitled to be treated as the equal of everyone else. For me to *recognize* that I have been insulted and to respond appropriately, I must have a sense of myself as a bearer of rights and a full participant. I must, at least for political purposes, identify with a specification of citizenship which has these as elements. What view of my citizenship must I have, what specification of citizenship must I identify with, if I am to recognize that others have or have not respected me when they comply with or violate the duty of civility and the proviso? What view of others and their citizenship must I have if I am to have the settled disposition to comply with the duty of civility and the proviso myself?

As we have seen, these require that when fundamental questions are at stake, citizens must be ready to offer certain kinds of values and principles for their position: values and principles that count as reasons because they can be seen to bear the appropriate connections with citizens' rational capacities. This implies that the rational capacities of citizens as such can confer the status of being a reason for settling fundamental political questions one way rather than another. Thus the fact that some law would violate my right to religious liberty counts as a reason against the law because rights and rights violations can be seen as the kinds of considerations that would be accepted by free, equal, reasonable and rational citizens as one of the bases for settling fundamental questions. If I am to recognize that I have been disrespected when someone else violates the proviso, I must think of myself – perhaps tacitly rather than explicitly – as someone whose rational capacities can confer this reason-giving force. If I am to have the settled disposition to comply with the proviso myself, I must think of others as citizens whose rational capacities can confer it as well. This must be seen as part of the authority citizens, as free, equal, reasonable and rational, have over their political world: the authority collectively to determine what considerations count as reasons for settling questions about the conditions which impinge most fundamentally on the autonomous fashioning of their own lives.

This answers the first of the two questions I said must be answered to determine whether Rawls's view of public reason succeeds:

(7.1) How must citizens think of their authority if they accept and comply with the duty of civility and the proviso?

What of the second?

(7.2) Is it reasonable for some citizens to reject this view of their own collective authority?

The answer to this question clearly depends upon the conditions under which a disagreement is reasonable. Therefore in order to answer (7.2), it is necessary to recur to the discussion of reasonable disagreement in chapter 5. There I said that there is reasonable disagreement about some subject if reasonable people reasonably reach different conclusions about it. Can reasonable people reasonably reach a different view than Rawls's about citizens' collective authority?

As in chapter 5, consider citizens who impute a common interest conception of legitimate aims to their liberal democratic government, think that government must respect the traditional rights and liberties, think government must be responsive to the will of the people and who, when deliberating about what measures to advocate and vote for, are guided by what they think their liberal democratic government may justifiably do. Such people seem, intuitively, to be reasonable. I have argued that many citizens realize their citizenship because of the actions of churches and other secondary associations. This, I have suggested, is one of the ways they acquire the religious political arguments that Rawls thinks need to be made good by appeal to public reasons. The activities of churches and secondary associations also encourage people to identify with different specifications of democratic citizenship. Some will think citizens are subject to natural law or to some other moral code that they think provides good reasons for action in politics as elsewhere. Whether these reasons can be presented as the outcomes of idealized choice or of acceptance by reasonable citizens is, for them, irrelevant to whether they count as reasons. It seems especially likely that different specifications of citizenship will be articulated and encouraged when the proper role of religion in democratic politics is itself the subject of political, philosophical and religious debate, as it now is in many of the liberal democracies of the west. The acquisition by some of non-Rawlsian views of citizenship may therefore result from the operation of mechanisms by which citizens are integrated into the political life of these societies. In chapter 5 I suggested that the proliferation of different views of citizenship among citizens who are reasonable is as natural as the proliferation of views of the good. If this is so, then citizens may reasonably disagree with Rawls's specification of citizenship. It is hard to see why disagreements about citizens' authority are any less reasonable than those disagreements about the good that are recognized as reasonable all around.

Furthermore, I connected the underlying motivation for Rawls's view of public reason with a view about the conditions under which, for political purposes, we can autonomously endorse and pursue our plans of life. Rawls thinks we can endorse and pursue our plans autonomously, I argued, only if they are formed under conditions of which we could approve when we are represented as reasonable and rational. It is because we must respect one another's interest in leading autonomous lives, I said, that Rawls thinks we must honor the duty of civility and the proviso. I have not challenged Rawls's claim about the conditions under which we can autonomously endorse and pursue our plans. I cannot examine it here except to note that the claim is one about political autonomy and that the claim is not obviously true. It may be that one's life-plan can be autonomously endorsed and pursued in a society characterized by a constitutional consensus[62] or a stable *modus vivendi* centered on a liberal constitution. Perhaps it could also be autonomously endorsed and pursued even under conditions supportable only by a liberal perfectionist conception of justice like that defended by Joseph Raz[63] or William

---

[62] For the notion of a constitutional consensus, see Rawls, *Political Liberalism*, pp. 149ff.

[63] Joseph Raz, *The Morality of Freedom* (Oxford: Oxford University Press, 1986).

Galston.[64] These are social possibilities about which we know too little, as I shall say again in the conclusion. If it is reasonable to think they are compatible with our political autonomy, then it is reasonable to reject Rawls's claim that we must observe the duty of civility to respect one another's fundamental interests in autonomy. The duty of civility and the proviso could then be rejected even when these important liberty interests are at stake. A moderate perfectionist view would, of course, carry with it a different view of the reasons which bear on fundamental political questions, and hence a different view of citizens' authority, than Rawls's view does. If we could endorse and pursue our plans autonomously in a society well ordered by moderate perfectionism, then this too supports a positive answer to my second question.

Some people might read Rawls as claiming that his specification of citizenship is the right one because it is a specification no one could reasonably reject. A positive answer to (7.2) would, on this reading, show that he is wrong about this and that his specification of citizenship is not the appropriate one for contemporary pluralistic democracies. If it is also thought that the duty of civility *is* a duty only if the Rawlsian specification of citizenship is right, then a positive answer to (7.2) would show that the duty of civility is not a duty after all. The real point of defending a positive answer to (7.2) is not, however, to support this line of argument. The premise the argument imputes to Rawls – that the appropriateness of his specification of citizenship depends on the fact that no one could reasonably reject it – is clearly too strong. Rather, the point of defending a positive answer to (7.2) is to show that reasonable people can reasonably reach different views about citizenship and its authority. Citizens can, I am suggesting, be reasonable if they do not take Rawls's specification of citizenship as regulative. The question is how that disagreement is best accommodated. I argued in chapter 5 that it is best accommodated by (5.1) and (5.2).

I do not deny that Rawls has identified a specification of citizenship that is latent in the liberal democratic tradition, one that citizens may aspire to when it is clearly articulated and presented to them. What I want to suggest, however, is that it is an ideal of citizenship properly so called and not a specification that imposes a duty. Affirming and acting upon it would make available valuable forms of trust, respect, civility, civic friendship and autonomy. Moreover, it provides a useful standard by which to assess, criticize and reform our political behavior.

[64] William Galston, *Liberal Purposes* (Cambridge: Cambridge University Press, 1991).

By making salient the features of public debate that would make trust, respect, civility, friendship and autonomy available, the ideal can help us to locate various sources of incivility in our political life. By reflecting on it, we can come to appreciate the value of self-restraint in political argument and to recognize ways in which our own political behavior could be more civil.

But it may be that the ideal cannot be realized without costs. Some of those costs will be costs to democracy itself if the self-censorship argument I offered at the end of chapter 5 is sound. Other costs are harder to calculate in advance. Citizens would have to identify with the Rawlsian specification of citizenship very strongly if the generalized willingness to comply with the duty of civility is to accomplish what it is supposed to. General willingness to comply with the duty is supposed to maintain mutual trust, mutual respect and civility. These responses depend upon citizens' thinking of themselves as persons who are owed and who owe reasons of the right sort. They are affective responses, or responses with significant affective components. Our affective lives are notoriously difficult to regulate. If a view of ourselves such as Rawls's specification of citizenship is to regulate them reliably enough to produce trust, respect and civility, it cannot be a view of ourselves whose hold on us is transient or episodic. It must be one with which we stably and reliably identify. This mass self-identification will not be brought about easily. Almost certainly it could not be effected by public institutions alone. As I have stressed throughout, secondary institutions of civil society play a large role in fostering and reinforcing the view liberal democratic citizens have of themselves. We know far too little about what changes in them would be required if citizens were to identify with a Rawlsian specification of their citizenship, and far too little about what the consequences of those changes would be. Without the ability to calculate the costs of these changes, we cannot say that Rawls's specification of citizenship is the most reasonable for us or that the answer to my second question is "No." The Rawlsian specification is an attractive liberal democratic ideal. It does not, however, capture a form our citizenship *must* take or a form of civility we are *obliged* to pursue.

Conclusion

I have argued that what I have called "the standard approach" to questions about religion and liberal democratic decision-making does not ground the obligations of citizenship that its proponents put forward. This approach fails because it does not take adequate account of the fact that citizenship is an achievement, nor does it take adequate account of the ways that achievement is won. Once we attend to the role of civil society in bringing about the realization of citizenship and to the important contributions it makes to civic argument and public political debate, it becomes clear that citizens have deep but reasonable disagreements about which specification of liberal democratic citizenship is the right one. The upshot is that liberal democracies with vital and politically active secondary associations are likely to be characterized by deep but reasonable disagreement about what reasons and arguments citizens owe one another when they debate and vote on important political questions. I argued in chapter 5 that citizens may rely on religious arguments and vote their religious convictions even if they are not prepared to make good their arguments or justify their votes by appeal to reasons of other kinds.

The obligations of citizenship that I have defended do not allow citizens to vote and argue on any conscientiously chosen basis whatever. To honor their obligations, citizens must have and be ready to apply standards to their own reasons for voting and to their own political arguments. They must, for example, have views – perhaps tacitly held and unsystematic views – about what their liberal democratic government may justifiably do. Their view of what government may justifiably do must impute to government the aim of promoting the common good. Despite the fact that (5.1) and (5.2) impose some discipline on citizens, they allow citizens a good deal more latitude than the guidelines defended by proponents of the standard approach. In defending these principles, I have drawn heavily on empirical data. I hope that my defense shows how empirical work can be brought to bear on pressing philosophical questions about the nature of citizenship and the extent of citizens' authority. I also hope to have provided a view of religiously inspired political activity that is more balanced than that presupposed by many philosophical discussions of religion and democratic decision-making. This I regard as especially important, since I have little sympathy for some items on the political agenda that religion is commonly assumed to support in the United States.

When I introduced the standard approach I said that it responds to a number of convictions that have a powerful hold on modern political thought. While I have argued that it does not give an adequate account of the duties of citizenship, I granted in the last chapter that the most sophisticated version of that approach – Rawls's – articulates a very attractive ideal. I have not denied the possibility of a society in which that ideal is realized. Readers sometimes overlook how much of Rawls's efforts have gone into showing that such a society is possible. To show that it is possible, he draws on what he takes to be reasonable laws of moral psychology and reasonable conjectures about political sociology to show how an overlapping consensus might develop among adherents of various reasonable conceptions of the good in a society whose public culture was already imbued with democratic values.[1] Establishing that possibility is a very important philosophical achievement. Seeing why it is so important an accomplishment shows how much work remains to be done by those who – like me – challenge the standard approach.

Citizens' attitude toward the liberal democracy in which they live can be one of anger at unrealized possibilities, cynicism about its unfulfilled promises, resignation, or principled affirmation of and commitment to it. Which of these attitudes we adopt obviously determines our attitude toward politics and our social world. More important, which of them we adopt affects our attitude toward humanity and the worth of life or, as Rawls says, toward "the world as a whole."[2] For example, the belief that human beings are too selfish or sinful to sustain a just liberal democracy is bound to have a profound effect on our view of and relation to others, on our conduct toward them and on our political behavior. Therefore a very great deal turns on determining which attitude toward our liberal democracy is the most appropriate.

---

[1] Rawls, *Political Liberalism*, pp. 158–68.
[2] *ibid.*, p. lxi; see also Peter deMarneffe, "The Problem of Evil, the Social Contract and the History of Ethics," *Pacific Philosophical Quarterly* 82 (2000): 11–25.

The principled affirmation of and commitment to liberal democracy, under conditions that are manifestly unjust, presupposes the belief in the possibility that liberal democracy can do better. Indeed, Rawls thinks, it presupposes the belief that a just social world is possible. It also presupposes the belief that such a world can come about because, as just, it is the object of intentional agency, so that its justice plays a causal role in its coming into being and in its longer-term stability.[3] The justice of society can play such a causal role only if human beings are responsive to moral reasons, including considerations of justice and, Rawls thinks, the political values of public reason. He therefore thinks we can believe in the possibility of an enduringly just society, stable for the right reasons,[4] only if we also believe that human beings have a moral nature and are capable of a very important form of human goodness.[5] That is why believing in the possibility of a just liberal democracy affects our attitudes toward humanity and the world. Establishing this possibility matters to Rawls in part because it can ground these attitudes.

Belief in the possibility of a just liberal democracy can help to sustain affirmation and commitment to actual liberal democracies, and the attitudes toward others that commitment presupposes, only if the possibility in which we believe is robust. If a just liberal democracy is too unlikely – if it is a mere logical possibility – then affirmation, commitment and the actions and attitudes which follow from them will be at best quixotic. There may seem little point in committing oneself to the pursuit of justice or to refraining from entirely self-interested political action. There is, of course, no way for philosophy to show that a just liberal democracy will be realized. Indeed there may be no way for it to show that the possibility of a just liberal democracy is as robust as it needs to be to sustain an enduring commitment to actual liberal democracies. Perhaps the view of this possibility that Rawls recommends is best described as one of "political faith," for faith typically entails a commitment or confidence that goes beyond what the evidence warrants.[6] But if philosophy cannot provide conclusive grounds for the articles of political faith, it can attempt to show that faith in the possibility of a just liberal democracy is reasonable, and hence that we can have faith in the moral goodness of humanity. This is precisely what Rawls tries to do. As he says at the conclusion of "Idea of an Overlapping Consensus":

---

[3] Rawls, *Political Liberalism*, pp. lxi–ii. For driving home the importance of this point and of its connection with what I call "political faith," I am indebted to Cohen, "Arc of the Moral Universe" and to Robert Adams, *Finite and Infinite Goods* (Oxford: Oxford University Press, 1999), pp. 375ff.

[4] The phrase "stability for the right reasons" is Rawls's; see *Political Liberalism*, p. xxix.

[5] *ibid.*, p. lxii. [6] See Adams, *Finite and Infinite Goods*, p. 385f.

These matters connect with the larger question of how political liberalism is possible. One step in showing how it is possible is to exhibit the possibility of an overlapping consensus in a society with a democratic tradition characterized by the fact of pluralism. In trying to do these things political philosophy assumes the role Kant gave philosophy generally: the defense of reasonable faith (III: 2, 2). As I said then, in our case this becomes the defense of reasonable faith in the possibility of a just constitutional regime.[7]

As we have seen, proponents of the standard approach attempt to lay down conditions of civility and legitimacy so that public debate which satisfies those conditions will be an exchange of reasons everyone can recognize as good ones and political decisions which satisfy them will be supported by reasons all can recognize as good. One proponent of that approach – Rawls – tries to vindicate our faith in the possibility that those conditions be satisfied. He does so to serve a much deeper philosophical purpose. Those who would challenge the standard approach as the right account of our obligations face the daunting tasks of providing alternative accounts of legitimacy and civility and of providing some grounds for political faith. Where are we to begin?

Rawls sometimes writes as if only two political possibilities are of philosophical interest for the societies he addresses. One is an overlapping consensus on a liberal political conception of justice, or on a family of liberal political conceptions. The other is a *modus vivendi* as exemplified by Europe just after the wars of religion. The way Rawls writes about a *modus vivendi* suggests that he thinks it would be marked by unremitting hostility, rancor and mistrust, that a known balance of power is its only stabilizing force and that it lacks equilibrating forces. But between Rawls's paradigm of a *modus vivendi* and an overlapping consensus lies a wide range of social possibilities. These include not only a stable *modus vivendi* centered on a liberal constitution, but also a constitutional consensus and what Avashai Margalit calls a "decent society."[8] If Rawls's phrase "*modus vivendi*" is elastic enough to cover this range, then it is clear that a *modus vivendi* can be stabilized by habit and by allegiance to institutions that are perceived to be decent and satisfactory if suboptimal.[9] It can be equilibrated both by cycles of liberalism and conservatism[10] and by social forces which, over a couple of election cycles, force adherents of extreme positions toward the political center.

[7] Rawls, *Political Liberalism*, p. 172.
[8] Avashai Margalit, *The Decent Society* (Cambridge, MA: Harvard University Press, 1996).
[9] For a subtle and sophisticated exploration of these matters, see John Haldane, "The Individual, the State and the Common Good," *Social Philosophy and Policy* (1996): 59–79.
[10] Schlesinger, *Cycles of American History*.

These are social possibilities about which we know far too little. For example, we know far too little about the morality of procedures for political decision-making in the face of deep disagreements about justice, including the morality of majority rule.[11] One reason for this is that we know far too little about the moral claims – the legitimacy – of imperfectly just institutions.[12] We also know far too little about the moral quality of relations among citizens under such circumstances and about what form civility should assume. This last subject is one on which I have tried to make a start in this book by asking what reasons citizens owe to each other when there is deep disagreement about exactly what reasons for political decisions are good ones and which specification of citizenship is the right one. As I stressed in the introduction, these conditions make it important to distinguish those whose political views and arguments we do not like from those who violate their duty as citizens. There may be many citizens who, without violating their duties as citizens, use religious and other comprehensive views to argue for political outcomes with which we are in very deep disagreement. In that case, we should argue, vote and organize coalitions to oppose them.

The pluralism to which I have pointed throughout the book entails that there are unlikely to be shared grounds for the faith in liberal democracy and in humanity that Rawls hopes to vindicate. This is not, I believe, as deeply troubling as it might initially seem. What each individual's affirmation and commitment seems to require is not that there be one social possibility in which everyone has faith but that, for every citizen, there be some attractive social possibility in which she has faith. Some might have faith in the possibility of a deliberative democracy, some in the possibility of a natural law republic, some in the possibility of a Rawlsian overlapping consensus. Provided each can explain why her faith is as reasonable as Rawls has shown faith in an overlapping consensus to be, then each person's affirmation of and commitment to liberal democracy will be reasonable when seen from her own point of view. This may suffice even if there are few shared reasons for affirmation and commitment. Similarly, the right attitudes toward others and toward the world might require, not that there be one ground for those attitudes which all can affirm, but that for each person there be some ground for them that she can affirm.

---

[11] We know far too little about it despite some very interesting work on the subject. See, for example, Jeremy Waldron, *The Dignity of Legislation* (Cambridge: Cambridge University Press, 1999), pp. 130–66.

[12] But see David Copp, "The Idea of a Legitimate State," *Philosophy and Public Affairs* 28 (1999): 3–45.

This points to another possible ground for the affirmation of liberal democracy. Different citizens with different views about fundamental human interests will view different political issues as most important. Under these conditions, citizens may assess political progress locally rather than globally. Their faith that political conditions will improve may depend, not on the possibility of a just and stable liberal democracy *tout court*, but on the possibility of improvement judged by their lights with respect to the issues about which they care most deeply. For some, the most important issues will be those that bear on the health and integrity of the traditional family. For others they will be those that bear on environmental preservation. For still others they will be those that bear on the equality of women. Perhaps what is needed to sustain commitment to liberal democracy is the belief that local political improvement, improvement on the issues they care most about, is possible.

In a pluralistic society, citizens will also have very different reasons for believing that human beings have a moral nature. Yet they may have little to do with the possibility of an overlapping consensus or citizens' responsiveness to public or accessible reasons. Some will believe that human beings have a moral nature because they believe that human beings are responsive to the natural law. Others because they believe human beings are created in God's image and likeness. Still others will point to instances of human heroism or saintliness as evidence of what women and men can be. These may be enough to convince them that they can cooperate with others for political purposes.

Select bibliography

Adams, Robert, *Finite and Infinite Goods*, Oxford: Oxford University Press, 1999.

Almond, Gabriel, "Rational Choice Theory and the Social Sciences," in Kristin Monroe (ed.), *The Economic Approach to Politics*, New York: Harper Collins, 1991, pp. 32–52.

Aquinas, Thomas, *Summa Theologiae*, Matriti. Biblioteca de Autores Cristianos, 1961–65, 3rd edn.

Arendt, Hannah, *On Revolution*, Harmondsworth: Penguin, 1990.

Audi, Robert, *Religious Commitment and Secular Reason*, Cambridge: Cambridge University Press, 2000.

Audi, Robert, "Liberal Democracy and Religion in Politics," in Robert Audi and Nicholas Wolterstorff (eds.), *Religion in the Public Square: the Place of Religious Convictions in the Political Debate*, New York: Rowman and Littlefield, 1997.

Audi, Robert, "The Place of Religious Argument in a Free and Democratic Society," *San Diego Law Review* 30 (1993): 677–702.

Audi, Robert, "The Separation of Church and State and the Obligations of Citizenship," *Philosophy and Public Affairs* 18 (1989): 259–96.

Audi, Robert, "The State, the Church and the Citizen," in Paul J. Weithman (ed.), *Religion and Contemporary Liberalism*, Notre Dame, IN: University of Notre Dame Press, 1997, pp. 38–75.

Bernardin, Joseph, *A Moral Vision for America*, ed. John Langan, SJ, Washington: Georgetown University Press, 1998.

Branch, Taylor, "Uneasy Holiday," in Dorothy Wickenden (ed.), *The New Republic Reader*, New York: Basic Books, 1994, pp. 419–48.

Brennan, Geoffrey and Lomasky, Loren, *Democracy and Decision*, Cambridge: Cambridge University Press, 1993.

Bryk, Anthony, Lee, Valerie and Holland, Peter, *Catholic Schools and the Common Good*, Cambridge, MA: Harvard University Press, 1993.

Buchanan, Allen, "Justice as Reciprocity vs. Subject-Centered Justice," *Philosophy and Public Affairs* 19 (1990): 227–52.

Carter, Stephen, *The Culture of Disbelief*, New York: Basic Books, 1993.

Cohen, Jean, "Rights, Citizenship and the Modern Form of the Social: Dilemmas of Arendtian Republicanism," *Constellations* 3 (1996): 164–89.

Cohen, Joshua, "The Arc of the Moral Universe," *Philosophy and Public Affairs* 26 (1997): 91–134.

Cohen, Joshua, "Deliberation and Democratic Legitimacy," in Alan Hamlin and Philip Pettit (eds.), *The Good Polity*, Oxford: Basil Blackwell, 1989, pp. 17–34.

Cohen, Joshua, "The Economic Basis of Deliberative Democracy," *Social Philosophy and Policy* 6 (1988): 25–50.

Cohen, Joshua, "Money, Politics, Political Equality" (unpublished manuscript on file with author).

Coleman, John, SJ, "Deprivatizing Religion and Revitalizing Citizenship," in Paul J. Weithman (ed.), *Religion and Contemporary Liberalism*, Notre Dame, IN: University of Notre Dame Press, 1997.

Copp, David, "The Idea of a Legitimate State," *Philosophy and Public Affairs* 28 (1999): 3–45.

DeMarneffe, Peter, "The Problem of Evil, the Social Contract and the History of Ethics," *Pacific Philosophical Quarterly* 82 (2000): 11–25.

Dworkin, Ronald, "The Curse of American Politics," *New York Review of Books*, October 17, 1996, pp. 19–24.

Easton, David, "A Reassessment of the Concept of Political Support," *British Journal of Political Science* 5 (1975): 435–57.

Elster, Jon, *Sour Grapes: Studies in the Subversion of Rationality*, Cambridge: Cambridge University Press, 1983.

Estlund, David M., "Democracy Without Preference," *Philosophical Review* 99 (1990): 397–423.

Finnis, John, *Natural Law and Natural Right*, Oxford: Oxford University Press, 1980.

Frank, Robert H. "Why Living in a Rich Society Makes Us Feel Poor," *New York Times Magazine*, October 15, 2000.

Franklin, John Hope, *From Slavery to Freedom*, New York: Alfred A. Knopf, 1947.

Franklin, Robert M., " 'With Liberty and Justice for All': the Public Mission of Black Churches," in W. C. Gilpin (ed.), *Public Faith: Reflections on the Political Role of American Churches*, St. Louis: CBP Press, 1990.

Galston, William, *Liberal Purposes*, Cambridge: Cambridge University Press, 1991.

Garcia Marquez, Gabriel, *Chronicle of a Death Foretold*, New York: Alfred A. Knopf, 1983.

Gilpin, W. Clark (ed.), *Public Faith: Reflections on the Political Role of American Churches*, St. Louis: CBP Press, 1990.

Greenawalt, Kent, *Private Consciences and Public Reasons*, Oxford: Oxford University Press, 1995.

Gutmann, Amy and Thompson, Dennis, *Democracy and Disagreement*, Cambridge, MA: Harvard University Press, 1996.

Haldane, John, "The Individual, the State and the Common Good," *Social Philosophy and Policy* (1996): 59–79.

Harris, Frederick C., "Religious Institutions and African-American Political Mobilization," in P. E. Peterson (ed.), *Classifying by Race*, Princeton: Princeton University Press, 1995, pp. 278–310.

Harris, Frederick C., "Something Within: Religion as a Mobilizer of African-American Political Activism," *Journal of Politics* 56 (1994): 42–68.

Hertzke, Allen D., *Representing God in Washington*, Knoxville: University of Tennessee Press, 1988.

Heschel, Abraham Joshua, *Moral Grandeur and Spiritual Audacity*, ed. Susannah Heschel, New York: Farrar, Straus, Giroux, 1996.

Hollenbach, David, SJ, "Liberalism, Communitarianism and the Bishops' Pastoral Letter on the Economy," *Annual of the Society of Christian Ethics* (1987): 21–39.

Hollenbach, David, SJ, "Politically Active Churches: Some Empirical Prolegomena to a Normative Approach," in Paul J. Weithman (ed.), *Religion and Contemporary Liberalism*, Notre Dame, IN: University of Notre Dame Press, 1997, pp. 291–306.

Jackson, Timothy, "Love in a Liberal Society," *Journal of Religious Ethics* 22 (1994): 29–38.

Knight, Jack and Johnson, James, "What Sort of Equality Does Deliberative Democracy Require?," in Jack Knight and James Johnson (ed.), *Deliberative Democracy: Essays on Reason and Politics*, Cambridge, MA: MIT Press, 1997, pp. 279–319.

Korsgaard, Christene, "The Reasons We Can Share," *Social Philosophy and Policy* 10 (1993): 24–51.

Kymlicka, Will and Norman, Wayne, "Return of the Citizen: a Survey of Recent Work on Citizenship Theory," *Ethics* 104 (1994): 352–81.

Larmore, Charles, "Public Reason," in Samuel Freeman (ed.), *Cambridge Companion to Rawls*, Cambridge: Cambridge University Press, forthcoming.

Leege, David C., "Catholics and the Civic Order: Parish Participation, Politics and Civic Participation," *Review of Politics* 50 (1988): 704–36.

Lincoln, C. Eric and Mamiya, Lawrence H., *The Black Church in the African American Experience*, Durham, NC: Duke University Press, 1990.

Lynch, Robert, "The Human Story Behind an INS Round-Up," *Origins* 26, October 3, 1996.

Macaluso, Theodore F. and Wanat, John, "Voting Turnout and Religiosity," *Polity* 12 (1979): 158–69.

Macedo, Stephen, *Liberal Virtue*, Oxford: Oxford University Press, 1990.

MacIntyre, Alasdair, "On the Essential Contestability of Some Social Concepts," *Ethics* 89 (1973): 1–9.

Madron, Thomas W., Nelson, Hart M. and Yokley, Raytha L., "Religion as a Determinant of Militancy and Political Participation Among Black Americans," *American Behavioral Scientist* 17 (1974): 783–96.

Margalit, Avashai, *The Decent Society*, Cambridge, MA: Harvard University Press, 1996.

Marshall, T. H., *Citizenship and Social Class and Other Essays*, Cambridge: Cambridge University Press, 1950.

McGreevy, John, "Thinking on One's Own: Catholicism in the American Intellectual Imagination, 1928–1960," *Journal of American History* 84 (1997): 97–131.

Meilander, Gilbert, "Begetting and Cloning," *First Things* (June/July 1997): 41–43.

Michelman, Frank, "Law's Republic," *Yale Law Journal* 97 (1988): 1493–1538.

Morris, Aldon D., *The Origins of the Civil Rights Movement: Black Communities Organizing for Change*, New York: Free Press, 1984.

Murray, John Courtney, SJ, *We Hold These Truths*, New York: Sheed and Ward, 1960.

Nagel, Thomas, *Equality and Partiality*, Oxford: Oxford University Press, 1991.

Nine Georgia Priests, "The Essentials in Reforming Immigration Law and Practice," *Origins* 25, August 10, 1995.

O'Neill, Onora, "Constructivisms in Ethics," in *Constructions of Reason*, Cambridge: Cambridge University Press, 1989.

Paris, Peter J., *The Social Teaching of the Black Churches*, Philadelphia: Fortress Press, 1985.

Paris, Peter J., "Comparing the Public Theologies of James H. Cone and Martin Luther King," in Dwight N. Hopkins (ed.), *Black Faith and Public Talk*, Maryknoll: Orbis, 1999, pp. 218–31.

Peterson, Paul E. (ed.), *Classifying by Race*, Princeton: Princeton University Press, 1995.

Pocock, J. G. A., "The Ideal of Citizenship Since Classical Times," in Ronald Beiner (ed.), *Theorizing Citizenship*, Albany: SUNY Press, 1995, pp. 29–52.

Pope John Paul II and the American Bishops, *Life Issues and Political Responsibility*, New Hope, KY: Catholics United for Life, 2000.

Purdum, Todd S., "California enacts expensive college aid program," *New York Times*, September 12, 2000.

Rawls, John, *The Law of Peoples*, Cambridge, MA: Harvard University Press, 1999.

Rawls, John, *Political Liberalism*, New York: Columbia University Press, 1993.

Rawls, John, *A Theory of Justice*, Cambridge, MA: Harvard University Press, 1971.

Raz, Joseph, *The Morality of Freedom*, Oxford: Oxford University Press, 1986.

Raz, Joseph, "Authority and Justification," *Philosophy and Public Affairs* 14 (1985): 3–29.

Reese, Thomas, SJ, *A Flock of Shepherds*, New York: Sheed and Ward, 1992.

Richardson, Henry, "Beyond Good and Right: Toward a Constructive Ethical Pragmatism," *Philosophy and Public Affairs* 24 (1995): 108–41.

Rosenblum, Nancy (ed.), *Obligations of Citizenship and Demands of Faith*, Princeton: Princeton University Press, 2000.

Rousseau, Jean-Jacques, *The Social Contract*, Harmondsworth: Penguin, 1968, trans. Maurine Cranston.

Santiago Nino, Carlos, *The Constitution of Deliberative Democracy*, New Haven: Yale University Press, 1996.

Schlesinger, Arthur M., Jr., *The Cycles of American History*, New York: Houghton Mifflin, 1986.

Schumpeter, Joseph, *Capitalism, Socialism and Democracy*, New York: Harper and Row, 1976.

Shklar, Judith, *American Citizenship: the Quest for Inclusion*, Cambridge, MA: Harvard University Press, 1991.

Shklar, Judith, "The Political Theory of Utopia: From Melancholy to Nostalgia," *Daedelus* 94 (1965): 367–81.

Simmons, A. John, "Justification and Legitimacy," *Ethics* 109 (1999): 739–71.

Simon, William E. and Novak, Michael, *Liberty and Justice for All*, Notre Dame, IN: Brownson Institute, 1986.

Smith, Christian, *American Evangelicalism: Embattled but Thriving*, Chicago: University of Chicago Press, 1999.

Stern, Kenneth, *A Force Upon the Plain: the American Militia Movement and the Politics of Hate*, New York: Simon and Schuster, 1996.

Strange, John, "Bishop Gossman urges Catholics to make the tough call on Nov. 7," *NC Catholic* 56.1, October 22, 2000, p. 14.

Sunstein, Cass, *The Partial Constitution*, Cambridge, MA: Harvard University Press, 1993.

Sunstein, Cass, "Beyond the Republican Revival," *Yale Law Journal* 97 (1988): 1539–1590.

Sunstein, Cass, "Naked Preferences and the Constitution," *Columbia Law Review* 84 (1984): 1689–1732.

Talking About the Death Penalty, Indianapolis: Indiana Catholic Conference, 2000.

Taylor, Charles, *The Ethics of Authenticity*, Cambridge, MA: Harvard University Press, 1991.

Taylor, Robert Joseph, Thornton, Michael C. and Chatters, Linda M., "Black Americans' Perceptions of the Sociohistorical Role of the Church," *Journal of Black Studies* 18 (1987): 123–38.

Verba, Sydney, Schlozman, Kay Lehman and Brady, Henry, *Voice and Equality: Civic Voluntarism in American Politics*, Cambridge, MA: Harvard University Press, 1995.

Wald, Kenneth D., *Religion and Politics in the United States*, Washington, DC: Congressional Quarterly Press, 1992.

Waldron, Jeremy, *The Dignity of Legislation*, Cambridge: Cambridge University Press, 1999.

Waldron, Jeremy, *Justice and Disagreement*, Oxford: Oxford University Press, 1999.

Waldron, Jeremy, "Religious Contributions in Public Deliberation," *San Diego Law Review* 30 (1993): 817–48.

Waldron, Jeremy, *Liberal Rights: Collected Papers 1981–1991*, Cambridge: Cambridge University Press, 1993.

Warren, Mark, "Deliberative Democracy and Authority," *American Political Science Review* 90 (1996): 46–60.

Warren, Mark, *Dry Bones Rattling: Community Building to Revitalize American Democracy*, Princeton: Princeton University Press, 2001.

Watson, Justin, *The Christian Coalition: Dreams of Restoration, Demands for Recognition*, New York: St. Martin's Press, 1997.

Weatherford, M. Stephen, "Measuring Political Legitimacy," *American Political Science Review* 86 (1992): 149–66.

Weithman, Paul J., "Citizenship and Public Reason," in Robert P. George and Christopher Wolfe (eds.), *Liberal Public Reason, Natural Law and Morality*, Washington: Georgetown University Press, 2000, pp. 125–70.

Weithman, Paul J., "Perfectionist Republicanism and Neo-Republicanism" (unpublished manuscript on file with author).

Weithman, Paul J., "Waldron on Political Legitimacy and the Social Minimum," *Philosophical Quarterly* 45 (1995): 218–24.

Weithman, Paul J. (ed.), *Religion and Contemporary Liberalism*, Notre Dame, IN: University of Notre Dame Press, 1997.

Wilcox, Clyde and Gomez, Leopold, "Religion, Group Identification and Politics Among American Blacks," *Sociological Analysis* 51 (1990): 271–85.

Williams, Bernard, *Ethics and the Limits of Philosophy*, Cambridge, MA: Harvard University Press, 1985.

Williams, Delores, *Sisters in the Wilderness*, Maryknoll: Orbis, 1993.

Wills, Garry, *Under God*, New York: Simon and Schuster, 1990.

Wilson, James Q., *Political Organizations*, Princeton: Princeton University Press, 1995.

Wolfe, Alan, *One Nation, After All*, New York: Viking Penguin, 1998.

Wolfe, Alan, review of Taylor Branch, *Pillar of Fire: America in the King Years, 1963–65* (New York: Simon and Schuster, 1997), *New York Times Book Review*, January 18, 1998, p. 13.

Young, Iris Marion, *Inclusion and Democracy*, Oxford: Oxford University Press, 2000.

Zielbauer, Paul, "Possibility of defection is met with anger and delight," *New York Times*, Thursday, May 24, 2001, p. A21.

Index

civic argument 48ff., 55f., 60, 66, 69, 71,
  76ff., 81, 86, 87, 91, 93, 137ff., 161, 212
civic friendship 7, 9, 10, 91, 162, 210f.
civic skills 41ff., 72, 73, 76, 80, 82, 90, 91, 141
civic virtue 150, 155f., 165f.
civil rights movement 46
civility 9, 40, 109, 132, 135f., 160ff., 180,
  210f., 215f.
Cohen, Jean 31n.15
Cohen, Joshua 8, 70n.4, 75n.9, 76n.19, 87,
  87n.21, 146n.12, 214n.3
common interest view of governmental aims
  125, 137, 208
communitarianism 51
comprehensive views (including
  comprehensive doctrines) 3, 93, 121,
  122ff., 180, 192, 200ff., 216
concepts
  concepts vs. conceptions 17f., 69
Cone, James H. 53n.59
conservatism, religious 1
Copp, David 216n.12

De Marneffe, Peter 213n.2
De Tocqueville, Alexis 43
death penalty (including capital punishment)
  35, 55f., 56nn.64–65, 65, 85, 114, 117, 139
deliberation (including public deliberation) 8,
  11, 20, 40, 54ff., 71, 75ff., 84ff., 88f., 90, 94
  broad view of public deliberation 8of.
deliberative basis condition 55
deliberative democracy 74ff., 86ff.
democracy 10
democratic theory 12, 15, 21, 28, 35, 39, 66,
  69, 70, 72, 75, 80, 82, 83, 85, 88, 91, 93,
  150, 161
desirability condition on norms 175ff.
disagreement 4, 5, 172ff., 216
  reasonable disagreement 4, 5, 132, 135ff.,
  142, 208ff., 212
domestic partnership benefits 4, 31, 94f.
Dukakis, Michael 118n.10
duty of civility (Rawls) 179, 180ff., 189, 191,
  194f., 201, 207ff.

eastern orthodoxy 37
Economic Justice for All 50n.50, 51ff.,
  51n.53, 59
effective identification with citizenship 14,
  20, 33, 36, 41, 62, 71, 76, 87, 91, 137
Elster, Jon 27n.10
employment, right to 4, 25, 27
equality 1, 2, 6, 7, 11, 15f., 24, 25, 26, 28, 31,
  39, 41, 44ff., 49, 71, 73, 75, 76, 78, 124f.,
  176, 194, 204, 206

Estlund, David 101n.6
expressive value 120

feminist movement 22
Finnis, John 196f.
Franco, Francisco 10
Frank, Robert H. 26
Freddoso, Alfred 152n.20
freedom of religion 1, 57
Freeman, Samuel 8n.8
full participation 4, 17ff., 23–24, 24ff., 29ff.,
  32ff., 35, 36, 40, 53, 54ff., 69, 84, 125,
  207
fundamentalism, religious 1, 64

Garcia Marquez, Gabriel 107n.8
gay marriage 4
gay rights movement 22
Germany 126
Glucksberg see *State of Washington v.*
  Glucksberg
Gomez, Leopold 45n.36
Gutmann, Amy 8, 178

Habermas, Jürgen 77
Habitat for Humanity 50, 90, 156
Hagar 53
Haldane, John 215n.8
Harris, Frederick C. 46f.
Heschel, Abraham 111
Hollenbach, David 40n.2

ideals 14, 67ff., 73, 75f., 80, 89f., 144f., 149ff.,
  153, 155f., 160f., 186
  ideals of citizenship 14, 103, 106, 156, 167,
  186f., 194, 210f., 213
identification with citizenship 14, 20, 35, 42,
  49, 64, 69, 71, 88, 91, 104f., 116, 132, 136,
  139, 207ff.
immigrants (including immigration) 4, 10,
  20, 27, 29, 58ff., 84, 85, 114f., 139
Islam 37

Jackson, Timothy 152n.19
Jews 10
John Paul II, Pope 55
Judaism 32
justifying reasons 6, 124, 131, 134, 166, 178,
  180, 188, 195, 197

Kant, Immanuel 151, 169, 190, 191, 206, 215
Kennedy, John 10, 111
Kennedy, William 25
King, Martin Luther 52f., 62, 111, 146f.,
  146n.12, 183f.